Richard Hooker Wilmer

Guy Averall

A Patriotic Sketch

Richard Hooker Wilmer

Guy Averall
A Patriotic Sketch

ISBN/EAN: 9783337306878

Printed in Europe, USA, Canada, Australia, Japan

Cover: Foto ©Thomas Meinert / pixelio.de

More available books at **www.hansebooks.com**

A PATRIOTIC SKETCH.

AS WRITTEN BY

A PRIVATE SOLDIER OF THE U. S. ARMY.

———— ——

PHILADELPHIA:
E. CLAXTON & COMPANY,
No. 930 MARKET STREET.
1881.

PROEM.

This Booke which is written by a Private Soldier of the United States Army, tells who Guy Averall was, where he has been, and also what training he received. It furthermore mentions the various kinds of patriots whom he met; and how these latter behaved themselves in a lively, agreeable, and interesting manner when before him. To all good enlisted men the work is dedicated.

CONTENTS.

PRELIMINARY.

I.

A GOOD many years ago, longer in fact than we think necessary to tell, a stately vessel, belonging to the Black Ball Line of Packets, then plying between Europe and America, was seen slowly approaching the harbor of New York. The ship, named the Imperial, had previously been boarded by a pilot, who now in conformity with maritime regulations, was making preparations for bringing his charge into port. The studding sails; the staysails; the spanker; the t'gallant sails, fore, main, and mizzen, had all been taken in; nothing, in fact, was now spread, save a jib and top sail, under which the vessel kept her course. Finally too these were clewed up; a number of sailors had previously heaved out the anchor by means of a tackle; Mr. Barr, the chief mate, was giving orders so that the chain which was ultimately to hold the vessel could not possibly get foul when the anchor was dropped; the Captain, a dark featured, weather beaten man, kept up the show of authority, by "overhauling" a sailor now and then; while the pilot, a bluff looking old son of Neptune, was so much occupied with his charge, that he seemed as calm and imperturbable as the great sea divinity himself. At length the word "let go " was given from the quarter-deck ; a splash was heard in the water : the immense iron cable rattled through its hawse-holes ; the Imperial swung round with the tide ; and before those on board, both passengers and sailors, was spread the magnificent harbor of New York. On one side lay Staten Island ; the slopes of which were covered with many picturesque edifices, painted generally, in accordance with established rules, a pure white : to leeward, at some distance, a couple of forts were to be seen, with tier upon tier of formidable looking guns ; further inland, a few rounded islets were observed, clothed apparently in a uniform tint of green ; a busy steamer, here and there, plied backward and forward through the waters ; while beyond all, the spires and prominent edifices of the mighty Gotham itself loomed up, in distant perspective, on the far off horizon. A cheer was at once given by the emigrants on board the Imperial, for now that their voyage was terminated, they all seemed gratified that the hope of placing their feet on *terra firma* would soon be realized.

Among the passengers who appeared on the deck of the Imperial at this time, was a youth of rather slim appearance as far as externals are concerned, and whose name we have already promulgated on our title page, Guy Averall. Guy's father was a man who had led a somewhat irregular life ; and who, as far his influence could possibly extend, intended apparently that his son should lead an irregular life also. When young the boy had the promise of a fair education ; but unfortunately for him his father, who followed the profession of gen-

tleman at large, could not sustain him in this career;
so the higher knowledge had to be abandoned, and
in its place was substituted such training as an ordinary National School could give. The elder Averall now resolved to emigrate to the Colonies, and
accordingly Guy was turned over to the care of a
widowed aunt, and the father set off for Australia.
How he prospered in that far off country no one
ever learned ; meanwhile, however, the aunt bestowed on the boy that care which most women will
exhibit to a woe-begone nephew and a sister's moth-
erless child. She accordingly gave Guy such instructions in morality and religion as his age seemed to
demand; permitted him, when not employed on
errands or working in her garden, to read such volumes of a devotional and theologic nature as her
house contained; saw that he was dressed for
Church on Sunday, and could repeat, in a creditable manner, the ten Commandments and the Lord's
Prayer; warned him against all boys of his age
who told lies or swore ; and if at any time, in sheer
waywardness, he evinced a taste for rowdying servant men, itinerant ballad singers or other low
company, the aunt endeavored to impress on the
youth a proper idea of his own station in life, telling
him that the Averalls after all, were not so degen-
erate a stock as they might seem, that some of them
actually kept out of jail and paid their debts ; and
that none of the breed ever came to disgrace, except
through the pressure of the hard times, when
coupled perhaps with their own extravagance, want
of foresight, or other accidental fault.

As to Guy himself, he listened to this recital over

and over again till he knew it all by heart, and
resolved within himself, to retrieve the fortune of
the Averalls, if he only had a chance of escaping
to the continent of America. He pondered on this
subject long and earnestly, but was nevertheless
afraid to broach the matter to his aunt, so much
was he fearful of the disapproval of his worthy old
relative. He however, kept the plan concealed in
his secret heart, and whenever he could gather any
scrap of information from some traveller who had
visited the great West, he was careful to hide away
the knowledge as so much "treasure trove," whose
use would depend on future opportunities. "If I
were only free from this state of servitude in which
I am now placed," he would exclaim, "how happy
I would be with unlimited freedom before me." At
length the wishes of our hero for rambling were
gratified, for one morning his aunt approached him
with tears in her eyes, saying she had just received
a letter from Australia, that his father, who had
recently been employed as assistant on a sheep
farm, was now dead; that what was worse, he bade
adieu to the world without leaving a penny to his
name; that the funds left in her hands belonging to
Guy were nearly all exhausted ; that she had nothing in the world but a mere maintenance for herself ;
and since the boy in the natural cause of events
must soon leave her side, she therefore recommended him to take his proper portion, seven
pounds, ten shilling and one penny, go to Liverpool,
secure a passage to Kamchatka, to Calcutta, to the
Straits of Babelmandel or anywhere else, provided
only he would get well out of the way, and never

trouble her in the future for clothing, advice, assistance or anything else. Guy received this news with fear and trembling; was sorry, of course, as all boys of sixteen are, to hear that his father was really dead ; cogitated for some time on his future prospects; told his aunt that America was the soil that had always been dearest to his heart; and then declared his resolution to follow the course that his guardian had suggested. "Never in the future," said he, "will I impose myself in any way on my relatives, even if the obligation should only entail the expenditure of half an hour's trouble, or the outlay of a groat, in ready cash, on their part."

As he stood on the deck of the Imperial the bosom of the young rambler was filled with a fine enthusiasm, while his meditations ran somewhat in the following way. "Well, here I am, with the vast American continent before me—a continent which some have abused and some have praised, but in which I am determined to earn an honest living, as far as the laws and my own strength will allow me. To be sure my purse is light, but what of that —as long as I have hands by my side, I need not be afraid for food and raiment. Friends and advisers I have none, but must not every one eventually become chief counsel to himself, and why may I not assume, at this instant, a task which in the long run becomes inevitable? As to books, I never have had any very regular instruction in them, and that, I suppose, is some loss ; still I have common sense, and two good eyes in my head, and that surely must count for something. Let the world then be my instructor, as it has been to many others ; let me do the duty that is set before me day after day; and as to the rest, let those who are blessed with worldly pelf, enjoy their future as they choose, but Guy Averall will remain satisfied provided he be allowed to earn his bread in decent guise, and suffered to live and die as an honest man."

II.

THE sentiments thus uttered by our friend Guy were commendable in the extreme, as every well disposed person will admit; how far his subsequent actions corresponded with his words will sufficiently appear in the sequel. The day after the arrival of the Imperial at her anchorage, a tug came alongside that vessel, the passengers got aboard, and in a couple of hours were transferred to one of the wharves in the lower part of New York. Guy found no difficulty in securing a boarding house, such as suited his humble means, and after performing his ablutions and examining the contents of his wallet, he determined to take a stroll around the streets of the metropolis. He accordingly sought the extremities of Greenwich and of Washington Streets, and wandered up and down them for a while. The first thing that attracted his attention was the number of signs in German letters, stuck here and there on the houses in that particular region, a fact strongly suggestive of the cosmopolitan nature of the residents of that particular locality. Guy entered one of these establishments in sheer listlessness, and forthwith began to note the various incidents that he saw. The inhabitants of the place, as far as he was able to observe, seemed to

be an extremely good natured race ; for three or
four stalwart looking fellows, with stomachs of comfortable dimensions, were congregated round a small
table in a "saloon ;" shouting, gesticulating, and
kissing each other over their glasses of lager, in a
way which utterly confounded our young adventurer. Guy now began to look around for some of
his own countrymen, nor were they hard to find ;
bold, haughty, independent fellows, with a certain
Erin-go-bragh air about them which did his heart
good ; and served on the instant to recall the warlike deeds of Wellington, Beresford, Meagher,
Mitchell and other illustrious heroes, who had made
the name of Irishmen illustrious in all quarters of
the globe, where the Hibernian accent is heard, or
the praise of the Hibernian people is spoken. Next
Master Averall wandered into Broadway, and in
spite of his best efforts to appear indifferent, the
youth found himself amazed and stupefied by the
noise and bustle which surrounded him on all sides.
What a wonderful place, to the stranger, this Broadway is ! How alert and withal how determined each
person appeared to be ; how eagerly each one
seemed to fulfil his particular errand ; how energetic
the accents with which all spoke ! Guy felt as
though he were a mere infant in such a busy throng,
and wondered if ever he would be able to hold his
own in such a bustling locality as this thoroughfare.
Walking on, his eyes were soon greeted by a new
sight. This was an edifice, four or five stories in
height, painted all over with the most grotesque
combination of mermaid, animal and woolly horse,
and supporting a balcony from which six stalwart

.musicians, with brass trumpets in hand, diffused celestial harmony on the breeze. It is needless to say that the house, now before our friend, was appropriated by the great Barnum, the prince of showman, the man who had exhibited Joice Heath and General Tom Thumb, and whose efforts in parading himself before the public, in a professional sense, had made him the idol and wonder of most young Americans. Still going onward, a church was next seen with outlying tombstones, and images of dear though half-forgotten saints; and after this other streets and other edifices, big with trade, were passed, and still the great tide of humanity swept onward, in either direction, on the sidewalks. The absence of the mere lounger was somewhat remarkable to the eye of the stranger, none of your well-to-do professional gentlemen, such as are met with in other capitals, appeared to be in sight; every one present seemed to have some object in view, and was anxious apparently to accomplish it, in as little time as possible. At length Guy became tired of this ceaseless activity, and stopping before a house in process of construction, he asked the Superintendent the time of day, and was duly informed it was about noon. As dinner with a youngster is a most important item, our friend now resolved to retrace his steps, and seek that part of the city from from which he had started a few hours previous.

On his way back, to his lodgings, quite a little incident occurred, for Averall was fortunate enough to encounter a most interesting acquaintance. As he sauntered along the foot-path, in the vicinity of the park, a gentleman in black broadcloth, with

white neck tie and patent leather boots, who looked
very much as though he were a clergyman of the
Episcopal church, overtook our friend, and asked if
an emigrant vessel had not discharged her passengers that morning near the Battery? Guy informed
the stranger that such was the case, when his reverence volunteered the information that he was in
search of some friends of his, whom he expected
on the Imperial that very morning. Guy now
asked the name of these expected friends when that
of Smith was given, and the question afterwards
put if our adventurer had heard of any person,
who had answered to that title, among the passengers? Now Smith being such an uncommon name,
it did indeed seem strange that any one answering
to that cognomen should have been on board. Guy,
however, made answer that two distinct Smiths were
known to him, as passengers on the Imperial; one
of them he believed had intended to emigrate to
the Far West; and the other, a young man, was in
search of a relative who was now a resident of New
York.

"That is he—that is he—I've found him out,"
said the stranger, glad evidently to get the information, "the young rascal shall soon be within my own
clutches. I've just had a letter from his sister-in-
law, my own cousin, telling me to look out for the
good for nothing scapegrace." And without more
ado, Master Averall and his new found friend, set
out in company towards the Battery.

During the ramble the stranger became very
communicative, and imparted a whole host of information about the United States in general, and him-

self in particular. It now appeared that Guy's friend was not in reality a clergyman, but simply a retired merchant, for, according to his account, he had emigrated from the town of Belfast some twenty-five years previously. His first employment he said, after landing in New York, was to roll a barrel of sugar into a cellar, for which achievement he received the princely sum of twenty-five cents. His next move was to open a small grocery store, where families were supplied with most excellent tea ; afterwards he sent out a schooner to the West Indies, with a cargo of flour on board, and in re-turn brought back a load of molasses. The follow-ing season he sent out two schooners instead of one, which fleet was subsequently increased to half a dozen. Thus he had gone on, sending out more vessels, year after year, till now he had no less than fifty full-rigged ships at sea, and was worth five million of dollars if he was worth a cent. "It is all owing to the spirit of enterprise and a protecting Providence," said the merchant with a sigh, "these things I look to as the efficient cause of my good luck—if young men would only exhibit the correct spirit of enterprise, and trust to Divine Providence, when they land on these shores, they might be all worth their millions, like me, before they reach the age of thirty."

Just at that instant the wayfarers approached a "store" in which a great clatter was audible, and looking in, Guy observed a man, standing on a chair behind the counter, repeating at the same time the words "twenty-five, twenty-five, twenty-five," with a sort of crazy volubility which was in

itself almost astounding. The youth was now about
to proceed onward, when the sugar merchant stopped him and said "hold on for a second or two, let
us see what this is." Young Averall accordingly
glanced in once more, and noticed the auctioneer,
for such he was, holding a watch in his hand, and
bidding it off at the same time, for the sum of six
dollars and twenty-five cents.

" Twenty-five, twenty-five, twenty-five only offered," said the seller of chronometers, starting forward once more in his mad career, " who says six
dollars and fifty cents for that beautiful Geneva
watch, made in the city of Paris, jewelled in four
holes, lever movement, compensation balance, and
all the modern improvements. Cost price eighteen
dollars and a half as imported by myself—selling
off the lot so as to make room for a new invoice—
determined to sacrifice them at almost any price.
Young man don't you wish to invest in this time-
keeper—just look at it if you please—worth twenty-
five dollars if it is worth a single dime at this instant.

Guy took the watch and examined it for an instant. It was a beautiful article, such as any young
man of sixteen might be proud of ; the back was
enameled with jet and gold, while the dial presented
the figure of a cupid surrounded by roses, the most
captivating picture that could possibly be imagined.
As was quite natural our friend Averall wanted the
watch, but recollecting he had but six dollars and a
half in his purse, he deemed it somewhat imprudent
to spend so much of his cash capital in a single
article of luxury. He accordingly was on the point

of handing back the time-keeper, when his friend,
the sugar merchant, stepped up to his side and whis-
pered *sotto voce :* " I'd recommend you to bid upon
that watch—cheap as dirt—nothing like commercial
enterprise—made all my money by investing, at
times in a proper way ; you'll certainly double your
capital on that watch before this day week."

This announcement was pleasant, and filled Guy
Averall with the highest hopes.   He certainly should
have liked to double his money in the course of the
ensuing seven days, but recollecting his means were
but small, he judged it somewhat imprudent to stake
his entire wealth on a single venture.   He accordingly hesitated for a while, and then informed his
friend that the contents of his purse at present, were
but limited, and therefore he did not care about
making the purchase.

"But nonsense, my dear young man," was the
answer, " you make a great mistake if you allow this
chance to slip.   Why, that beautiful gold watch with
the enameled back·is a treasure, and is offered for
one-third of its real value."

" That may be," was the response, "but a bird
in the hand is worth two in the bush, as my grand-
mother once said, and at present I am inclined to
hold on to my money."

"Oh pshaw ! nonsense," said the merchant,
"these are only your old-fashioned conservative
notions.   Enterprise, my dear sir, is the only thing
one requires to succeed in New York.   Won't buy
it !   I'm really sorry you hav'nt more discernment.
But stay, I'd like to purchase that watch myself, so
I'll make a bid.   Six fifty, Mister Auctioneer, if you

please." The auctioneer accepted the additional sum, and commenced rattling off the words "six fifty, six fifty, going at six fifty," in the same mad tone as before.

This seemed all right, but in another second an additional quarter of a dollar was offered, and the chance of getting the chronometer seemed to be against our friend.

"I'll have that watch or I'll die," said the ship owner in apparent desperation." Here take my pocket book and bid for it. Hold on, though, I've nothing on hand less than a ten thousand dollar check and they cannot change that here. Just bid for the watch and hold on to it, till I come back from the Bank, when I promise to refund your money with interest."

"But stay," said Guy, "I don't——"

"Nonsense, man," said the sugar merchant without permitting Guy to finish the sentence. "I'll have that watch in spite of fate. You can even bid seven dollars for it, rather than that I should miss it when away."

The auctioneer now saw proper to take up the cry of seven dollars, as if really bid, and before Guy had time to bless himself, the beautiful Swiss watch, manufactured in the city of Paris, and jewelled in four holes, was knocked down to our friend for the aforesaid sum.

"There now, it's a bargain; I'm glad of it," said the shipowner. "Just pay the seven dollars and take the watch, and I'll be back with you in ten seconds."

"But," said Guy, by way of expostulation, "there

surely is a mistake in this thing. I certainly did not bid for the watch. You yourself are responsible for the bargain."

"So I am—responsible for anything I say—just settle with the clerk yonder, and we will soon make the matter all right."

"But, my dear sir, you are in error," said Guy.

"Nonsense, man, nonsense," was the response, "I'm not in error. I know very well what I'm about."

Guy now found that there was no use in trifling any longer with his acquaintance, and although somewhat sorry to differ from the sugar merchant, he nevertheless did look that individual straight in the face, paused for a second or two, and then remarked that he would neither take the watch nor pay a penny towards completing the bargain.

"Who is to settle for this?" shouted the auctioneer, who meanwhile seemed tired of the noisy altercation.

"You are," said the sugar merchant, pointing to Guy.

"No I'm not," remarked our hero quite boldly.

"Yes you are," was the response.

"I deny it," was the rejoinder.

"We heard you bid for the watch," shouted a gentleman with a large gold ring on his finger in the opposite corner of the room.

"Who?" said Guy.

"You," was the answer.

"I never did such a things in the course of my life, never on my word of honor," responded Guy, who was now pretty well frightened at the predicament in which he found himself, and only wished he was rid of sugar merchant, auctioneer, the man with the large ring on his finger, and every one else in the establishment.

"We'll carry you off to jail," shouted the auctioneer who forthwith laid hold of Guy's coat.

"Police! Police!" shouted Guy. But no police were to be found, for as soon as the tumult became audible, the members of that efficient force all took to their heels and fled.

A grand uproar now followed. The auctioneer taking hold of Guy, dragged him in one direction, while the sugar merchant, who still seemed his friend, undertook to pull him in another. They hauled and twisted Guy about in various directions, and it is possible that Master Averall would have been torn in pieces among them, when luckily a *deus ex machinâ* appeared at this instant in the person of a man, of about twenty-eight or thirty years of age, who possessed a handsome, well-formed figure and erect bearing, and who seemed to be passing down Broadway at that instant. Hearing the noise, the stranger came to a halt; when Guy, after a little delay, contrived to inform him of all that had happened, how he met his clerical friend up town, how the latter pretended to be in quest of a relative whom he had expected that morning, how Guy had been induced to attend the watch auction, and finally how an attempt had been made to force an article on him that he neither desired nor felt himself able to purchase. As soon as this recital was finished, the stranger paused for a second or two, looked at the auctioneer, sugar merchant and clerk;

revealed the letters U. S. on his cap, and then coupled the demonstration with a tirade, which certainly was not unmerited when applied to the personages before him.

"You contemptible set of fellows," said he, "have you no way to exist except by defrauding every stranger that falls a victim to your clutches? Why do you not go and earn an honest living in some fashion, rather than exist as miserable cheats?" Then turning to Guy the lecturer continued. "You are a stranger here, I see, let me therefore give you a word of advice. Leave this place in as little time as possible; for older personages than you have been swindled in New York. And, if at any time you visit this city in the future, beware of these large sugar merchants whom we meet occasionally on Broadway. They may be honest, for Heaven forbid that I should deny that honest men may not be found even here; but when a big millionaire, with thirty ships in the ocean, chooses to exhibit the profound interest in you that this gentleman has shown, it is ten to one he has a design on your purse, and the sooner you get out of his way the better."

Such were the words of the speaker, which Guy received open-mouthed, not knowing what answer to attempt, although feeling somewhat ashamed at the time of being caught in such a ridiculous situation. Guy would have thanked his protector for his good offices on the occasion, but somehow or other his tongue stuck to his palate, and he could not find a single word to say, either by way of excuse, thanks or justification. The stranger seeing the lad's embarrassment, did not care apparently to add

to it by prolonging the discourse—he simply made
Guy a bow, and then took the opposite direction on
the street. Going away, Guy looked at him for a
while, as if he were a veritable saviour, and then in
a demure and very quiet manner, the young man
sought the retirement of his own " hotel." Recall-
ing the events of that day, he thought he had
discovered a great deal that was admirable and
interesting in the metropolitan city of America.
He commended the length of its streets, the height
of its houses, the width of its avenue, and above all
the spirit of enterprise and industry that was everywhere displayed. But how a respectably dressed
gentleman, with a clerical necktie, and patent leather
boots, should so far demean himself as to be impli-
cated in an attempt to palm off a trumpery, worthless watch on a poor emigrant, was more than he
could exactly determine.

III.

WE have it on record, that when that eminent
philosopher, Benjamin Franklin, first visited the
city of Philadelphia, he bought three large loaves
for a penny a piece, ate one of them for breakfast,
and putting the others, each under an arm, he carried them round several squares in the city of Broth-
erly Love, and finally gave them away to some destitute person whom he met on his travels. Now
although we cannot pretend to the same degree of
circumstantial exactness, in describing the adventures of young Averall, yet this much appears certain, that on the morning following his encounter
with the sugar merchant, Guy did eat his breakfast

in seasonable time ; and after yawning and cogitating and perambulating around, as a good-for-noth-
ing fellow is apt to do. he finally resolved to take
the advice always proferred, and seek his fortunes
in the country. "Yes, yes," said he to himself, as
he strolled around and thrust his hand contentedly
into his pocket, "my adviser of yesterday was right,
I see quite distinctly the way the land lies in this
vicinity. New York, I have no doubt is a very captivating place, and I should love very dearly to take
another promenade in Broadway, yet if I venture
there, some other sugar merchant or large millionaire might come across my path, and if I should be
so unfortunate as to fall into his clutches, then lack-
a-day, what would become of Guy Averall? No,
no, I wont trifle with this Delilah any longer, I will
take my bundle in hand, cross the broad and majestic Hudson, seek the quiet of a country life
among the glades and sequestered by-paths of New
Jersey, and as soon as I get settled down to the
enjoyment of my new existence, I will laugh at all
the sugar merchants and ship owners that ever set
foot on Broadway. Gracious! who knows, in the long
run, but I might find that chief treasure that every
man is seeking, a wife, in that very land on the
opposite side of the river. There is luck in store
for Guy Averall as yet, even admitting that his first
adventure in America was somewhat unpropitious.
Yes, yes, I have it; the great object I should aim at
is simply a quiet farm nouse, with rural simplicity
and rustic ease, and a "maid who is lovely to soul
and to eye," as my countryman Moore sings—ah,
yes! that indeed would be felicity. And here

Guy Averall, who was not by any means entirely destitute of poetical sentiment, began repeating the words of the author just mentioned.

"I knew by the smoke that so gracefully curled
  Above the green elms that a cottage was near,
And I said if there's peace to be found in the world
  For a heart that is humble, it should seek for it here,
  A heart that is humble, should seek for it here."

Just as Guy had finished this beautiful lyric, from which the foregoing verse is an extract, his meditations were cut short, for three or four gentlemen in military uniform passed him in the street. Guy, of course, had seen soldiers before—British soldiers, in red coats, if you please, and at times had even felt a sort of enthusiasm for the fife and drum; but with the prospect immediately before him, does any one imagine he should seriously adopt the profession of arms! Certainly not, the thing was impossible, his own heart told him there was better things than a musket and bayonet in store for him among the corn fields, and green capped woods of America. So without reflecting any further on "battle shout, and waving plume," our friend once more sought the interior of his lodging house, where he instantly completed such preparations as were necessary before leaving the city.

In due time after this, Master Averall sought one of the ferry boats which cross the North River, and before many minutes he found himself on the opposite bank of the Hudson. Entering the railway car, which was to convey him for some distance into the Jerseys, he picked up an old newspaper, lying on a seat, and began to read. The first thing

that attracted the attention of our adventurer was a
paragraph about the respective merits of the Whigs
and the Democrats, the two parties who then controlled the destinies of the country. But as Guy, at
this time, was totally uninformed respecting the
characteristics of these factions, he found it impossible to decide on their respective claims. Further
on, he came to a leading article, in which the subject of slavery was discussed, and wonderful as it
may now seem, that old wretch, Horace Greeley, was
delivered to all the pains of purgatory, because forsooth he advocated the strange and monstrous doctrine that the institution of slavery was shameful in
itself, and that no person had a right to sell another
person, just as if he were a beast of the field, even
supposing the skin of the unfortunate victim were
black. Now Guy was not an abolitionist at this
time, he never had attempted the *rôle* of liberator
of the human race, his own necessities in fact, were
so urgent, just then, that he had hardly time to
think of freedom or liberty or emancipation or anything of the kind. Still it did seem to him, that the
tone of the article he had been reading was sadly
out of place in a Christian land, and was utterly at
variance with the best thoughts and instincts of the
age in which he lived. But here was something
which pleased him much better. It was a long
article, written on Ireland, in which the rascally
oppressions of the English were mentioned with
appropriate comments; and then the virtues, the
valor, the generosity, the bravery and the beauty of
the down-trodden race were eulogized in terms
which we need hardly quote in this place, but whose

fervid style of eloquence was well calculated to arouse one's inmost heart. The breast of Guy Averall warmed with sympathy as soon as he glanced over this article; he was an Irishman himself, and felt an Irishman's sympathy with his country, he was glad to see that here, on the western side of the Atlantic, the wrongs, the sufferings and the merits of his native land were fully understood; and although scant justice was given to an Irishman at home, in this country he was properly appreciated. "I see, I see," said he, "the generous tone of sentiment which prevails in the western world—I see that even here in the vicinity of New York, the down-trodden patriot has a welcome, such as is rarely accorded him in other places. My success in America is certainly assured; those bright anticipations in which I indulged this morning will all be realized. I'll rise like a phoenix from my burning nest; and watch like an eagle or turkey buzzard for my prey, the whole of New Jersey will be spread under my observing eye, and zounds when the proper time comes, and a fair and virtuous widow, for instance, with a few hundred dollars in her own name, is seen far beneath me, as my quarry, I'll descend from the sky above her, in one fell swoop, and never will cease billing and cooing, till I can claim her as my own personal perquisite and plunder."

Such were the sentiments that found place in the mind of Averall at that instant; do not, however, kind reader, set him down as a mere picaroon on that account, for many a man as lofty and generous as Cæsar himself, would under similar circumstances have acted and felt in the same way.

IV.

THE iron horse travelled onward, and Guy kept
cogitating and laying out plans for the future ;
finally the engine gave a screech, the bell on it
began to ring, the train came to a halt, and in less
than five seconds, our friend found himself standing
on the railway platform at Newark. "Hack, sir, do
you want a hack," vociferated half a dozen voices
as Averall moved to the street outside. But Guy,
like another Gloriana, passed unharmed through the
surging mass of his countrymen who endeavored to
entrap him, and ere many minutes he emerged safe
and sound into the street.

Yes, there he had it ! Those red brick houses
and those green window shutters, the usual concom-
itants of an American town, what a sermon could
be preached on that theme ! But we forbear, since
some critics choose to characterize the combination
as beautiful, picturesque and even grand, so we
have no desire to destroy the pleasing illusion.
Guy doubtless thought Newark a very fine place, so
on he went, wondering at everything he saw, yet
anxious meanwhile as to his possible chance of
obtaining employment. The chief enigma with him
then was, in what direction he should seek for work ;
for Averall, owing to the lazy, half-gentlemanly way
in which he had been brought up, had never thought
it necessary heretofore to apply himself to any given
occupation.   Just as he was passing a livery stable,
however, a man hailed him, and asked him if the
" greenhorn " wished to earn a few dollars. Guy
was only too glad to get the opportunity, and made

answer accordingly, when numerous questions were
put as to the lad's previous training, to what labor
he had been accustomed, and other inquiries of a
similar nature. These questions having been answered in as satisfactory a manner as possible, a
bargain finally was struck, and it was agreed that
Guy was to be taken on trial for a month by his
employer. "All right," said Averall. "I am content. I'll endeavor to do my best. What is your
name, may I ask?"

"Gore," was the answer, "no matter, however,
about that, for it wont affect the bargain in any way.
If you are inclined to take me at my word, get into
this wagon, and before very long you'll find yourself in East Greenville."

According to command, Guy got into the vehicle
as directed, and while driving on, he entered into
conversation with the farmer, and found him to be
quite a companionable man. "How much is land
worth in this vicinity?" said Guy, who seemed to
be animated with a laudable desire of gaining information on all subjects of general interest.

"From fifty to seventy-five dollars an acre, more
or less, some of it is probably worth a hundred.
How much is land worth in Ireland, may I ask?"

"Don't know exactly. I can only guess by the
rent that is commonly paid. This rent, at present,
may be as much as one pound, or one pound ten,
the English acre."

"Well, let me see," said the farmer. "A pound
is equal to five dollars, is it not, so one pound ten is
seven dollars and a half. Allowing five per cent.
interest as a fair equivalent for the purchase money,

3

your land in Ireland then must be somewhat higher
in price there, than it is here, though after all the
difference is not so very great."

"Yes," said Guy, who now spoke as a native,
"but if it was not for those rascally landlords who
always oppress us, we might have it much cheaper.
These scoundrels rack and harass their tenants, in
every possible way, and finally drive them out of the
country. If it were not for the landlords we might
all live like princes in Ireland. In a certain sense I
must say I have been the victim of landlord oppression myself."

"Sorry to hear you say that," said the farmer,
"but every Irishman I have met for the last ten
years complains in the same way." So with these
and similar discourses both parties contrived to pass
away the time, while they travelled along the common country road which leads from East Greenville
to Newark.

In less than a couple of hours from the time he
was engaged, our friend reached the farm of his
employer. The homestead was situated just under
a spur of the Orange mountains, and was a place of
rural simplicity, at the time of which we write;
although latterly it has been invaded by a host of
people from New York City, who have taken up
their residence in East Greenville, and have somewhat demoralized the early training of the inhabitants. At the time spoken of everything in East
Greenville was free from the contamination of the
city, and as a consequence there were none of the
bickerings, rivalries, and evil comparisons which we
are told now exist there. The immediate neighbor-

hood of Mr. Gore's habitation seemed pleasant
enough, and everything around the farm appeared
to be in excellent order. The house itself was surrounded by a neat white-washed paling; at a short
distance from it was a large wooden barn, half filled
with hay, and between these two was the barnyard,
which contained a number of sleek looking cattle,
no very unpleasant looking objects, be it remembered, to the thrifty agriculturist. Dinner was ready
in some ten or fifteen minutes after the arrival of
Mr. Gore, when master and man, as is the custom in
America, sat down to a very plentiful meal. There
was ham and eggs, potatoes and choice butter, a cup
of coffee and a pumpkin pie, all provided in regal
profusion. The farmer's wife, a very neat looking
woman, was present; and to crown all her niece,
Miss Jones, a young lady somewhat older than Guy,
made her appearance, and with a most engaging
smile she actually sat down and commenced to sip
her coffee. The youth now thought that his lines
indeed had fallen on pleasant places, and that before him lay a goodly heritage. After the repast
was over Guy got up, and assisted his employer in
attending to some outside work till evening; and
when all was over and supper was finished our
friend sat down and penned a most dutiful and
respectful epistle to his aunt, telling her of the success that had already attended his steps in life; and
expatiating at great length on the simplicity, the
good manners, and the absence of anything approaching to aristocratic pride, that was to be found
among the rural population of the State of New
Jersey.

V.

For the next month or two following his engagement with Mr. Gore, our friend and adventurer led
a truly contented and happy life. He rose up early
in the morning; chopped wood; fed the hogs,
horses and cows about the establishment ; carried
water from the pump into the house ; and now and
then, by way of variety, he started a fire in the
kitchen. At six o'clock precisely he marched in to
breakfast ; an event, by the way, which was always
heralded by the music from a big tin horn, said
instrument being usually blown by the sylph-like
Miss Jessie herself. The breakfast over, Guy took
the field and amused himself in sundry innocent
ways—ploughing corn, pitching hay, hoeing potatoes, and so forth, till dinner. Sometimes the pro-
prietor accompanied him in these toils ; sometimes
Guy Averall was left alone at work while his employer started off for Newark. In almost every
respect there seemed to be perfect harmony between
the two, all of which was in happy contrast with
that "come-here-my-man" system which Guy had
occasionally witnessed in the plains and valleys of a
certain old island. At twelve, the big tin horn
sounded once more as the signal for dinner ; and as
Guy was blessed with a glorious appetite at this
time, it is needless to say he did ample justice to the
cheer that was habitually set before him. On one
of these occasions Mr. Gore asked Averall " if there
were any common schools in Ireland ? "

"Plenty of them, " said Guy.

" Then why should the inhabitants of your isle be

accused of such deplorable ignorance?" inquired the one.

"That," said Guy, "is a question which I cannot properly answer."

The dinner over, both parties usually sought the field again, and amused themselves in muscular exertion of various kinds, till the horn gave the signal for supper. After dispatching this meal, the cows were again milked, the hogs and horses were duly fed, the necessary amount of wood was split for the ensuing day, and at the hour of half-past seven or eight, our friend and adventurer had permission to retire to bed. As to sleep, Guy rested like a top, he usually closed his eyes in ten minutes after he lay down, and never opened them till the usual trumpet awoke him from his slumbers in the morning.

As to Guy's educational progress at this particular epoch, it was in mere book matters decidedly slow. Except indeed for an hour or two each Sunday afternoon, he found no time for reading whatever. A good many little scraps of information were nevertheless picked up now and then by our friend as a peripatetic philosopher, for Mr. Gore, although desirous of a good day's work, was not a Sphinx by any means when employed in the fields, and as far as his knowledge went, he was always happy to give Guy the benefit of his information. Sometimes they discussed politics ; when the master generally saw fit to give his opinion on current events as a New Jersey whig, sometimes they chatted away on farming, when the advantages of each particular crop was discussed, then George Washington and the Mexican war came in for a turn ; and Guy Averall was duly enlightened on these subjects. And thus it came to pass that our young friend came to consider his employer, on the whole, as a very intelligent and well informed man, and did not see the slightest objection to him as a possible relative in the future. And indeed this admiration seemed mutual, for Mr. Gore on one occasion, saw fit to flatter the self love of Averall, by telling him that he was the most intelligent and conversable young Irishman that ever he had seen in the course of his whole life, an encomium doubtless rather high flown, even supposing that Guy was somewhat anxious to merit the compliment. Sunday afternoon, the only portion of the week he had to himself, hung somewhat heavily on Averall's hands, for outside the regular supply of newspapers, and an old gazetteer, there was rather a dearth of reading matter in the house, and Guy was too tired with his efforts during the week, to relish anything approaching mere muscular exertion. One day however a book peddler came round, and on looking over his stock, Averall was fortunate enough to discover a brand new life of Napoleon. Now Napoleon is almost certain to be a favorite with most young persons—indeed there is a certain halo about your ideal conqueror which no juvenile can resist, so long as there is a particle of youthful daring about him. Whether it is the young Alexander taming Bucephalus, or David attacking the giant Goliath ; or Bruce riding out at Bannockburn, in front of the troops of King Edward—the effect is still the same. We all admire the hardihood evinced on these occasions, even should we feel disposed, at a more mature age, to criticise the moral aspect of their actions.

Now Guy, being an Irishman, had of course a due proportion of this valorous sentiment about him; and when he opened the volume, and saw all the beautiful pictures that the book contained, he instantly concluded that a wonderful treasure was within his grasp, and fumbling in his pockets for a dollar, he purchased the volume in an instant. Gracious goodness! What delightful wood cuts were scattered, here and there, through the production. In one place were chargers neighing, and horsemen with drawn swords; and Prussians and Austrians stretched on the ground, like so many sheep, while Napoleon the grand, with an aspect more than human, sat calm and imperturbable in the midst of the conflict. Need we characterize any further the leading features of this far seeing and highly interesting work? It was printed in New York, it was published by a strictly moral house; the name of its author was the Reverend John S. C. Abbott; and begging pardon of all connected with the volume at the time, we have here only one question to ask, how could any one purchase such a treasure as this, and at the same time remain one of your ignorant, stupid, whiskey-loving Irishmen, such as we occasionally see depicted in the Harper periodicals?

VI.

But it was not only with simple inhabitants of the county, that Guy was brought in contact at this period; for on a certain occasion he was fortunate enough to meet with a fine lady. One day when our hero was at work in the fields, a somewhat antiquated looking dog-cart, drawn by a couple of mules,

came thundering down the road that passed in front
of Mr. Gore's house. Guy, who had reached the
fence at this instant, was on the point of turning his
horse, so as to run a furrow in the opposite direction, when suddenly the vehicle came to a halt, and
some person or other, from one of the seats, made a
motion as if to beckon the young agriculturist. Guy
paused a moment so as to be certain that his impression on the matter was right, when the hand was
waved even more rapidly than before, and the words
"farmer, farmer" were enunciated in very distinct
tones from the equipage. This demonstration
seemed to imply the desire for an immediate conference, so Guy accordingly left his plough, and leap-
ing over the fence he walked quite leisurely to the
speaker. On approaching nearer, he discovered that
the individual who thus addressed him, was a woman
of decidedly majestic proportions, dressed in a
somewhat faded suit of black silk, with a red shawl
on her shoulders, a brown straw hat on her head, and
armed in one hand with an immense cotton umbrella. Guy wondered in the world who this strange
nondescript could be, when the latter once more
thrust her head out of the vehicle, and commenced
a regular oration : "Oh farmer I'm so glad to see
you, and how do you do this morning? Quite well,
I'm very glad to hear that ! And how are the fields
this morning, and how is the horse you plough with,
and how is everything also in the country ! Farmer
I very seldom ask questions of strangers you know,
but at the same time my curiosity is somewhat excited on one point. Is not that vegetable you now
are ploughing called Indian corn ; and if so is it not

occasionally used as food for cows, horses, oxen and other animals such as we usually find in the rural districts?

"Why yes, ma'am," said Guy, somewhat puzzled by this strange question, "we occasionally make use of it in that way. Sometimes however it is turned to higher and better uses, for the fruit of that plant, as I am creditably informed, is transferred in some localities to certain large buildings with vats and other curious things in them, and there it is manufactured into first rate whiskey."

"The dear good buildings," exclaimed the lady, "with the vats and the other curious things in them, how much satisfaction it would afford me, if I could have the pleasure of looking at them for an instant. But farmer, I have one further question to ask. Is Indian corn considered a farinaceous vegetable?"

"Indeed, madam, I don't know whether to consider it farinaceous or not. We feed it night and morning to both horses and hogs, and they all seem to relish it heartily."

"Relish! do you say. Then it must be farinaceous or live animals such as horses and swine could not possibly fatten on it. But farmer, one further question if you please. Do you love to work in the fields?"

"Don't object," said Guy, "I consider it my business to do so, as long as I am paid for it."

"So it is, so it is, it is your business to plough, just as it is the business of those who are more fortunately situated to paint, to dress, to observe the beauties of nature, or if they happen to be an Emperor of *la belle France*, to crush the haughty Austrians. But, farmer, how long each day do you work in the field ?"

"From six to twelve, and from half past one to seven" said Guy, "about ten or eleven hours in all."

"Why dear me! that is terrible," was the rejoinder. I could never continue at any occupation for more than half an hour at a time. But do you not feel tired when at work in the fields? "

"No I cannot say that I do," answered Guy, "ploughing corn is, after all, but light work ; beside which I have permission to give the horse a rest, once in a while, whenever the weather is more than usually warm."

"The poor dear horses, I do love them so very much" said the lady, with a sympathetic sigh. "The horse indeed is a noble animal; and was created by the god Neptune, according to the heathen conchology, who struck the earth with his trident. But farmer, I have one further inquiry to make—how long have you followed this occupation of tilling the soil ? "

Here Guy was on the point of making an appropriate answer, when the driver of the vehicle, who did not seem in the least to appreciate this talk about agriculture and the animal kingdom, saw fit to interpose with the remark, that their time was but limited, and they must go, " else," said he " I'll be durned if you don't be left behind, by the train, which shortly will be due for Newark."

"Thank you, thank you, coachman," said the lady with the most exalted air imaginable, as if utterly unconscious of the style of address which her Jehu saw fit to adopt. "I declare if my servants and others did not remind me of my duties now and then, I'm afraid that some of them would be sadly neglected. I'm sorry farmer, that I have not time to stay—if I remained with you I should have a great many questions to ask on the subject of agriculture. Coachman you can now drive on, for I would not miss, on any account, the train that is now starting for the city. Good bye, farmer, good bye."

And with these words the lady raised the big cotton umbrella over her head, and the dog-cart started off at a gallop, leaving the astonished Guy in complete ignorance as to the real character and station of the strange catechiser with whom he had just came in contact. He afterwards discovered, however, that the personage in question was simply a woman of magnificent proportions, such as we occasionally discover in the highest and best circles in America.

VII.

The attentive reader will meanwhile enquire how Guy Averall was progressing in that deep design which he at a previous period had formed to lay claim to the heart and hand of the first fair maiden that came across his path, so as to erect a home and habitation for himself in the middle of that sovereign State, of which he then was a resident. In reply to this inquiry, let us answer in brief, that master Averall succeeded in this matter as well as any young man of his age and endowments could reasonably expect. One Sunday afternoon, having already finished a chapter or two of Napoleon, a brilliant idea entered the mind of our hero; to write a love

letter.   He accordingly took pen ink and paper, and
commenced his billet doux in the following style :

GREENVILLE, State of New Jersey,
September 12th, 18—.

Dear and most estimable Miss Jones :—

"He jests at scars who never felt a wound," and
none but those who have experienced the pangs of
love can appreciate the feelings by which I, for a
long time, have most grievously been tormented —."
But having written thus far Guy came to a sudden
halt.   "Oh pshaw!" said he, "if I write to the girl
in this way, she will only giggle at me as a perfect
fool, and then all the chance I have with her will be
lost.   It wont do to attack the citadel by force ; I
must rather make my way to it by slow approaches."
So on a sudden Guy threw the letter that he had already
begun into the fire ; and inwardly resolved to bide
the issue for some time, and be governed in his general course by subsequent events and appearances.
Nor in truth was he without a warrant for indulging
in some expectations.   At this period in his history,
our friend was on the whole, a rather comely looking
fellow.   His form indicated good bodily strength ;
his face was expressive of a bright open disposition ;
his sunny locks, curling round his temples, had
something positively bewitching in them ; while his
eye, so full of hope, seemed the synonym of health-
ful, boyish activity.   Nor was Miss Jessie on the
other hand, without her attractions ; bright, cheerful
lass that she appeared ; our friend, in the long run,
began to look on her as an almost absolute piece of

perfection. As to the previous history of the young
lady, it may be briefly told. Miss Jones, or as the
neighbors chose to call her, Jess Jones, had been left
an orphan by the death of her parents some six
years previous ; and hence, in lack of a more fitting
guardian, her bringing up had devolved on her aunt,
in whose house she was accordingly installed as a
member. And well and dutifully did Mrs. Gore discharge the trust thus reposed in her; for after Miss
Jessie had been subjected to the regular curriculum
of the district school, she was brought home, and
then initiated into all those useful arts, without which
no family can prosper in the country, and which
stand for a good round sum in the rural parts of
America. Talk of your piano threshing and parlez
vous francais, and stuff in which ladies, now-a-days
lay so much stress !—Miss Jones, of course, ignored
such follies as these ; but as far as the baking of the
whitest and nicest bread, and the washing and iron-
ing of the cleanest and snowiest linen, and the man-
ufacture of tarts, jellies, and pumpkin pies, she could
hold her own against any young housewife in the
country. With all these manifold accomplishments
in her possession, is it any wonder that the praise
of Miss Jessie should be on every tongue, and that
Guy Averall, tuft hunting young miscreant that he
was, should in reality and sincerity, cast a longing
eye towards her.

After disposing of his first love letter in the way
already described, the condition of affairs remained
for some time in *statu quo*. Master Averall loved
the girl, there was no doubt about that, the difficulty
with him was to find an appropriate way of convey-

ing his sentiments to his inamorata. He thought of
asking permission to escort her to church, but that
as a proper strategic movement, might possibly have
been too bold; the thought of writing another love
letter and then quietly dropping it into the post
office, but that might subject him to a rebuff, he
thought of fifty other things in succession, but in
the end he gave them all up. So the utmost he
could do was to assist Miss Jessie in some of the
delicate little tasks that fell to her lot, such as hanging out the clothes to dry after they were washed, or
in shelling a few pease for dinner on Sunday, or in
taking hold of a pail of household slop intended for
the hogs, and emptying it himself into the swill
barrel, or better than all, if chance were given, of
applying his own mouth to that big tin horn, which
Miss Jessie usually blew, and summoning the family
together, in proper form to dinner. Once indeed
he had thought of telling Miss Jessie that he should
consider himself the happiest man alive, if he were
the owner of a small farm in the Jerseys, and had
such a wife as she to share his lot, but when the
opportunity presented itself for making this speech,
the tongue of Guy Averall clave to his palate, and
he slunk away, just as if he had been apprehended
in the crime of petty larceny. Oh woman, woman!
what a magical power thou hast, once we yield ourselves to thy influence—you frown, you smile, you
coquette, you command, and in all your varying
moods, we are nothing but your slaves and humble
servants.

At length a grand opportunity came. One day
towards the end of October it was announced that

the great showman, P. T. Barnum, was to visit the
town of East Greenville with a circus, and would
exhibit an infinite number of lions, tigers, and other
wild animals for the amusement and edification of
the inhabitants of that vicinity. Master Averall
now thought that this was his chance, he would com-
bine the useful and agreeable in one act, equip himself in fitting apparel, and ask Miss Jones to accompany him to the exhibition.

He meditated on this subject for a while, and in
due time found a fitting opportunity of stating his
case. The young lady was just leaving the garden
with a big cucumber in her hand, when Guy Averall
broached his project in the most polite and fitting
terms of which he was master. " Would Miss Jessie
be so kind and condescending as to accompany him
to the show—if so he would do his very best to
make the occasion agreeable." Miss Jessie snick-
ered and smiled, in the first instance, when the
request was made, and then a calm expression of
placid delight passed over her own angelic face as
she prudently made answer that she was very much
obliged to Mister Averall for his kind offer, but indeed
she must speak to her aunt on the subject. The aunt,
as Guy was informed that evening after tea, had no
objection whatever to make—Miss Jessie was willing to place herself under his protection—Guy Averall was now in the seventh heaven of delight, so
away he went, the very next day into Newark,
invested all the money he had in a brand new suit
of clothes, and then and there he took a solemn
oath that although these garments had cost him a
goodly sum he was bound and resolved to look

every whit as respectable as any young man of his
age within the limits of " old Essex," the very fore-
most county in the State of which he was a resident.

At length the time for the representation came,
when lack-a-day ! what an amazing display of
bucolic elegance was to be seen, as the citizens of
the said " old Essex," poured into East Greenville
from all directions. Some were on foot and some
on horse, some rode in buggies and some in wagons,
but all alike were bent on seeing that prince of
showmen—the great Barnum. How jovial looking
some of the young sparks from the mountains west
of Orange were,—one could distinguish them at the
distance of half a mile, by the red and green neck-
ties which they wore. Guy put up his horse at a
livery stable, and after resting for a while, he sallied
out in company with his Dulcinea, to view the sur-
roundings. The usual crowd of peddlers, mountebanks and quacks that accompany one of P. T.
Barnums exhibitions was in sight. The first person
who attracted the attention of our friend, was a
cheap Jack near a corner—this eloquent citizen was
mounted on a stand, and was willing to sell the
entire lot of jewelry which he held in his hand,
watch chain, wedding ring, gold sleeve-buttons made
of brass, along with that elegant topaz breast pin
for the insignificant sum of twenty-five cents. What
a stream of glib nonsense the fellow has at his command—no wonder an occasional auditor here and
there, is persuaded to purchase from him. Further
on, an operator in thimble rig offers you the chance
of becoming quite rich, provided you are willing to
take the risk—" you put down one dollar, gentle-

men, and receive back eight, and there is no nonsense about it either." Yonder a professor of leger-
demain takes a number of rings, hands them to the
crowd, so that every one can satisfy himself that there
is not a flaw in the series, and then *presto*, he tosses
them up in the air, joins them in a chain, and afterwards snaps the chain in pieces and presents each ring
separately to the audience. To older persons than
Guy this all seems marvellous, and they really wish
that the sleight-of-hand man would make them the
confident of his wonderful secret. But hark! what
noise is this! the band playing! yes, and I vow
behind it comes the giant procession, headed by the
great Phineas himself. There we have it all ; the
lion, the tiger, the dromedary, the hippopotamus, the
woolly horse that John C. Fremont chased for three
whole days and nights on the top of the Rocky
Mountains, the Japanese mermaid compounded of a
fish and a monkey, the old colored woman who
nursed our venerated Washington when a child, as
well as the thousand and one other curiosities. Guy
immediately purchased a couple of tickets, and
after a little pushing and squeezing, he finally succeeded in escorting his charge into the tent where
the exhibition took place. Here all was wonder
and novelty to Master Guy, for indeed it was the
first circus he ever had attended in the whole course
of his life. Was it not wonderful how that man
walking on stilts could pick up a handkerchief by
leaning backward ; and how the tumbler could
make the somersault over twenty-five horses ; and
how that young lady, with the short skirt, could
stand on the back of a horse going at full gallop,

and afterwards jump through a hoop, covered all
over with tissue paper ! She did it all, however,
quite gracefully ; and what is more, alighted on her
feet, and then bounded into the side tent. And
after all this came the explanations.

" This animal, ladies and gentlemen, as you will
perceive, is the hippopotamus. He differs from all
the beasts of the field and the fowls of the air, in
breathing exclusively through his skin. He is
found along with the crocodile and other wild quad-
rupeds at the bottom of the river Nile, and was
purchased by Mr. P. T. Barnum for the sum of
twenty-five thousand dollars in cash." Here the
crowd signified their approval by the words "well
done," " he knows what he is talking about," " he
is none of your wild Irishmen at any rate," " he is
able to show us the beast in a respectable and intelligent way."

" This personage, ladies and gentlemen, whom I
now bring out before you is a descendant of the
Egyptian priest Manetho. You perceive he wears
a long beard, and is dressed in loose flowing robes.
'He was discovered inside of the pyramid of the
monarch Cheops, by an agent of Mr. P. T. Barnum,
who was engaged at the time in oriental research.
He speaks no language but the Coptic, and writes
no characters but the ancient hieroglyphics, such as
were employed in the valley of the Nile, more than
thirty-five thousand years ago." The priest makes
several figures on the ground, and Guy, at the same
time thinks that his reverence bears an uncommon
likeness to that identical old rascal who met him six
months previously on Broadway, and who almost

forced him into the purchase of that worthless trumpery watch.

"These, ladies and gentleman," continued the instructor are two savages, who were imported some time ago from the island of Timbuctoo. Their history is this, they were caught in a piratical expedition, and were sentenced to be eaten by the king of that country ; but an agent of Mr. P. T. Barnum, who happened to be present, at the time fortunately secured them for exhibition for the space of three years, by giving bonds in the sum of ten thousand dollars for their safe return at the end of that period, when the monarch intends to follow out his original design of making a feast for his court. But any one who is acquainted with Mr. P. T. Barnum is thoroughly aware that he never will submit to such an outrage as that. He has accordingly dispatched a messenger to the king of Timbuctoo to state that he is willing to pay the ten thousand dollars, just as he stipulated, by way of forfeit at the end of the three years, but he can never agree that such innocent strangers as these poor savages are, should swell the hungry gullet of wild cannibals."

This interesting trait of benevolence on the part of the showman, seemed to produce a great effect on the crowd ; and amidst the cries of " Barnum" " Barnum" " Barnum," the head of the establishment was finally induced to come forth.

"Ladies and gentlemen," said the manager, " I feel flattered at receiving this mark of attention from the large and highly interesting audience now before me. I say interesting, for to me there is nothing more satisfactory than seeing a goodly array of

pleasant faces when I happen to visit your own
beautiful village. And here I wish to indulge in a
boast, namely that during my professional career as
a manager, it has been my aim on all occasions, to
furnish my patrons such amusements as would tend
to the elevation of their taste, and their moral improvement also, whenever they saw fit to visit my
show. I say all this emphatically, for no one, either
here or elsewhere, can instance an occasion where I
have catered to a prurient taste, no matter what
might be the tempation. In furnishing you, therefore, with a series of cheap and popular amusements,
I think I have enabled you to pass an hour or two
in an agreeable manner, and at the same time have
done some little service to myself and my country.
But perhaps some one will object that Barnum is an
old humbug. Well perhaps he is, but even admitting that to be the case, still there are other hum-
bugs in the world much bigger than himself. Why,
my dear friends, if the actions and motives of one
half of the great statesmen who figure in history
were analyzed, what a pitiful array of aims, purposes
and proceedings would we have! you yourself would
not like the dissection any more than I, and therefore it is better that the scrutiny should never begin.
Further than this I believe we all admire a little
humbuggery, now and then in a good natured way,
and provided the penalty inflicted is not an exorbitant one, we laugh, and feel more contented with the
world and with each other in consequence. For
myself, I can only say, my desire has always been to
amuse my patrons as well as I possibly can; and
provided I succeed in this, my aim in visiting your

very beautiful and interesting village will be more than accomplished."

Here an immense cheer was given for Barnum, and after witnessing the rest of the performance the crowd separated.

VIII.

BUT let us dismiss these minor topics and proceed with the main current of events. Guy Averall was indeed a happy youth after his return from the town of East Greenville that evening. He had seen the great showman, on whom all agriculturalist far and near do most fondly doat ; and better than that he had the pleasure of accompanying the bright cynosure of his eyes to the place of meeting. As to Miss Jessie he loved her more deeply than ever, and almost vowed in his heart of hearts, that she was simply the very dearest piece of perfection that ever existed. Yet it must not be supposed from all this that there was anything mean or servile in the bearing of Guy Averall, either to his Dulcinea herself, or to those relatives under whom the young lady was placed. On the contrary our hero, on all occasions contrived to sustain his dignity as a man ; and instead of being wholly mercenary as regards Miss Jones, he proposed in an open-hearted manner to do his very best to support her himself, nay further than this, he even saw fit to enter into some very elaborate calculations as to the cost of living in case Miss Jessie and he should actually get married. Let us see—the girl was healthy, industrious and accustomed to work, so instead of being a dead weight, as many young ladies in America now unfor-

tunately are, she would rather be a helpmate and
assistant. Then suppose Guy in the first instance
should rent a small farm on "shares," all he would
have to do would be to provide a couple of horses
and a plough to begin work, and provisions sufficient to last a year—three or four hundred dollars
at the utmost would be sufficient to secure these
articles. Need any young man, in America, who
contemplates matrimony, hesitate for such a trifle
as this ? Certainly not, the thing was a mere baga-
telle, and as to personal clothing and kitchen utensils, that much would come in as Miss Jessie's pro-
vision toward housekeeping. Yes, yes, the course
open to Guy Averall was plain, he was to continue
working with Mr. Gore for the next two or three
years, save his money, invest it like another Jacob
in live stock, and as soon as the increase of these
proved sufficient for his requirements, he was to
purchase that pair of horses of which we have already
spoken, and then he could press his suit as a man
and a citizen of the most lofty intentions. The
only obligation on him just now was not to be too
hasty in speaking of his future plans, especially as
there was no need in disclosing them to any one
just yet, even supposing they were all finally fixed
and determined on.

This programme although feasible and well ma-
tured required nevertheless much time for its accom-
plishment. Meanwhile Guy Averall resolved to
observe a discreet silence in regard to his intentions,
especially as he became somewhat suspicious eventually, of a certain member of the family with which
he now sought to be domesticated   As to Mr. Gore,

he was a hard working, well meaning and independdent Jerseyman in every respect ; but as to the old lady, his wife, Guy thought at times she was slightly supercilious. What was the use of her watching him like a hawk, for instance, every time that he and Miss Jessie were together, even for a few minutes. Bless her heart, Master Averall had talked to fair maidens before now, and was not such a bandit as to whisk off the girl without speaking to her relatives on the subject. But one evening Miss Jessie told Guy a somewhat pitiful tale. She said her aunt, the very day previous, had called her aside into their only parlor, and then and there had uttered due words of caution against all Irishmen. She recounted a very pathetic story of a certain young friend of her's, who lived on the other side of the mountains and who allowed a strange Patlander to approach her with insinuating and deceitful words. This man induced the girl to leave her home and go west with him, where they worked for a while on a farm ; but eventually the husband, after the manner of his countrymen, took to democratic politics and strong drink ; beat his wife and was hauled up before a civil magistrate ; and finally to cap the climax, he forsook his home and companion ; joined a set of strolling play actors who were going through the place ; and is now, if reports be correct, the associate of the worst possible class of criminals and mountebanks. Master Averall felt puzzled, at first, when this strange adventure was recounted ; he however made answer that any person who acted in that way, was deserving of a very severe censure, but hoped nevertheless that

Mrs. Gore did not consider every Hibernian a scape-grace, because one of them proved a black sheep, and a casual acquaintance of hers was the victim. To this very pertinent suggestion, Miss Jessie made answer that she really did not know; she only felt certain that her aunt had taken great care to impress the whole recital on her, and had evidently some very particular reasons for doing so. Guy said nothing further by way of extenuation, except that he was sorry for the mishap, he resolved never-theless to be very careful for the future in his beha-viour, and above all things to give no occasion of offense either to Mrs. Gore herself or to her husband.

For the future, therefore, Master Averall resolved to remain quietly to himself. Sometimes in the evenings, when his usual tasks were over, he pro-duced his Life of Napoleon, and pondered and mused over the deeds and achievements of that amiable and interesting hero. Sometimes the far-mer, when disposed to be communicative, would enlighten Guy as to the true intent and meaning of those old Whig doctrines in which he had been nur-tured; and how Andy Jackson, the hero of New Orleans, had promised on a certain occasion to hang the obstreperous John C. Calhoun of South Carolina as high as Haman. Then the Revolu-tionary war, and mad Anthony Wayne came in for their share of attention; or General Scott and the war with Mexico were duly brought on the carpet. One thing which occasioned considerable surprise to Guy Averall at this time was the unrestrained and apparently unwarrantable abuse which Mr. Gore, now and then, heaped on certain ex-Presidents.

It was nothing but "old Martin Van Buren" or "old Polk of Tennessee" or some other epithet equally irreverent; although, after all, it is to be presumed that both these gentlemen only obeyed the will of the popular majority who elected them. At any rate this constant abuse of ex-Presidents in America, appeared to Guy Averall, in the first instance, as extremely singular. After all, is it not true that there is this objection to making the chief authority of a country elective to wit:—that let his intentions be ever so honest, he never, even at the best of times, can be more than the *chief of a party*, instead of commanding that universal loyalty, to which an executive otherwise ordained might be entitled? This feature of Presidential forms of government, has been noticed in a very distinct manner by one of the most able of modern writers; and certainly the judicial impartiality of Mr. Mill, when speaking of these and similar themes, entitles him to a candid hearing on the part of all who are interested in political science, either in our own or in other countries.

But a truce to this theme ; let us go on with our story. After the warning given him by Miss Jones, the behavior of Guy was in itself truly admirable. He went to church, but it was alone ; he attended an evening spelling school, on one occasion, but remained very quietly in a corner ; he even endeavored to disarm suspicion by allowing Miss Jessie to hang up the washing herself, without offering in a single instance to take the clothing from her delicate little hand and place it on the lines stretched in front of the kitchen. But it was all to no purpose—the eyes of the gods were upon him. The story is a pitiful one but it shall be brief. One morning Master Averall arose at a seasonable hour so as to haul a load of coal from Newark, After feeding his team and attending to his chores in the usual manner, our friend, as was his wont, strayed into that part of the house devoted to culinary operations. Miss Jessie was there grinding the coffee for breakfast, when Guy in an unguarded moment took hold of her hand, gave the mill a turn or two, and then vowed that the lady in question was the prettiest little coffee grinder in existence. Hereupon Miss Jessie laughed and made reply that she considered Guy Averall the biggest humbug in the State of New Jersey. This speech was too much for poor Averall, he really liked the girl, and at the same time felt indignant on account of being the subject of so much suspicion. So he popped down on his knees, and began delivering a speech, on which he had been meditating for the last fortnight, when all in a sudden, he thought he heard a rustling behind him, and on looking round, oh horror of horrors! there stood the old vinegar-faced aunt, Mrs. Gore herself, who unobserved by either party, had been quietly listening to every word that had been uttered. The situation, to say the least, was a very embarrassing one; so Guy in an instant dropped the hand of Miss Jessie, sprang to his feet, hurried back into the barn, and only reappeared when the usual summons was given for breakfast. That meal was consumed in moody silence. Mr. Gore spoke a few words it is true, but as to the other members of the family, they hardly opened their mouths during the time they were together. When dinner came the situation of affairs did not seem to be much different—the " boss " was now absent on business, and as to Miss Jessie and her aunt they both seemed perfectly dumb. This silence was ominious, indeed Guy already suspected his fate. It came in due time, for that very evening, Mr. Gore called the offender aside, paid him his wages, and then remarked that he considered him a very interesting and intelligent young man in many respects, yet as the year's work was about completed— the corn was all gathered, the potatoes had long since been dug, the wood for the winter was mostly chopped—everything finished, in fact, he thought he himself would attend to whatever little tasks might be necessary till spring, and therefore, for the present, he would dispense with Guy Averall and his ervices.

This is the first phase in the education of the principal personage of this history. Its subsequent development will appear in successive Chapters.

I.

Next morning Master Guy bundled up his effects, and in rather thoughtful mood, he once more took the road to Newark. As he sauntered along, his cogitations ran in something approaching the following :—" Well, what an unlucky dog I am—fated, it seems, to be constantly in trouble. A few weeks ago, I was ready to presage for myself all sorts of felicity, when suddenly the ground gives way under my feet, and I am plunged into an abyss from which I scarcely know how to extricate myself. It was an unfortunate thing making love to Miss Jessie so early in the morning; if there had been the smallest particle of common sense in my composition, I might have known that her old hatchet-faced aunt, was likely to be stirring about at that time. I do not see, though, why Mrs. Gore should have taken such a stand against me—I really loved Miss Jessie, and would have done anything in the world to make her comfortable. Well, well, the fates that rule the sky have seen fit to deny me that privilege. Some persons seem born to good luck, and some are not—now there is that fellow Blasedell, whom I saw sneaking round the house, night before last, and who by the way is no more fit to be Jessie's husband than I am fit to be President, and yet because he owns fifty acres of land, and has

a little money in bank, I suppose Mrs. Gore will be
inclined to assist him as far as lies in her power.
Still, I don't know after all why I should care so
much for Miss Jessie—I saw her standing in the
garden, this very morning, and although I was walking away from the house, she never once cast a
single glance towards me. Now that in a young
woman, such as she, was certainly uncomplimentary,
so confound the whole thing—let it go,—for the
present I must look out for myself. I'm sorry I
invested four months wages in this suit—if I had
the price of it just now, the cash would remain in
my pocket till I got something or other by way of
employment. I'm lucky, however, in one respect—
I have no distinguished relatives in this part of the
world to chide me for my misdoings, and read long
homilies in regard to the perversity of the present
generation. I wonder, by the way, if that venerable
aunt of mine, that I left behind me, some time ago,
ever deigns to think of me—if she does, I suppose
she imagines I'm riding in a coach and four with a
liveried servant behind my back, and all this because
I'm here six months in the United States of America! What a delightfully imaginative people, by
the way, these Irish are—bless me! they fancy that
gold dollars can be picked up, like pebble stones, in
every other part of the world except their own.
Hard times with me just now, yet I don't know,
after all, that I can blame Mrs. Gore so much for
what she has done—I suppose she thought it necessary that Miss Jessie should have an adviser at
present rather than a protector. Still it is very
unpleasant to be thrown out of work at this time of

the year, when employment is scarce—especially in
a part of the world where you have rather a slim
acquaintance. Some of the people, though, who
are better off than I, don't seem to realize the goods
within their reach ; on the contrary they grumble
continually, just as if they were the mere puppets
of fortune. Well, well, let the worst come to the
worst, I'll endeavor to be content, for a walking philosopher saw fit to inform me, on one occasion, not
many years ago, that in our own breasts we can
make or mar felicity."

As Guy pondered on these themes he proceeded
onward, and was already within a short distance of
his destination when suddenly he heard a footstep
behind him, and on turning round a somewhat
sprightly specimen of humanity, of apparently thirty-
five years or thereabouts, hailed him with the classical formula *quò te Mæri pedes ? an quo via ducit in
urbem ?* Guy, whose classical knowledge was not
sufficient to enable him to catch the sense of what
was said, was somewhat surprised at this singular
style of address, and after saying something or
other by way of response, he took a deliberate sur-
vey of the stranger. The personage, now before
him, was somewhat below the middle stature, with
chest and shoulders well developed; his complex-
ion, never very fair, was much tanned by exposure ;
his upper lip was garnished with a moustache ;
while a pair of restless black eyes, sunk under his
brows, seemed to be in constant motion, as if in
search of some object on which they might rest for
a second. The dress of the wayfarer was a common suit of Scotch tweed, and an ordinary felt hat

was stuck, with a sort of mock dignity on his head, while a bundle, held in one hand, and a stout stick, carried in the other, seemed to complete his outfit.

"Heigh ho! young fellow," said the man as he approached, and spoke at the same time in an excellent Tipperary accent, "and which way are you bound? To Newark, eh? Do you know what, I have noticed you pondering before me for the last half hour. That is bad—you must not think too much, for as Cæsar says of lean Cassius, such men are dangerous. Why, by the hole o' my coat, if you go on meditating in that way, you'll reduce yourself to the thickness of a wafer; and wafers, you know, serve no other purpose except now and then to fire off a gun, and once in a while to close an envelope. Do you know, sir, that there is a law to be passed by the State of New Jersey, at the next meeting of the legislature, against any person, unless he has passed the age of sixty, who shall presume to hang his head down, and indulge in solitary speculative cogitation! Just think of that law, if you please, and think of your fate in like manner if ever the enactment is put in force against you."

Guy was forced, in the first instance, to smile at this very absurd statement; and then made answer that he, for one, was entirely aware of the power of the state in which he lived; and in case the law were passed he should take notice thereof, and govern himself accordingly.

"Because if you dont," was the remark, "the state, or some of its officers may take the case in hand, indict you before one of its judges for a serious misdemeanor, sentence you to pay a heavy fine,

and in case the amercement is not met—why, by
the powers above, they will consign you to the lock
up at the capital city of Trenton, or what is still
worse, they will turn you over to some of the con-
solidated Railways that now rule this part of the
country, and once you are in the power of these
corporations they will grind you to powder."

Guy smiled once more at this sally, and seeing
that his acquaintance was a fellow of humor, he determined to avail himself of the opening thus accorded, so as to ascertain if there were any possibility of
obtaining employment in that part of the State.

"Employment avick! Is it employment you
are after," said the other, "well, sir, let me inform
you that this word employment is a very indefinite
term. There is plenty of work to be obtained both
here and elsewhere, but the question is, are you
ready to take hold of it? In plain terms, have you
a trade—are you a harness-maker, saddle-maker,
trunk-maker, coach-maker, have you in short been
educated to any specialty? If you have, and the
business has not been stiffled by some accident, you
can doubtless obtain work in Newark. If, on the
contrary, you are nothing more than a gentleman of
elegant leisure, such as I, ready to turn your hand
to anything that comes in your way, then woe is me!
—I'm afraid you're going to have a somewhat hard
time of it. Your case, in short, will resemble that
of the cat and the fox."

"The cat and the fox," said Guy, "what is that?"

"Well," said the stranger, "as I'm a gentleman
and poet, and not overburdened with much business
just now, I'll tell you the story. The cat and the

fox were once travelling together, when the former
remarked she had only one way to get clear of the
dogs. 'Oh nonsense,' said the other, 'I have ten
such tricks in hand, and ten times ten in a bag.'
Soon after the hounds were heard. Puss ran to the
top of a tree and was safe ; while Reynard, in spite
of all his resources, was caught and mangled by the
dogs. The story is a short one, but I wish I could
impress the moral of it on all those who contemplate trying their fortune in America."

"In plain terms," said Guy, "you would not
advise them to come to this part of the world, unless
they have a special training, or else are willing to
rough it till they find their proper level. Well, I am
no flatterer, but permit me to say you talk like a
philosopher."

"Philosopher, pooh," was the answer, "I beg
your pardon. I never made any pretension to that
dignity. My father intended me for the church,
and gave me a tolerable education, I believe, as far
as it went; but I was too big a fool to profit by his
intentions. I got into an ugly scrape, ran away from
home, threw theology to the dogs, and have ever
since been content to remain as a layman. In
fine, as to this charge of being a philosopher, I have
only one word to say, and that is this, if ever I
appear sage-like or didactic, I most humbly ask your
pardon for the offence, for it most certainly was not
intended."

"What a happy frame of mind you seem to possess!" said Guy, "I only wish I could indulge in
the same mood on all occasions."

"There is no reason who you should not indulge
5

in it," was the answer, " My panacea for this melan-
cholic feeling is to enjoy the present and let the
future take care of itself. Did you ever read the
song in Gammar Gurtin's Needle, which I take special pride in, since it was written by a priest ?

> ' I cannot eat but little meat
>   My stomach is not good ;
> But sure I think, that I can drink
>   With him that wears a hood.
> So back and side, go bare, go bare,
>   Both foot and hand go cold ;
> But belly, God, send thee good ale
>   Whether it be new or old.'

That is pretty well quoted, is it not, by one of
your perambulating plebeians ? "

"You impress me more and more every instant,"
said Guy, "for I find you are not only a philosopher
but a wit. But here, without wishing to appear
inquisitive, I would ask one question ? If you are
a poet and gentleman of leisure, how does it happen
that you are not able to gain a livelihood in such a
place as the United States, where every one who
makes the slightest pretensions to learning or literary taste is sure to be amply appreciated."

The stranger came to a pause, suspended his
bundle on the end of his staff, and then placed the
latter very carefully on his shoulder. " Well sir,"
said he, "there is a secret connected with the affair
which I do not care to impart except by saying that
shortly after I landed in these United States, I accidentally came across a good natured relative of
mine, a very respectable old gentleman by the way,
who took me into his family, treated me very well.

and on his bounty I have lived ever since. His
name I wont mention at present, but perhaps I will
find an opportunity of presenting you to my uncle
one of these days. You will like him exceedingly,
I have no doubt, when you see him ; for I assure
you he is as honest and kind-hearted an old gentleman as ever you met in the course of your life.
But a truce to this matter—there is one subject on
which my mind is greatly perplexed at present, that
is to say the precise value of beans."

"Of beans," said Guy, "I don't understand.
Why in the world should you interest yourself particularly in beans."

"Ah pardon me my friend," was the immediate
answer "the bean is a plant which has a mighty
influence on the life of a hero, especially in America.
Sometimes I think long and devoutly on my uncle,
and then beans go up ; sometimes I suffer him to
escape my mind, and as soon as I do, beans go
down. It is one of those occult principles which
philosophers have endeavored in vain to explain ;
and which I, for my part, shall not attempt to
unravel. At present the words of the Sage Pythag-
oras, $\alpha\pi\acute{\epsilon}\chi o\upsilon$ $\kappa\acute{\upsilon}\alpha\mu\tilde{\omega}\nu$, beware of beans, are sounding in my ear, but whether I shall take heed of his
warning or not, is more at present than I can answer,
So adieu ! adieu ! for the present I must hie onwards. I'll determine the value of beans, before
many more hours are over. Meanwhile let me add
one word of advice, don't wear such a melancholy
countenance, my dear young friend, or you will
greatly distress me. We will meet again, I know we
will, although not at Philippi."

And shifting his bundle to the other shoulder, the stranger started off, leaving Guy to the solitude of his own reflections.

II.

MASTER AVERALL enjoyed his liberty during the whole of that day. He wandered around Newark, asked a few questions here and there in regard to employment; was told that work, at that season of the year, was somewhat scarce, and then in lack of anything more definite he stuck his hands in his pockets and said nothing. Once he sauntered into a lodging house, called for something to eat, and afterwards sauntered into the street. Here a couple of musicians attracted his attention. They were Italians, a little boy and a little girl, one carried a harp and the other a fiddle, and to these as an accompaniment, the lad gave the following words, which by a happy circumstance we are able to translate.

> Ho l' arpa al collo, son viggianese;
> Tutta la terra è il mio paese,
> Come la rondin che lascia il nido
> Passo cantando di lido in lido :
> E finchè in seno mi batte il cor
> Dirò canzoni d'armi e di amor.

which may be thus rendered :—

> My harp on my shoulder, I wander and roam,
> No nation is mine, for the world is my home,
> Like the warbler that flies from its parent birds' nest
> I sing in each clime, without pausing to rest.
> And while a true heart in this bosom beats strong
> Of arms and of love shall be ever my song.

" Happy souls ! " said Guy as he stood and listened for awhile, " you Italians are greasy and dirty looking, no doubt, but nevertheless seem contented and happy as you twang your instruments through the streets. I wish I understood Italian. It is a beautiful language, at least so I've been told by those who are instructed in it ; judging *per contra* by the persons who speak it habitually, in this part of the world, I cannot conceive why so much romance should be connected with its sounds, while our noble tongue, the Irish, is altogether contemned and neglected. There is no accounting for tastes in this matter—all we know is simply this, that Ferrara and Fiesole are supposed to be very fine places, while no one in America even wishes to acknowledge he has ever dwelt in Birr or Ballyraggat. Well, well, people will discover in the long run that the Irish are not such a nation of savages as some suppose them to be ; still it will require time and and good conduct on the part of such exiles as inhabit this part of the world, before the old prejudice is indicated." And with these sage comments running through his head, Guy Averall soon sought some other locality.

He sauntered up Market Street, and there saw two butcher boys driving a bargain for a dog; he purchased a copy of the *Newark Advertiser,* and noticed that those old Whig doctrines, which Mr. Gore commended, were thoroughly expounded in that sheet ; he wandered into a tavern and read the advertisement for a negro minstrel entertainment stuck on the wall; he then sought the repose of another establishment, of a similar kind, and was

happy to discover that back of it was a bowling
alley, and that for the sum of twenty-five cents, any
person present had the privilege of participating in
that game. Guy took one of the balls, whirled it
down the alley, made a four stroke at one time and
a six stroke at another, and finally after rolling and
whirling with all his might, the boy who kept the
count told our friend that he had won the game.
His opponent paid the forfeit, and Guy left the
place, but all this did not bring Master Averall that
employment which he sought. The truth was Guy
was somewhat more inclined to speculate than to
work at that particular instant, for at one place he
was offered his board and a couple of dollars a
month, provided he would drive team all winter,
but having already earned three times that sum
while under the protection of Mr. Gore, the young
man did not care to submit to such a terrible reduc-
tion in what he chose to consider his proper wages.
Had he been an ardent enthusiast in this matter of
money making, just then ; had he adhered to those
high resolutions with which his mind was filled when
he proudly trod the deck of the Imperial, Guy
Averall might have commenced his career in this
good city of Newark, toiled at all sorts of ignoble
occupations for ever so many years, and then perchance ended, in due solemnity, by becoming one
of your big millionaires. But a kind providence
reserved him for a different fate. The day following
his arrival in Newark he happened to pass a small
house in the vicinity of the Railway Depot on
Centre Street, and there he observed an advertisement. " Wanted for the United States Army able-

bodied men, to whom will be given good pay, clothing and subsistence." And then followed a statement of the amount paid each grade in the service, with the full sum that Private, Corporal, and Sergeant would receive during the full enlistment of five years. Guy read the account very attentively, asked himself if he would like to be a soldier, and feeling somewhat undecided on the matter was on the point of proceeding onwards, when his attention was attracted by the voice of a person, engaged apparently in scrubbing and singing inside the premises. The individual thus employed, although hid by an intervening wall from the gaze of the public, seemed nevertheless to be as industrious as if the eyes of the whole world were fixed on him. He rubbed away apparently very contentedly, while at intervals his labors were enlivened by a song, which ran in something approaching the following strain :

"Oh the boys in Kilkenny are sweet roving blades "—"a little more wather here if ye plaise " —"whenever they meet with a pretty fair maid "— "that's it Sullivan, down here "—"they kiss her, and they court, spind their money quite free "— "bad luck to it, here is a spot of dirt as big as a plate "—"oh, of all towns in Oireland, Kilkinny for me—oh of all towns in Oireland, Kilkinny for me."

"Well," said Guy to himself, this is no uncertain sound, I rather opine that the singer of these verses is none of your sentimental Italians, at any rate. I'll see who he is." And in an instant Master Averall, who had been completely captivated by the music, entered the room, and was somewhat surprised to see his acquaintance of the previous evening in soldier's uniform, with trowsers tucked up to his knees, his feet bare, a flannel shirt on his back, and a corn broom in his hand, the whole man being engaged apparently in cleaning out the premises in the manner already indicated.

"Heigh ho! young fellow," was the salutation after Guy had made the customary obeisance. "I told you we would meet again; although not at Philippi."

III.

MASTER AVERALL at first felt somewhat disconcerted at this free and easy style of address; but recovering himself he made the usual greeting; and then on glancing round discovered that the person he heard addressed as Sullivan was a broad-shouldered, stout, little Irishman; in shape somewhat resembling his friend, but possessing, in the whole a countenance of less intellectual character than that with which his assistant was gifted. At one side of the room was a plain wooden table, with a couple of chairs; while near the window stood an ordinary office desk, whose pigeon hole compartments seemed to contain a number of official papers. No other furniture was in the room beyond the above articles; unless indeed we except an old coal scuttle, which was artfully secreted in a corner.

After a pause of a few seconds Guy's interlocutor again began, "yes, yes," said he as he shook the broom he held in his hand, "I knew well enough, my dear friend, we would meet before long; although I did not care to specify the exact locality in which the encounter would take place. I knew well enough by the cast of your face, yesterday morning, that before long you would drift into this receptacle for the unfortunate. Still, there are worse places in the world than this, let me assure you. Don't look so hard at that mud puddle before us. Here we are, sir, on the banks of the Styx, waiting for old Charon to ferry us over. Troth that water is black enough and dirty enough in all conscience, but when you have swept out as many barrack rooms as I have, you will cease to wonder at the circumstance."

Without waiting for any reply to the foregoing observations, a vigorous application of the broom to the floor once more took place, and mingled with an occasional splash of water, the chant was again renewed.

"Though the town of Kilkenny there flows a clear straim—Faix, Sullivan, it wasn't like the one now before us at any rate—In the town of Kilkenny there lives a fair dame—I suppose there does, the dames are all fair, both in Kilkenny and everywhere else—Oh her cheeks are like roses and her lips much the same—Sullivan we must hurry up or else we'll not be ready for inspection. Like a dish of sweet strawberries smothered in craime—like a dish of sweet strawberries smothered in craime."

"Why," said Guy, by way of observation, after the last vestige of the black liquid was swept out of doors. "I hardly expected to find any troops in this vicinity. I thought that United States Soldiers were kept on the frontier; excepting, of course, the few who are stationed in permanent forts."

"So they are, but this you see is a peculiar case" said the other. "We are here after recruits. Do you want to join the noble Twenty-sixth Artillery, one of the best Regiments in the service—a regiment, by the way, that numbers among its officers the gallant Captain Daisy, Major by Brevet in the United States Army, as honest an old fellow as ever drew a sword, while his wife is a lady of rare excellence, able to take care of herself and a whole garrison beside. Willing to enlist, eh! Just think of the noble profession of arms, sir, a calling that any young man might be proud of. Or, if you are of a practical turn of mind and eschew romance, let me privately assure you that you cannot do a better thing in the beginning of winter than to turn soldier."

"Is the service of the United States an agreeable occupation?" said Guy.

"Faith that it is, and profitable too," was the answer—"the very greatest service for promotion in the world. You enlist for instance one day. The next, in all probability, your captain takes notice of you as a handsome, well-behaved young fellow, and in an instant you are made Corporal. You continue a Corporal for a few months, for you see it wont do to hurry matters too rapidly, and forthwith you are made Sergeant. War is declared with some foreign power, Mexico for instance, and before you have time to bless yourself, your commission as Lieutenant is forwarded to you from Washington. Once an officer you have nothing but plain sailing before you, for in our Army, the person who lives the longest is sure to rank the highest, even if he should attain to the age of Methuselah. All you have to do is not to waste your opportunities by falling into bad habits; for by my conscience, if I were not an unmitigated blackguard myself, and a constant imbiber of a bad article of whiskey, Private Hogan at your service, might at this moment be a Colonel commanding a Department, or what is still higher, a Brigadier General."

"I'm sorry for you really," said Guy, "if such be indeed the case; mend your manners, however, and you will be all right. One question, meanwhile, let me ask—how does it happen that you have selected Newark as the theatre of your operations. New York, it seems to me, is the proper place to obtain recruits."

"The story is briefly told," was the answer. "About three weeks ago, our Company, then stationed in New York Harbor, was reduced by deaths, desertions and persons discharged, to less than its proper complement of men. I saw at once that this state of things could not be tolerated, so one morning I wrote a letter to the Adjutant General of the Army, asking permission to open a recruiting office in this place, and for the form of the thing I brought the letter to the Captain of our Company, who immediately signed it. Now the Adjutant General and I are great friends; we correspond once or twice a month at the very least, and indeed there are few requests that I make, provided that they are at all reasonable, but sooner or later he sees fit to allow me. In the present case Colonel Jones was particularly gracious, for by return mail there came an official letter granting me all I desired. The whole affair was now settled—Ernest Heidenrick our first Sergeant, who by the way has a flourishing regard for me, was ordered to pack up the company effects, the desk with its official records was assigned to my care, our cook, Mr. Sullivan—allow me to present him—took charge of the camp kettles, and so in the end we all started for Newark, hired this house, put out our advertisement in due form, and here we are, ready to welcome any one who will evince his patriotism, by laying aside the habiliments of a civilian, and assuming the clothing that properly is connected with the glorious Stars and Stripes which float resplendently over our heads."

"Then if I understand you correctly," said Guy, "you are at present engaged in recruiting for the Army."

"Recruiting, why yes, and also cogitating on the value of beans. Delicious vegetable, I assure you, possessed of the most wonderful properties when duly administered to the soldier. Whenever a batallion or two for instance are sent pell mell against the enemy, they are always treated to a plate of soup, concocted in a hasty manner from the esculent. Sullivan give the pot a stir. *Hic coyuus scitè ac munditer condit cibos*—Plautus my boy ; a fine old dramatist, full of archaic spelling. But perhaps I am worrying you with my Latin—if so, I can only offer as an excuse the fact that now and then a few phrases from that tongue will drift through my head, just to remind me of the time when I repeated my *Ave* and *Credo*, with due solemnity, among the boys and black heaths of the old soil itself. But enough on this subject—the Sergeant, God-bless him, will be here before many minutes, and as we are to have an inspection this evening, I must proceed with my work, so as to have every thing neat and respectable in anticipation of the event."

IV.

A FEW flourishes of the broom completed the process of sweeping, after which Mr. Hogan appeared once more in the room ; and remarked that after all he believed he had been in too much of a hurry, that he had full twenty minutes as yet, at his disposal; and therefore he deemed it proper and right to indulge in a " whiff of a smoke." He then lit his pipe with great dignity, stuck his hat on three hairs, asked Guy if he indulged in the weed, and after receiving an answer in the negative, he seated himself on the table, crossed his bare feet in front of it, and then began to puff away with all the solemnity of a Pacha.

"Would you advise a fellow, like me, to enlist," said Guy after a pause of a few seconds.

"I wont advise you either one way or the other," was the answer, " lest at some time you should blame me for urging you to accept what might possibly seem a bad bargain. Still, this much I will, say, that in certain respects the United States deals in a very liberal manner towards its servants ; and as far as pay, clothing and allowances are concerned, there is probably no army in the world so well provided for as our own. Of course there are some hardships and annoyances connected with the service, as every one must admit, but still after trying both citizen and soldier life, I give the preference to the latter. You saw me yesterday morning with a bundle on my back ; well, sir, I was just on

my return from an expedition in the country. The
story is as follows,—it may save to illustrate what I
have said. About three weeks ago, my term of
enlistment had expired, when as luck would have it,
I happened to see an advertisement in the papers
saying that an assistant was required at a celebrated literary place known as the " Laurel Hill
Institute of Gentlemen Cadets " near Newark. This
name " Institute " rather captivated my fancy, so in
default of anything more definite I thought I would
apply for the place. Away accordingly I started.
Without much difficulty I found the principal of
the school, and after a little conversation and examination of some length, I was formally accepted as
tutor. The bargain was this, I must teach the boys
ten hours a day, live on cabbage and Graham rolls,
like the rest of the fraternity, watch the students
from morning till night, report their delinquencies
to the head of affairs, superintend such drills as they
had in the establishment, blow the organ on Sun-
days, and dress like a gentleman beside on the small
sum of twenty-five dollars a month. I stood the
thing for a while ; but in the end the constraint of
the place was too much for me. One morning I had
a quarrel with an insignificant scrub of a boy, son
of the Principal, who seemed to think, Heaven save
the mark, that the care of the entire place rested on
his shoulders. He reported a boy for taking half a
biscuit from a plate that stood in the pantry ; the
boy, who was hungry and afraid of getting a whip-
ping, began to cry—I seeing the affair took the lad's
part, and said it was a mean, insignificant piece of
business to report such a trifle. The young gentle-

man whom I had taken to task then began to make
faces at me, and call me a Paddy of an Irishman,
an insinuation which I am sorry to say I could not
deny. I repaid the compliment by giving the youth
a slap, the father came in and took his son's part,
one word brought on another, till finally I went to
my room, bundled up my effects, demanded my
wages, came into town and enlisted once more, and
and am now Private Tim Hogan of the Twenty-
sixth Artillery, at your very good service."

"And so you like the Army, after all," said Guy,
somewhat amused meanwhile at Mr. Hogan's account
of his efforts at school-teaching.

"Like it! certainly," was the answer, "else I
would not be in it. Glorious place for promotion as
I told you before. Only eschew a bad article of
whiskey, as I already have hinted, and you will be
a Brigadier General, at the very least, before you
die. Of course there are some annoyances—I and
the Sergeant, for instance, have an odd spat now
and then, just by way of amusement; but what of
that,—it is all a sort of by-play. Heidenrick is a
good fellow at the bottom of his heart, and I like
him, at this instant, even in spite of his little pecca-
dillos and faults. But speak of old Satan and he
will appear—in the passage I hear the footsteps of
the great Ernest himself."

In a few seconds a long, lanky, cadaverous looking Teuton, with a squint in one eye and a nose
slightly inflamed, entered the room, and after gazing
around him for some time, he commenced his oration in the following manner.

"Hogan—I vants you to hurry up—get de room

vixed so as to be ready for de Major. Vere are dose babers I dolt you to get ready. Eh! not ready yet. Dunner and blitzen they ought to have peen two hours ago. I zuppose you were talking und gabbling here ven you ought to have peen attending to pusiness."

"I have been attending to business as closely as you," said Hogan, who in spite of the Sergeant's reprimand, did not seem at all abashed.

"No you hav'nt, I huve peen overrun mit pusiness all de morning, bud dunner und blitzen again, vat does dis ere veller vant here?"

"I don't know, you can ask him yourself," responded the clerk.

"Ask him yourself! ist dat de respects you show to your superior non-commissioned officer," exclaimed the Sergeant. "For what you not know petter un that?"

"My education in some respects was rather neglected," replied the other with admirable *sang froid*, "I suppose I must learn an accommodating style of address from you."

"Address—vell I'll improve your address. Go und finish dose babers, as soon as we gets dru de inspection. Und zee that before evening you don't get trunk."

"If I do, I know my fate," was the answer, "but at present I have no relish either for the guard house or for a general court martial. The papers will be finished before evening."

"Und you knabe, vat wants you here, eh?" said the Sergeant, who having disposed of Hogan in the first instance now turned his attention to Guy.

"I have a free foot in this part of the world," responded our friend, " and as a necessary consequence I have made up my mind to enter the Army."

" Vot you enlists—ist dat vot you say. Free man, eh? Land of the brave and home of the free, eh! who taught you dat?"

"I learned it myself," said Guy.

" You learned it yourself,,vot in New Jersey! Vell den you knabe, let me ask you one question. Do you expects to be any more free vonce you enlists?"

"I don't know" was the anwer.

" You don't know just now, but before long you will find it out. However, I enlists you. Come here to-morrow morning at nine o'clock, und we vill see vat we can do mit you. I vill talk to the Major."

While this dialogue was progressing between Guy and the Sergeant, the clerk Hogan saw fit to retire to a back room which contained his accoutrements ; and in a few minutes afterwards he re-appeared in clean boots, clean trousers, and clean jacket, his tout ensemble being the very personification of military neatness. How any person could change his habiliments in the few seconds that Hogan required for that purpose was a mystery which Guy Averall could not comprehend. Having, however, completed his examination of the clerk, Master Averall sauntered out of the premises. As he was going down the hallway, a very quiet looking little man in uniform passed him ; and shortly afterwards the voice of the Sergeant was heard giving the word "attention," a polysyllable which is always pronounced in military circles, when an officer of the United States Army enters a room that

6

is occupied by enlisted men. Guy Averall immediately surmised that the inspection, to which reference had been made already, was now going on;
and that the personage who had passed him, when
making his exit, was neither more or less than that
gallant Captain Daisy.

V.

DURING the evening Guy Averall retired to his
lodging house, and while there began to cogitate on
the career now open before him. He thought of
that wonderful history which he had been reading
a short time previous; he though of Austerlitz,
Jena, and the terrible passage of the bridge of Lodi,
he thought of the possibility of rivalling these feats
of arms in the United States of America; enlisting,
in short, as a simple private, and finishing his course
as chief of some brigade in the Republican service.
Was there anything impossible in this. Certainly
not;—did not Ney, Victor, and a score of others,
all originally rise from the ranks, and can it be said
that such a country as the United States, the
chances of promotion are less than in the older
nations of Europe! The thing is preposterous,
Guy Averall will be Brigadier General yet—that's
settled. But here a slight suspicion passed over
the mind of our hero—perhaps, after all, the chances
for elevation in the American Army were not so
brilliant as at first sight they may seem—perhaps
the man who enlists under the Stars and Stripes is
uncertain, in default of patronage, to attain the
higher grades, and that when the clerk Hogan spoke
of rapid promotions the words were uttered in pure

irony. Well, even so—the life of a soldier, after
all, is not to be despised. The changes from station would afford an excellent opportunity of seeing
the country, and as to the mere act of enlisting,
there was certainly nothing disreputable in it.
Yes, a soldier's calling, let people say as they may,
is an honest, and as the world is now constituted a
necessary one ; and although sentimental humanita-
rians may preach, it will be a long time before we
can dispense with a uniform. As to the individuals
in the Army, it is only natural to suppose that there
are the good, the bad and the indifferent among
them, just as we have these several classes everywhere else. A truce then to this hesitation—to-
morrow our adventurer will enter in a new career—
perhaps the step he is now about to take may be
attended with good luck; but even if the contrary
should happen, Guy Averall will surely inflict no
injury on any one but himself.

Next morning, therefore, according to command,
Master Averall appeared at the recruiting office,
where the usual formalities pertaining to enlistment
were dispatched. Guy underwent a medical examination, took the customary oath, signed his papers
before a notary public, and now stood a full private
in the United States service. At first an objection
was made on account of his age, but when Guy
stated that he was his own master, and consequently
no officious relative could claim him as a runaway,
the demurrer was withdrawn. It is but right to say
that in this entire transaction, even in spite of
Hogan's exaggerated statements, there was nothing
but fair dealing exhibited on the part of the govern-

ment. The amount of the private's pay, which was then seven dollars a month, was clearly stated ; the clothing given to him was mentioned ; while no attempt was made to conceal the fact that the engagement itself was a somewhat lengthy one, and could not be terminated on either side by mere caprice. In fact all efforts at misrepresentation, in order to induce young men to enlist, is steadily dis-countenanced at Washington; and indeed the good Captain Daisy was by nature too inert to extol the service to anything beyond its merits. When Guy had taken the required oath, he simply contented himself, as Hogan had already done, with adminis-tering some seasonable advice on the prevailing offence of intoxication.

"When you get into the Darmy," said the official speaking through his nose, and looking at the same time very earnestly at Guy, " when you get in the Darmy, be careful to avoid pad trink. Young men ruin their constitution by too much stimulant, now a days—pad trink causes fights after bay day and garrison court martials and that sort of thing—whiskey, my dear young man, is the source of an infinite amount of trouble."

" I never, as yet, have been guilty of any excess in that way," said Guy.

" Yes, I know, I know," was the answer, " but still the temptation is too much for young men, even in spite of their good resolutions. Let pad trink alone, and you will be all right. Dat will do. Sergeant, if a good strong man, fit to look after a horse and work a bangle should enlist, send him to me or Mrs. Daisy by all means. I want a man of that sort, but see that he is regular in his habits, at the same time; for this thing of pad trink has given me more trouble than all the other evils in the Army put together."

At this instant the clerk Hogan appeared with some papers requiring the Captain's signature, and Averall stepped out. Five or six other recruits were accepted that morning in due form; for in truth the cold weather seemed to have a magical effect on New Jersey patriotism, as far as one branch of the service was concerned. Of those enlisted on the present occasion, two were Irishmen, two were Germans, one was an American and one was a native of Canada—these members indeed may serve as an indication of the different nationalities which are found under ordinary circumstances in the Army. The Irishmen and Germans were like Guy fresh importations; the Canadian had been drifting around Newark for some time; as to the American, whose name was Petersen, he was a good-natured whimsical fellow, who at one time had been a printer in the interior of Pennsylvania, more recently a lecturer on phrenology, and now seemed resolved to turn soldier as he expressed it "just for a lark." One appendage which he carried in his hand must not be forgotten in this place—a box containing a collection of skulls, and on these, as fragments of phrenological science, an immense value seemed to be placed. Guy, nevertheless, in talking with Petersen found him a man of considerable information, and hence he determined to cultivate his acquaintance as thoroughly as possible. In return, the printer gave Guy a long description of such manners and usages as were prevalent among the Ger-

man population of his native state; told him of the
Mennonites, Dunkards, and other religious bodies
found among them; and finally, wound up with an
account of that curious custom called "bundling,"
which permits a couple who contemplate marriage
to occupy temporary the same nocturnal couch, but
visits with the most condign punishment any violation of the seventh commandment.

AFLOAT.

I.

THE morning after the enlistment of Master Guy a grand discussion took place in the recruiting depot on a point to which the mind of the military man naturally reverts; namely, the composition and character of the armies of the different countries of Europe at the present time. The place of meeting was the mess room; the speakers were the more verdant recruits, who had joined the service the day previous, and the particular theme which engaged their attention, in the first instance, was the famous battle of Waterloo, and the part that was borne in it by the several contestants, French, Prussians and English, who were there engaged. A profound admiration for barbaric force was evidently the prominent trait during the debate, while each interlocutor spoke according to his individual predilection, and endeavored above all things to uphold the honor of that nation which he was inclined to claim as his own.

"The Frinch, I maintain, are the best troops that the world has ever seen," exclaimed one speaker, an Irishman from the County Cork.

"In steadiness and discipline, they cannot for a moment be compared to those under John Bull," was the appropriate answer, as given by a Canadian.

"Yes, but by gar, when the old Brussians came in, both Vrench and English have to submit," was the rejoinder, put forward by the German.

" Bosh, nonsense, the Prussians were whipped again and again, during the wars with Napoleon; while the English under Wellington were never beaten," said the Canadian.

" How do you account for Wellington's exclamation about wishing for night on Blucher, during the progress of the fight ? " asked the Irishman with a proud look.

" How do you account for the repulse of the old guard, with the shouts of *tout est perdu* which followed ? " was the reply.

" The Frinch took one of the positions in front of the English, even in spite of their teeth," remarked the one.

" The English held the chateau of Hogoumont, notwithstanding the best efforts of their adversaries to dislodge them," replied the other.

" During the last hours of the fight, the British reserves were all in line, and even then they were almost used up."

" The French outnumbered their opponents in the beginning of the affray, and were repulsed again and again by inferior forces."

" Yes, but if it had not been for the old Brussians what could Wellington have done ? Napoleon would have renewed the attack, and would have whipped the British, spite of their teeth."

It is not known how long this discourse would have lasted, or where it would have ended, had not the amiable Heidenrick appeared at this juncture and cut it somewhat short. " Dunner und blitzen," said he, as he thrust his head into the room, "for what are all you vellers making this tammed noise

for. You two Irish yellers, I can hear your voice
all over de house, und you tammed Dutchman too,
you are every pit as pad as the rest. For what you
not know that I expects peace and quietness in
these quarters till I gives you leave to speak. Zo
you learn good manners and keep quiet at once."

The peremptory style in which these words were
uttered, served as a damper upon any further debate ; after all was quieted however, an old Scotchman, called Moldwell, who had formerly served in
the Twenty-sixth Artillery, and who had re-enlisted
that very morning remarked : "Is there not something senseless," he said, in this exaltation of human
slaughter, as the most sublime of earthly qualities.
Some of the greatest pests the world has ever seen
were remarkable for their love of fighting, but in
spite of the pyramid of skulls which they erect, here
and there, every one despises and abhors them. As
to Napoleon Bonaparte, he was undoubtedly a very
great man ; but it is not the number of persons
that he killed that constitutes his claim in our admiration, but rather the skill he evinced in commanding men and in bringing his own country under the
dominion of order, at a time when it was completely disorganized. Without these qualities he
would have been nothing better than a Gengis Khan
or an Attila."

"I understand your meaning," replied Guy, "but
after all, your conqueror, be he good or bad, is a
mighty interesting fellow ; and in addition it seems
to me that a people who do not advocate a proper
sentiment of honor in the profession of arms leave
a poor legacy to their successors. I have lately

been reading one of the greatest work on history, that probably ever was written, and as long as I have Abbott and his narrative at my back, I care little for these petty cavillings." And having delivered himself in this truly oracular manner Guy Averall made his escape from the recruiting station, and in company with the clerk Hogan, he afterwards sought the street.

"Thank Heaven we are free from the tongue of that old boor, at any rate—I mean Heidenrick of course," said the scribe as soon as he had gained the outer air, "we can now go round the city, like free men. Wont you come along with me, till we see some of the sights?"

To this proposition Guy immediately assented, but they had not proceeded very far before Averall noticed a couple of rather rough looking fellows, of the Irish persuasion, coming out of a whiskey shop, and swaggering before him down the street. They were both dressed in a half-ragged, half-careless style, but seemed to be in the best possible spirits, for after proceeding a few paces they struck up the following chorus:

> Where'eer we go we make a noise,
>   Paint blue eyes black, and flatten noses,
> Kick up a row among the boys,
>   And level those who dare oppose us.
>   Bow, wow, wow. Yankee Doodle now,
>   Give us a chance for a while to maltreat you.
>   Bow, wow, wow.

"Humorous certainly," said Guy, "our country is occasionally honored, in the representatives that are thrust before the public."

"Honored! of course it is," was the response.
"There is no Irishman, in these United States, who
does not feel proud of the fact that he has such
compatriots as these. But listen once more to the
music."

After a while the swaggerers continued,

> No Tory Judge in the land of the free,
>   To hang, draw, quarter and abuse us,
> No Justice of the Peace, save those that we elect,
>   To souse a bully boy, if he happens to abuse us,
>   Bow, wow, wow. Yankee Doodle now,
>   Give us a chance for a while to maltreat you.
>   Bow, wow, wow.

"What an unmitigated couple of ruffians," said
Guy, speaking in this instance from the bottom of
his heart. "Do you find many such as these in the
United States service?"

"Why no," was the answer "military discipline
hardly agrees with them. Such fellows as these
prefer the freedom of citizen life, where they can
roam at large. They run to fires; act as repeaters
at election time; vote the democratic ticket; and,
generally speaking, contrive to pick up a living in
all sorts of ways, provided they can get clear of
continuous, steady work. In this particular locality
we call such fellows as these the 'livelies;' a word
which expresses the free and easy disposition which
is habitual to them. All Irishmen, my dear friend,
in these parts, are divided into two classes the
'livelies,' and the 'dulls.' The last contrive to
save a little money, now and then, and do not differ
essentially from the great body of citizens by whom
they are surrounded. The others manage to spend

even more than they earn; yes, and what is still better, spend it with considerable eclat!"

"Eclat! that may be," said Guy, "but somehow or other, I cannot say that I admire their free and easy style of living. Still, let us not be too hasty, perhaps they may not be as bad as they seem, and therefore it would be wrong to prejudge them."

At this instant the two worthies were joined by a confederate, somewhat bigger than either, and the three remained together in consultation respecting some question of local politics which then engaged their attention. After a few seconds, a woman who was peddling oranges, came into the street; and as an orange to the mobocracy is a fruit somewhat distasteful, it was resolved forthwith to attack her. No sooner said than done, in a trice the poor woman was upset, her fruit was scattered over the pavement, and while two of the rowdies ran away, the third began to pick up the contents of the basket and transfer them instantly to his pocket. But he had hardly proceeded any length, when the woman bethought her of her remedy; and began screaming "police, police" at the top of her voice.

There was a long pause before any policeman appeared, but finally a gentleman, in citizen attire, with a star on his breast, became visible, and asked the woman what was the matter?

"What's the matter, is it, yer after axin" was the response "Faix plinty iv matter, I assure you. Look at that hangdog looking ruffian, who has just ran round the corner. He has upset me basket iv daicent oranges into the gutter; and that other main looking villain, with the dirty brown coat, has

stolen the half of them, och hone! och hone! that
iver I should see this day! Here are all my savings
and scrapings, after struggling for tin long years in
Amerikay, scattered abroad in an instant."

"Well, what do you wish me to do in this matter?"

"Wish you to do in the matter! And are ye
after axin me such a question as that. Why arrest
the bloody villian of course; and put him in jail;
and let him be tried for insultin and abusin as daicent
and respectable a woman, as ever trod the streets of
Newark."

"It is your fault, not his," said the Policeman
with a grunt.

"Well did I ivir—" said the woman. But just
at this moment the official began to reflect that perhaps, after all, it was better for him to put the law
in force, and arrest the plunderer, who was now proceeding leisurely up the street.

He started forward in order to put this design
into execution, but hardly had he touched the first
offender, when one of the other confederates appeared on the scene. This man seemed to be an
adept in the arts of the street; for just as the policeman was on the point of making the arrest, he came
behind the latter, tripped him up very skilfully with
one foot, hit the official a blow on the neck when
falling, and then both he and his friend scampered
off, as fast as their feet could carry them. Meanwhile the unfortunate woman, on whom the assault
had been made, collected such remnants of her fruit
as she could secure, and then started home, mutter-
ing her discontent as best she could.

" Well, well," said Guy when the whole thing was over, " this certainly is one of the most wonderful affairs I ever saw in the whole course of my life. Is this the popular government which we have in America ? "

" Speak reverentially of the gods " said Mr. Hogan with a look which defied criticism, " else their majesties will visit you, on a sudden, with Nemesis at their heels. You are now in a part of the world where valor is supreme, accompanied with occasional flashes of wit and humor. Democracy makes us all happy. This is what is known as the buily sixty-fourth ward ; and we are now standing in the city of Newark."

Mr. Hogan was facetious; his parts indeed shone out on several occasions, during the day; and towards evening, as they were returning together to the recruiting station, Guy Averall took the liberty of suggesting once more that a gentleman of the varied attainments of the clerk, could readily find more profitable occupation than in the Army. At first Hogan made no direct reply to this remark, but after both friends were seated in the company office, the scribe heaved a sigh, and then observed that there was indeed a fatality connected with the service, for once a person had joined it he was doomed again and again to re-enlist. " Still," said he, " I enjoy the army heartily, spite of Heidenrick, and following out this notion, I on one occasion, composed a few verses on the subject, which with your kind permission I should like to sing, as expressive of the feelings of an old soldier like myself, after he has taken refuge for the third or fourth time under the United States flag."

" Let us hear them," exclaimed Guy.

And in accordance with this invitation, the bard, after sitting down on a chair, crossed his legs, and when his cap had been adjusted in proper style, he favored Private Averall with the following ode.

Where'er I've wandered, and calmly pondered,
   On back pay squandered, 'twixt me and you,
There comes a twitching, mild and bewitching,
   That urges me for to don the blue.
Whether kissing, courting, or drinking, sporting,
   With chums consorting, the same is true,
For some gentle spirit, that I inherit,
   Whispers, " Hogan, boy, put on Army blue."

I've oft resisted, and turned and twisted,
   And still insisted, for some other hue,
But the thing's so taking, there's no forsaking,
   That piece of cloth they call Army blue.
Since then I'm fated, thus to be mated,
   To the dear coat is full honor due,
I long have known it, ne'er will disown it,
   That piece of cloth they call Army blue.

These stanza's sung to that well-known air, " The Groves of Blarney," were received with fitting applause, and after the conclusion of the ode both parties proceeded to their supper.

II.

In a couple of days after the foregoing events, the men already enlisted were assembled, and put into uniform, after which Sergeant Heidenrick informed them that he had orders to dispatch the party without delay to their ultimate resting place, Fort Columbus, New York Harbor. A grand bundling of effects now followed; and as Sullivan, the cook, had shown himself to be a man of mettle, in a dispute with a noisy recruit, the day previous, he was accordingly put in charge of the party. As to Guy Averall the news of this transfer to a regular military station delighted him exceedingly; he longed, in fact, to buckle on his armor, and show himself a soldier, ready for fight. Respecting his old flame, Miss Jessie, he had already banished her from his mind, and was resolved to maintain a warlike attitude towards her, and also to the rest of her sex, as long as he remained in the service. So he strapped on his knapsack, slung his haversack over one shoulder, and in company with the rest of the recruits, he marched to the Market Street Depot in Newark, so as to take the cars for his ultimate destination at as early a period as possible.

On their way across those salt marshes that lie on the road to New York, a very pleasant conversation took place among the members of the party, for after the battle of Waterloo had been again discussed, and the Prussian, English, and French armies had all been arranged in their respective order of merit, the bard Mr. Hogan, saw proper to prefer a request to the phrenologist Peterson, so as to obtain a glance at the box which contained the collection of skulls belonging to the latter. "My dear sir, won't you let us have a look at your curiosities?"

"With all my heart, with all my heart," was the immediate answer. "Glad, sir, to find that you take an interest in the form of heads. Phrenology, let me assure you, is really one of the most sublime and useful of the sciences." And, in an instant, the box which contained the craniological specimens, under charge of the printer, was dragged from its resting place, under his seat, and a very fine sample of the upper portion of the human frame was placed in the hands of the speaker.

"Why may not this be the skull of a lawyer ?" said Hogan, who chose to quote Hamlet, after he had obtained possession of the relic. "Where be his quiddits now, his quillets, his cases, his tenures, and his tricks ? Humph ! This fellow might be in 's time a great buyer of land, with his statutes, his recognizances, his fines, his double vouchers, his recoveries. Is this the fine of his fines, and the recovery of his recoveries, to have his fine pate full of fine dirt ? Will his vouchers vouch him no more of his purchases, and double ones too, than the length and breadth of a pair of indentures ? The very conveyance of his lands will hardly lie in this box ; and must the inheritor himself have no more ? I presume, Mr. Peterson, you have studied Shakspeare ?"

"Gad, I have," said Peterson ; and what is better have acted him too, and just as soon as we get established in regular quarters, I propose that some of us gentlemen of taste, should form a Thespian society, so as to give a proper representation of Hamlet. Can I count on you, sir, as one of our members. Glad to see you have an appreciation of that noble science of which I am a devotee ; although in point of fact, that head over which you have been spouting, did not belong to a lawyer at all, but to a French carter, a man of an enormous appetite, just feel his bump of alimentativeness, if you please, who died in consequence of eating a large quantity of watermelons. Indeed, I secured his skull on ac-

7

count of his untimely end, and now consider it one of the most precious relics in my collection."

"I understand," said Hogan. "Meanwhile let me ask has it not been objected to phrenology, that while there may be some general truth in the science, it is folly to suppose that there are so many minute divisions in the brain, each one connected with a particular faculty, as its advocates suppose?"

"Such an objection as that savors of ignorance," was the reply. "The truths of phrenology, my dear sir, rest on a basis which cannot be shaken. Observation and induction are all we rely on, in support of our claims; the philosophy of Bacon, neither more or less, if you please. The world has seldom seen two greater men then Doctors Gall and Spurzheim, to whom we are indebted for the formation of this new system. Here sir, in this part of the head, we have the animal propensities; while the intellectual faculties such as comparison and causality are found in another. For ages men have been groping in the dark, with the so-called science of metaphysics, and what is the result? Why simply a conglomeration of systems, in which each philosopher says all his predecessors are wrong, and he alone is right. But with phrenology the case is different. Nothing is assumed till it is proven, and as a consequence we have positive results, instead of mere speculation, as is the case with the earlier metaphysicians. At present, gentlemen, the subject of phrenology is only half appreciated by the general public; the time will come, nevertheless, when its claims will be better understood, and I verily believe, that the day is not far distant, when instead of

selecting officers for public trusts, by random elec-
tions, as we now do, the candidates for office will
have their heads submitted to a college of experts,
who after handling their bumps, in due order, will
decide which person among them is best fitted for
public confidence."

Hogan was on the point of protesting against
the grovelling view of human life and human actions
which the phrenologist had enunciated, but just as
he was entering his objection the train reached
Jersey City. In due time the party got out of the
cars, crossed the North River in a ferry boat, marched
to the Battery, and getting into a barge that seemed
to be awaiting them, they were soon conveyed to
Governors' Island. This place as is well known, is
situated at the distance of about one thousand yards
from the southern extremity of New York city, and
is separated from the shore of Long Island by a
channel of considerable depth. According to official report, its whole extent is something over sixty
two acres, all of which is devoted to military purposes. On the north-western extremity of the
Island, a somewhat conspicuous object is presented in
a structure known as Castle Williams, a circular
stone building, with three tiers of casemates and a
battery in barbette. The Fort itself occupies the
highest points of the Island, and is described as an
"old-fashioned, four bastioned Fort, with a deep
ditch." During the summer months the surface of
the Island is covered with a green sward, and presents a very pleasing appearance, when viewed from
the deck of vessels, going into or leaving the Harbor.
In one portion of the place is the ground appro-

priated to the Ordnance Department, and as Guy
Averall proceeded from the boat which conveyed
him to his final resting place, a curious feeling came
over him, for the piles of shot and shell which he
passed, the rows of guns placed on skids awaiting
shipment, and afterward the grim outline of the fort
itself, all served to fill him with a sort of military
awe which even his best philosophy was not able to
conquer. At this particular juncture, however, Private Sullivan, the soldier in charge, was graciously
pleased to remind our friend that he need not be
gaping around, just as if he had never heard of a
Fort, to close up the ranks, and take the proper
step, instead of staring around him like a wild "om-
hadoun."

After disposing of their effects in a suitable manner, the squad was marched to the kitchen, where
the orthodox dinner of bread, meat, and that bean
soup which Hogan had already eulogized, was
served. After this, the recruits were turned out and
put through the first principles of the drill—"by
the right flank"—"about face"—and above all
"the position of the soldier." As to marching forward in line, that at present was beyond the power
of any one individual of the party, for in spite of
all the explanations which Sullivan made, some
would face to the right when the command was
given to the left; and *vice versa* the left would be
mistaken for the right on some other occasion.
There is a legend current at most military posts of
a certain tyro in arms, who was so stupid that all
efforts to teach him his drill were futile, so a rope of
hay was fastened round one foot, and a rope of

straw round another; and then by giving the commands "hay foot," "straw foot," "hay foot," "straw foot," in succession, the young man was finally taught to march. But not one of Guy's party, we are happy to say, was so dull as to require anything of this kind. In the course of three or four weeks indeed, they were all adjudged to be competent soldiers, and were accordingly assigned to the same duties as the other members of the command.

III.

AFTER his transfer to Governor's Island, Guy Averall remained on the whole in a very contented and happy frame of mind. He walked around the Island, watched the steamboats and shipping as they moved up and down the bay; cast a wistful eye, now and then, at the big city which lay on the opposite side of the harbor, and when in company with some friend he discussed such questions of morals and metaphysics as the circumstances or the times might suggest. As to the reading pursued at this time by Master Guy, it is only necessary to say that for the present the Life of Napoleon was laid aside, and in its place was substituted such knowledge as could be gathered from the daily press. The *Sun*, the *Herald*, and the *Tribune ;* all of them New York papers, were laid under contribution. And here we would forewarn your terribly wise and terribly learned personage, not to affect the bearing supercilious, when this particular description of reading matter is mentioned. It plays a very important part in modern life ; and for that very reason, if for no other, we cannot afford to either despise or ignore it. Newspapers, we grant, in many cases, are anything rather than oracles ; indeed, as far as public events are concerned, the opinions expressed in them, are often hastily formed ; and are frequently forgotten as soon as uttered.   Yet after all they form the best vehicle, by all odds, that has yet been invented for informing the general public respecting current events.   What a treasure to us a series of Athenian newspapers, for instance, would be ; what an insight they would give us regarding the every day life of the violet-crowned city.   How much might an opinion be modified, of this or that public character, if only their actions and speeches were periodically reported ?   Some newspapers may be mercenary, but at the very most, a mercenary press is surely much better than a muzzled press.   No country can long preserve its liberty where a free expression of opinion is not at all times tolerated.

So much on this subject, let us now proceed to another.   As to the officers then stationed at Fort Columbus—Master Averall, of course, saw them every now and then.   Sometimes he met ·them on parade ; sometimes he passed them on the sidewalk, and on such occasions he touched his cap, in a dutiful and respectful manner, as each and every soldier in the American Army is bound by Regulations to do.   But to criticise them, even in the smallest matter, he found himself utterly incapable of doing, and therefore he never attempted anything of the kind.   To be candid, however, they all seemed to be well behaved, well conducted gentlemen, who attended to their military duties day after day ; and if there were any exceptions to the rule, it certainly did not appear upon the surface. Indeed, in the favorable opinion thus formed, Guy Averall was happy to find that the notions of other enlisted men coincided exactly with his own, for they all spoke in praise of their officers, considering them evidently the finest set of young fellows that drew the breath of life at that instant. One evening, for instance, as Guy Averall was walking round the Island, in company with the old Scotchman whose name has already been mentioned, he enquired the title of the present commandant.

"Why Captain Le Froy," was the answer " as gallant and polite a gentleman as ever lived. He comes from an old French family, in the State of South Carolina, and has embraced the military profession, from pure ardor and love of country. He graduated very high in West Point, I am told, has an immense amount of scientific and other lore, and is always devising some new improvement in tactical manœuvres. If a quarrel were to break out with Mexico, or any other foreign country, I'll venture to prophesy, that Le Froy, line officer although he now is, will be a full Brigadier-General before many months are over."

"And the Lieutenants of our Company, who are they?"

"The senior, a very good man by the way. is at present absent on detached service ; those present are two young gentlemen, recent graduates of West Point, the name of the one is George F. Spruce, and the name of the other is Theophilus Z. Taper, Esq., both as handsome and polite young men, as ever wore shoe leather. The knowledge that these officers

have is immense.   Calculus, the science and art of
war, grand strategy, and the most recondite principles of engineering, are all on their finger ends like
so many chopsticks.   For one thing, however, I will
give them credit ; namely, that they are both excellent drill instructors, as indeed most of our young
officers are ; and in a couple of years, when they get
rid of their lady love notions, and have a little more
practical experience of us rough soldiers, they will
both become very useful and valuable men."

"The course of training at West Point is quite a
severe test; at least so I have been led from newspaper stories to believe," said Guy.

"In a certain sense it is," was the answer.   "Of
course it is purely technical, as is the case in all military colleges, yet to master it thoroughly, in the four
or five years allotted to study, requires both capacity
and considerable powers of application.   The moral
training at West Point is also, in my opinion, much
superior to that which prevails in most American
colleges, where the students prevaricate, and play
dirty, nasty litle tricks on each other, in a way that is
almost beyond belief.   I shrewdly suspect, however,
as far as West Point is concerned, that while great
credit is due a portion of each class, for their technical skill, another section, per contra, are extremely
slip-shod in their acquirements.   It is the old story
of the really good student, and the one who has just
sufficient ability to pass.   Why it is only a few days
since I had to show a West Point man how to perform a very common arithmetical computation.   The
case, no doubt, was an exceptional one, and yet the
circumstance in itself served to suggest, either that

the mind of this functionary was not much given to exact formula; or else that a very large portion of that mathematical lore, on which so much care is expended, is very soon forgotten after the student leaves the Academy."

"Are young men ever sent to West Point through family influence?" said Guy, who really was then ignorant of the usual mode of appointment.

"My dear young friend," was the answer," this thing of a family possessing hereditary influence, in political affairs is one of your wild uncultivated notions, and is almost entirely unknown in America. Even an Adams or a Washington, could hardly rally at the present time a score of followers, by virtue of his name, with us personal merit, or perhaps I should say personal exertions at election time are every thing; and since each representative in Congress is vested with the power of nominating the cadet to which his district is entitled, the appointment is made from political considerations alone. Hence the young aspirant for military honors may belong to a family in which mental culture is hereditary; or on the contrary he may belong to one in which the opposite is the case. But in either contingency his treatment is precisely the same as at the Military Academy, once he is admitted there; indeed I know an instance, which occured not long ago, where the son of a great millionaire, was at the foot of his class, and as a consequence was consigned to the Infantry; while the son of a working miller graduated first and became an Engineer. This is all as it should be, and is certainly an improvement on the usages which obtain in other departments of public life. Further than this,

the number of men under military rule is sufficiently
large to constitute a society, with its own code of
propriety and usages, and to this code, which is in
the main I think, an honorable one, all the members
are bound by general opinion to conform. Among
the officers of the Army we have occasionally one, it
is true, who now and then ventures on some extraordinary thing; but these wild birds, as a general
rule, are not found among those who graduate in a
regular way. The deficiency then falls upon the
other subdivision who receive commissions; I mean,
of course, those appointed from civil life; for as to
the few persons at present promoted from the ranks,
their number is so small as to be left entirely out of
the count. In our political system, indeed, promotion from the ranks, in ordinary circumstances is
almost an impossibility."

" Then Hogan was merely quizzing me when he
stated that any well-conducted youth, who enlisted
in the United States Army, might ultimately expect
to reach the position of Brigadier General," remarked Guy.

" I imagine so," was the answer.

Just at that instant, in the shade of the evening,
two nice little dandified fellows passed Guy, and
commenced humming an air which Master Averall did
not very well understand, but which seemed to have
the words, " cigars " and " cogniac," mixed together,
pell mell, with each other, and which he afterwards
understood ran in the following way:

> When we march into a country town,
> Prudes may fly from us, and dames may frown,
>   But that's absurd.

When we march away, we leave behind,
Prudes and dames who've been vastly kind,
Pray take my word.

CHORUS.

Off, off, we go and say we're on duty,
Smoke our cigars, or flirt with some new beauty,
Vive, vive l'amour ! cigars and cogniac !
Hurrah ! hurrah boys ! Vive le bivouac !

As they passed him, Guy touched his cap to the young officers, and then asked his friend who they were, and was told in reply that they were neither more than less, than his own Lieutenants ; Messrs. Spruce and Taper, now out on an evening stroll. Guy paid them the compliment of being very handsome fellows, and then added that with such officers in the rear of his company, and the good Captain Daisy in front, he felt certain the honor of the service would be upheld on each and every occasion. But hardly were these words out of his mouth, when two more officers passed him, one of whom he noticed was swearing quite violently " by Jupiter," that they might all talk as they pleased, but he understood more about military law, and the theory and practice of general court martials than all the other officers in the service put together. Guy looked at this individual very attentively, while giving him the customary salute, and then asked who his serene highness might be, who spoke of himself in such mild and modest terms.

"Why is it possible, sir, that you don't know !" was the response. " That, sir, is the greatest genius in the whole wide world, under guise of a Second

Lieutenant. He is a citizen appointment recently made. His name is Blodgett."

IV.

MASTER AVERALL kept cogitating on the information thus furnished, for some time; and to say the truth it rather upset some of the notions he hitherto had entertained concerning promotion in the Army. "I see the case plainly," said he, "that confounded scribbling fellow has indeed been making fun of me, when he mentioned the word Brigadier after I met him in Newark. Still, five years is not the whole of one's lifetime; and provided I am dissatisfied with the service, it is easy to leave it, on the expiration of my enlistment. Meanwhile, it will cost nothing to behave myself properly; and that under all circumstances I am resolved to do. One thing, however, I hardly approve of; the nonsensical baggy clothes which they issue to recruits at this place; confound it, was the author and finisher of the habiliments in which I am at present encased, in dread that Guy Averall should feel snobbish In the suit? Just look at these trowsers—they have seats in them big enough for a couple of men! And this jacket too—I imagine the pattern by which it was cut must have been neither more nor less than a meal sack! Well, well, in a few weeks, at the very farthest, I'll get a brand new uniform from the tailor, and never mind, Private Averall of the gallant Twenty-sixth, will yet be as handsomely dressed a young fellow, as ever found place in the Regiment." And following out the idea thus enunciated, our friend. in due time, appeared in trim uniform, and inwardly vowed that for the future he would present a picture of neatness, and good order, such as would do credit to that particular organization of which he found an integral part.

But while improving his outward appearance in the way described, Guy Averall did not neglect his. manners, by any means, and in forming these, he found very material assistance by observing the habits and customs of the better instructed portion of the community, with whom his lot was cast. One day it was rumored that some of the officers were going over to New York City, a boat's crew was in requisition, and as Guy had the reputation of being a good, stout, healthy recruit, he was ordered out for that purpose. Hogan was designated as coxswain, and with that worthy at their head, the party sallied out, got the port barge in readiness, and drawing it alongside the principal wharf they quietly waited for the passengers.

They were not long in coming—the two young graduates singing their song about " vive l' amour " and " cogniac," as usual, while behind them appeared the irrepressible Blodgett, running at full speed. As soon as the latter approached the boat, it became painfully evident that neither his linen nor his coat was of the neatest ; but who in the world pays any attention to such a trifling circumstance as a clean shirt, when he happens to encounter a man of genius? As Blodgett approached, both Lieutenants cast a somewhat reproachful glance at their irregular look-ing associate ; but Blodgett, scatterbrain animal that he was, did not apparently pay much attention to these indications of dislike, for as soon as he got on board the boat he began to talk

"Gad, Spruce—almost too late—just in time however. Have been very busy this morning. Studied a little tactics at first, and then turned my thoughts to electricity. Have just been inventing the greatest machine that ever was known; it will run by means of a galvanic battery, and I prophesy that before five years are over, it will revolutionize the whole of Europe and America. Worked it all out in my head last night, while awake in bed, and reduced it to paper in an hour and a half this morning. Will show the whole thing to you, as soon as we come back from the city, and if you don't acknowledge it is the most perfect invention of the kind, I'll give you my head for a halfpenny." The other officers still glanced at Blodgett, as he thrust his greasy looking fingers, through his fiery wisps of hair, and inwardly wished that the electrican would discard inventions for the present, and pay a little attention to the rules of ordinary neatness. But who, as we said before, can account for the aberrations of genius?

After a pull of some fifteen or twenty minutes, the boat reached the wharf, when the officers started up town, having previously given orders for the crew to remain at the landing, and Guy, in the absence of anything more important, purchased a newspaper, sat down on the steps, at whose foot the barge was moored, and began to read. Meanwhile the bard Hogan, having stuck his cap on one side of his head, saw proper to observe, that one officer might speak of "cigars" and "cognaic"; and another might expatiate on the wonders of electricity; but for his part there was only one subject which troubled him at that instant.

"What is that?" said Guy.

"The real nature of beans." And hereupon the clerk burst into one of those absurd rhapsodies in which he now and then saw fit to indulge, mentioning among other things, that both Theophrastus and Pliny had recommended the bean very highly as a proper eatable, that Horace, anticipating no doubt the fare of the United States soldier, had spoken of beans and fat pork as an article of diet, and it was undoubtedly from reading the line *faba Pythagoræ cognata* and so forth, that the Commissary General of Subsistence, gave three-quarters of a pound of pork, and two and a half ounces of beans, more or less per diem, to each young Artilleryman, and commanded him to eat accordingly. But in the midst of this dessertation Guy Averall glanced toward the head of the wharf; and there, wonderful to relate, he espied the image of his own Captain, while in front of that officer walked the self-same lady who had puzzled him by her questions, some three months previous, when at work in the corn field; armed, as usual, with a big cotton umbrella. Guy would willingly have extended his observation, especially as the lady seemed to be engaged in earnest conversation with the gay and festive Taper, who accompained her down the wharf, and who bowed and smiled at every word which his protectress uttered. But on a sudden, up came Hogan, who in a very unceremonious manner took hold of Guy's unmentionables, and jerked him into the boat, with an expression the reverse of ceremonious. "Get out of the way, get out of the way, confound it," said he, "else the whole crew will be exposed to the glance of the Brigadier General."

"The who!" exclaimed Guy, somewhat puzzled at this movement on the part of the bard.

"Why, Mrs. Daisy," was the answer, "confound it, don't you see her coming down on the top of us. I understand her like a book. If she happens to notice a single soldier loitering about the wharf, we all know our destiny. She will order us away, on some fool expedition or other, and we possibly won't get back to our quarters till nightfall."

"Is that really her custom?" asked Averall.

"Of course it is," was the rejoinder. "Get out of the way at once, else she'll be down on us in five minutes."

In a few seconds after this, the sound of footsteps could be heard overhead; and Mrs. Daisy, for such she really was, seemed engaged in earnest conversation with her protegé. And certainly if the Brigadier was patronizing and inquisitive when addressing a "young peasant" at work in the fields; she surely was not a whit less benignant when speaking to a subaltern of Artillery, for the conversation between Mrs. Daisy and the young officer, was carried on in the following style.

"Oh Mr. Taper! Mr. Taper! you're so handsome this morning! How delighted I am to see you. I just brought you down to the end of the wharf, so that I might ask a few questions. I always take a certain interest in any one connected with the Island. How are you all over there. How is that dear man the Doctor? And how is that excellent soldier, the Ordnance Sergeant, and how are his two children, Alice and Jane? How is the cook in the Hospital, and how is the sutler's secretary, and how is every-

body else at the Fort? All well you say—my dear
Mr. Taper I'm so glad to hear that. I never interest
myself about the affairs of a garrison—never, never, as
you well know—all I do is to simply ask for the few
friends I have in the army, and once I find they are
well I remain content. As to the management of the
military department, I leave all that to the proper
authorities, to the officer in charge of the guard; to
the surgeon as guardian of the sick ; to the sutler as
vender of bread, butter and cheese; and to my own
husband, as commandant of the station, the best and
dearest man that ever existed. Is not that so Tom?"

"Don't know," was the answer on the part of
Captain Daisy, who at the same time took occasion
to rub the end of his nose with one hand, as if he had
heard that particular phrase about the 'best and
dearest man' so very often, that the words to him
had really lost all particular significance.

"I have been wandering round the world to the
sound of the drum," continued Mrs. Daisy, "for the
last eighteen years, packing up my knapsack whenever
I was told, and camping wherever the law would allow me, and during all that time I have never had
occasion to find fault with my own good husband—
no never, never, for a single instance. He took me
very young and very early, I never was in love with
any one but him, and to him my heart has since been
resigned on each and every occasion. But where are
all the soldiers by the way—the poor dear children. I
just came here to hunt them up, so that all of us
might have a little excursion among the vessels of the
harbor. Would you not like, Mr. Taper, to proceed
down the bay, for a little distance, just by way of di-

8

vertisement? Do you know I have the greatest curiosity to see one thing—an oyster boat. I wish to see how people on oyster boats live, and ascertain beside if the bivalves in their original state are the same sort of animal that is usually set before one in the city. Does not that strike you as a proper subject for enquiry."

"Why no, I don't see why it should be a subject for enquiry at all," said Taper. Indeed I never heard that the point was doubted."

"Well then we'll say the point is not doubted, but even granting this much, I am nevertheless resolved to have my excursion. I hold it to be the true and undeniable right of any woman, who follows her husband in the Army as I do, to insist on all reasonable indulgences in a general way, provided of course they do not involve too much expense or fatigue to those directly interested."

"I declare, I never thought of that," said Taper. "I'll go with you madam, after oysters or anything else."

"I'm so glad to hear you express your willingness to do so," responded the lady, "for do you know what, I have been arguing the same point into my own dear Tom, for the last half hour, and he still seems as unwilling to subscribe to my notions as ever."

"I'm very much surprised to hear that," said Taper, who spoke at the same time with a truly engaging smile.

"My good Tom is a very excellent man," continued the lady, "and I love and obey him as a wife and helpmate ought to do, still there are some theoretical subjects, such as oysters, on which we occasionally

differ. Still, in the present case I have no doubt that
Major Daisy will accede to my wishes. If we only
had those dear children, the soldiers, we could all
start off at once, make our examination, and then I
could return in a seasonable hour to the city, where I
am engaged at present in the study of general science,
French, literature and painting. I wonder, by the
way, where the men are—up Washington Street, I
suppose, in some of the filthy places where they sell
that abominable whiskey. Do you know, I really
never understood what soldiers did with their money,
till one evening, a few weeks ago, my principal cook
saw proper to inform me that after pay day, they frequently get drunk, and then the poor dear children
are thrust into the guard house, and are subsequently
tried by genuine court martial."

"I'm somewhat surprised you did not know that
much before," was the immediate answer on the part
of the officer.

"How could I though," was the reply. "You
understand I never, never concern myself in the affairs
of a garrison. My home and my husband are the only
objects that possess any interest to me, and in my
opinion that is all any woman, with a well-regulated
mind, should think about. I was brought up in the
lap of luxury, as everyone knows, but when I met
Tom I surrendered it all for his sake."

"Only what we should expect from your goodness of heart," was the reply with a bow.

"Oh my dear Mr. Taper, my dear Mr. Taper,"
said the lady, "don't talk in that way, or you really
will expose to a cruel world my dearest and best affections. In some respects my situation when young,

was very unfortunate, for I was never denied anything that I desired or wanted. I could go to the largest and best furnished store on Broadway, ordered whatever I wished for, and all I know, in addition, was simply this—the bills were sent to our home on Twenty-Fifth Avenue, and poor dear papa would instantly settle them all. I don't have many luxuries in the Army just now, for Tom and I are too poor for that, still I glory in the uniform that my husband wears, and would follow him from one end of the world to the other."

"Oh mother of Moses," said Hogan at that instant, *sotto voce*, "if ever there was a persecuted mortal in this world, the same good natured Tom is the individual. Well, well, this will all do as part of my essay on beans. But thunder and turf here she comes. She will soon find us out under the wharf."

"Where are the children, where are the children" continued Mrs. Daisy. "I declare I must look for them down here below." And in a few seconds, the somewhat stout looking pedestal of the Brigadier, was seen descending the steps toward the place where the boat lay concealed, and shortly afterwards the lady's own melodious voice was heard, giving the customary salute. "Oh Hogan, Hogan, I'm so glad to see you. And how are the rest of the children, and how is the cook at the Hospital, and how is the sutler's secretary, and how are you all on the Island. All well! glad to hear that!" Then the crew were ordered to bring out the barge, the party got into it, and directions were next given to let the oars fall. In due time they reached the object of the Brigadier's solicitude, an old schooner lying up the East River, when Mrs.

Daisy went on board, and after worrying the life out of the commander of the craft, in regard to the real nature of acephals, she finally bade him adieu. Then other Captains and other oyster boats had to be visited, Mrs. Daisy climbing over the bulwarks in a very suitable manner, and questioning and examining as before. Meanwhile, the men began to feel the pangs of hunger, but still the gallant Brigadier continued her persecutions, for several ships in the harbor had to be next seen. That brig from Genoa must be boarded ; that barge from Monte Video, with the beautiful ensign must be approached ; finally an inspection must be made of that old schooner, from Key West, which had a load of sponges on board. In the end, however, the lady was forced to give up her examination ; and then with strong arms but empty stomachs, the crew pulled back to the Island.

V.

IN a week or two after this adventure, the recruiting rendezvous at Newark was broken up ; and Captain Le Froy having been ordered to take charge of the Light Battery belonging to the Regiment at another station ; his successor, the good and amiable Major Daisy, assumed command of the military establishment at Fort Columbus. His wife, of course, accompanied him, and as soon as she arrived on the Island, her presence was instantly felt ; for a number of men from each of the companies, then in garrison, were sent to the quarters of the commanding officer, so as to assist in cleaning rooms, whitewashing entries, putting down carpets, and other work of a similar nature. In all these operations, it may be noted, our friend Averall bore an honorable part; and acquitted himself in this work with more than ordinary ability. As to Mrs. Daisy, just then, she was as gracious as any person in the Army could possibly be; indeed on one occasion, she was pleased to recognize the hero of this narrative as the "agriculturalist" she once saw on the farm in New Jersey; and then after styling our friend a "fine young recruit" she hoped he long would remain in that regiment with which she and her husband were so closely connected.

Being now a member of a regular command, Guy Averall had an excellent opportunity of observing the usual routine of garrison life. In reorganizing, Messrs. Spruce and Taper still remained as Lieutenants with Company "E"; that model soldier, Ernest Heidenrick, held his position as First Sergeant; Sullivan was made full Corporal, the phrenologist Peterson was detailed as Hospital Steward; such other non-commissioned officers, as were then appointed were selected from the old soldiers belonging to the organization. At the same time, the former list of calls was continued in the Garrison; which as near as can be recollected ran in the following way:

Reveille, ...	Day Break.
Fatigue, . . .	Immediately after Reveille.
Breakfast, ...	6:45 A.M.
Surgeon's Call, . . .	7:00 A.M.
First Call for Guard Mount, . .	8:15 A.M.
Guard Mount, ...	8:30 A.M.
Drill, ...	9:30 A.M.
Recall from Drill, . . .	11:00 A.M.
Dinner and 1st Sergeant's Call, .	12:00 M.
Fatigue, ...	1:00 P.M.
Recall from Fatigue, . . .	4:00 P.M.
Drill for Recruits and Awkward Soldiers,	Same Hour.
Recall from Drill, . . .	5:00 P.M.

Parade, 1st Call,	.	30 minutes before Sundown.
Retreat, . .	.	. . At Sundown.
Tattoo, . .	.	. . 9:00 P.M.
Taps, . .	.	. . . 9:15 P.M.

This list of signals explains itself sufficiently; and will enable any one who is versed in military matters to understand how the day at Fort Columbus was passed. To those who are novices in such affairs we might explain that in a regular garrison the most insignificant transaction seems sufficient to evoke something of that pomp, pride and circumstance on which the soldier doats; and hence the bugle, or drum and fife are in constant requisition. The reveille obliges the men to get up, the tattoo to lie down ; the fatigue call to go out to work; the doctor's call to report to the Post Surgeon. Then there are calls for going to meals ; calls for coming away from meals ; calls for going to church, calls for returning from church, and numberless other calls beside ; but to extend the list any further would simply be worse than useless. As an excuse for these, however, as well as for that severe and somewhat ceremonious discipline which obtains in the Army, let us quote the words of the great Shakspeare :

> Degree being vizarded,
> The unworthiest shows as fairly in the mask,
> The heavens themselves ; the planets and this centre,
> Observe degree, priority, and place,
> Insisture, course, proportion, season, form,
> Office and custom, in all line of order ;
> And therefore is the glorious planet, Sol,
> In noble eminence enthroned and sphered
> Among the others ; whose med'cinable eye
> Corrects the ill aspects of planets evil,
> And posts, like the commandments of a king,
> Sans check, to good and bad.

But enough on this subject—let us here end the quotation and say that on Governor's Island, just as in Newark, the good and amiable Heidenrick preserved his urbane manners on every possible occasion. One morning Guy Averall made arrangements with his chum Moldwell, for a day's absence, so as to visit New York city. A pass was accordingly written and presented to Captain Daisy, by the 1st Sergeant of the Company, when the latter carried in what is technically known as the "morning report." As the Captain seldom refused an indulgence of the kind, unless indeed he, or Mrs. Daisy, required the performance of some job of work around his own quarters, the permission was accordingly signed, and in due time was handed to the applicants. Guy and his friend now began to felicitate themselves on a day's enjoyment in the city; but just as they were ready to start, Sergeant Heidenrick came into the room, in a great hurry, and said "your bass is revoked—your bass is revoked—I vants you fellers to get ready for inspection. Dere is a Sheneral here from Ni York to-day, to inspect the command—all the basses are revoked, and no one is to leave the Island till it all is over. Hurry up, hurry up, donner und blitzen as quick as you can, and get everything in order." The usual commotion that exists under such an announcement now began; the cook commenced putting things to rights in the kitchen; the non-commissioned officers, in charge of squads, gave directions as to the cleaning of their respective rooms; here one private was sweeping a pile of dust into a hall; there another was pushing a torrent of black dirty water down a stairway, by means of a broom; yonder, a dormitory,

having undergone its purgation, the occupants were
walking around in bare feet, some engaged in whitening a set of belts, others in rubbing a musket with
buffstick and emery, while probably the Corporal in
charge amused himself by shouting every now and
then to some unlucky wight that happened to approach
the sacred precincts, in dirty boots. " Oh blast yir
soul, take those things off your trotters, don't ye
see the place is clain." Meanwhile Sergeant Heidenrick, as if fully conscious of his burdens, was all
anxiety that Company " E " should present as neat
an appearance as possible. He accordingly went
round in every direction, giving orders as to the
police of the place, here he detects a pair of old
shoes in their hiding place ; yonder a pair of socks
is discovered secreted in a bunk ; anon a couple of
blankets are noticed as improperly folded, and so on
to the end of the chapter. Next the Sergeant has a
word or two with Hogan, as to having the Company
records all ready ; afterwards the cook in the
kitchen is reminded that a certain set of knives and
forks, purchased from the savings of the Company
some six months previous, and which are usually kept
at the bottom of the mess chest, wrapped up in an
old shirt, should now be laid on the table, as if for
every day use. At length everything is completed ;
the squad rooms, office, and dining hall look sufficiently fine ; Sergeant Heidenrick's mind is at rest,
so he dons his parade uniform and belts, puts on a
pair of white gloves, takes his musket in hand, in a
few minutes after this the " assembly " is beaten, and
the order is given to " fall in."

Well, as we have advanced thus far, and as these

minute details of garrison life may possibly interest
some who are not soldiers, we may as well complete
our description of this ceremony.   The words " fall
in," having been enunciated, the men belonging to
Company " E " now form in line, in front of their
quarters, and are arranged according to size, so that
the tallest man and tallest Corporal should be on the
right ; and the smallest man, and smallest Corporal
on the left.   The command " in two ranks form company " is next given, which is executed by each person in succession taking alternately the place of a
front and a rear rank man.   Next the roll is called,
when each soldier answers his name, and brings his
piece to an " order "; after all this is over we have a
" rest," and an " attention "—the last command being
given on the approach of the good Captain Daisy,
going out to the parade ground, who strange to say, is
armed cap-a-pie, as a soldier should be, with both of
his epaulets actually on.   Soon the band is heard,
and Mr. Spruce, as superior to Taper in point of
rank,takes charge of the Company, the word "shoulder
arms " is given, the Company is marched out, takes
its place in line, is " dressed " by its commander, and
brought to a " support arms," the irrepressible Blodgett as Adjutant takes his place on the right of the
battalion, and after waiting there for some little time
the work of inspection now begins.

The first feature in this part of the programme is
the approach of the inspecting officer, and without
disparagement to present inspectors let us say, that a
finer, or more noble-looking, fat, plethoric old fellow
than the one in sight, probably never stood in front
of a Regiment.   Then Captain Daisy as post com-

mander draws near; the Adjutant brings the battalion to a "present," and reports it formed, afterwards he takes his place in line, Captain Daisy draws his sword and exclaims "prepare for review---to the rear open order---march." The ranks are then opened, another "present" takes place, followed by a "carry arms," and the inspecting general, in company with the commanding officer approaches the right of the line. Then the band strikes up some martial tune, such as "See the conquering hero comes," as if to signalize the achievements of the warlike personages then present. This part of the ceremony being accomplished, we have the words " close-order march ; companies right wheel, march." Then the column, in due form, steps off ; and the requirements of Scott on the subject of reviews are implicitly followed. Next the column trots around, once more, in double time, fat officers puffing, lame officers halting, and young and gallant officers shining in all their glory. After all, the companies are wheeled into line, then comes another "present," then a " carry," then a "wheel," with other directions too numerous to mention. Finally the real work of inspection begins. The " Ni York General " comes to the first company, looks at its arms and equipments, afterwards arms are stacked, knapsacks are unslung, and examined, and after being again repacked, the arms are once more taken, and the company is marched back to its quarters. Here another examination takes place, when bunks, bedding, cooking utensils and company records all undergo a scrutiny. The inspecting officer may then offer, if he sees fit, a word of comment on the appearance of the garrison, but if the contray should be the case, the circumstance is not noticed. In the present instance Captain Daisy being somewhat of a personal favorite with his superior, was fortunate enough to receive a very generous approval ; for the inspecting officer pronounced Company " E," of the Twenty-sixth Artillery, to be in excellent order ; its arms well kept ; its clothing clean ; its instruction exact; its discipline good ; and its Captain, as a matter of inference, one of the most energetic and discerning officers in the service. This complimentary description puts every one in good humor, the " Ni York General " marches off, telling long stories about the fields and fights in which he participated during the war of 1812, while Guy Averall obtains his pass, and is allowed to visit the city on the following day.

FURTHER PROGRESS.

I.

MEANWHILE that educational training, on which our young friend was bent, and which he had fully resolved to accomplish, was not by any means neglected. As to history, the subject of course was exhausted in the person of Napoleon ; and as to political knowledge, Guy Averall, after reading the New York *Herald*, could really contain no more. Hence it became necessary to seek out some new field of investigation. At this crisis polite literature naturally suggested itself, and Averall finally determined to attack the novel. Now novels may be regarded by many as very trifling affairs; books to be read one day and consigned to their resting place the next; still, in the present instance our hero contrived to unite the useful and agreeable in a manner which did him infinite credit. His first purchase in imaginative literature was a book well calculated to advance his knowledge in that noble profession which he had selected for his career ; for the volume was one which had long been a favorite with both civilians and military men, and was neither more nor less than " Charles O'Malley," the ' Irish Dragoon.' The hero of this book, it is hardly necessary to say, is a most wonderful fellow, he is a gentleman, born in the West of Ireland, where his father is the owner of a landed estate, he joins a regiment of English Cavalry, goes out to the Peninsula, fights and is wounded under the Duke of Wellington, encounters the great Napoleon the night before the battle of Waterloo, and finally comes home to the land of his birth, where he is duly married to Miss Lucy Dashwood. The plot is not very regular, and some of Charley's adventures are rather improbable, it is true; but what of that— in company with such personages as Webber, or Major Monsoon, or the renowned Mickey Free, can any young reader presume to be hypercritical? Guy Averall certainly was not, this composition of Doctor Lever's he simply considered the greatest effort of genius that mankind probably ever saw, and only wondered why the united voice of mankind, did not assign to that volume the very highest place in the world's literature.

The next novel that our friend read, was also by the author of "O'Malley"; and the book beside has this attraction that the principal character in it was a hero after Guy Averall's own heart, while his adventures and encounters were not dissimiliar to his own. Con Cregan is a sort of Scapin or Gil Blas, and is invested with that interest which belongs to all persons who rise in the world through sheer pluck and perseverance. His origin is very humble, for his father is nothing but the inhabitant of a little cabin on the border of Meath and Kings County; yet in spite of this, the subject of the story rises to great eminence; he flirts with Spanish beauties, becomes an officer in Africa hobnobs with ambassadors, and on one occasion is honored so far that the Princess de Verneuil, daughter of Louis Phillippe, actually " pours out tea," for him in the Tuileries itself. As to that " pouring out tea," it is a stroke of genius, only to be expected from an Irishman, like Doctor Lever; meanwhile let us assure our readers, that the history of Mr. Cregan is not by any means destitute of a certain touch of humor, now and then, and as to the pathos of the work, let the following passage speak for itself. The father of the hero, it must be premised, was the owner of a small estate on the border of two counties, which circumstance enables him to vote in both localities, without paying taxes in either. The way Mr. Cregan gets possession of the land is characteristic.

"The farm," says the author, speaking of the place where Con was born, "belonged originally to an old farmer called Harry M'Cabe, that had two sons, who were always fighting with each other, as to who was to have the old man's money. Finally, the younger one, Mat, grew tired of the struggle, and in a fit of disgust started off for Dublin and enlisted. Three weeks after he sailed for India, when the old man, overwhelmed by grief, took to his bed, and never arose from it again.

" One evening after midnight a knock came to the door of the cabin occupied by Mr. Cregan. 'Con Cregan, Con, I say, open the door, were the words heard outside from the mouth of the elder brother.

'Oh, Mr. Peter, what's the matter? Is the old man worse?' said the senior.

'Faix that's what he is, for he's dead!'

'Glory be to his bed, when did it happen?'

'About an hour ago,' said Peter in a voice greatly agitated, 'he died like an old haythen, and never made a will.'

' That's bad,' said Mr. Cregan, who being a very polite man, never said anything that could possibly offend the present company.

' It is bad,' said Peter, ' but it would be worse if we couldn't help it.   Listen to me, Con ; I want you to assist me in this business, and here is five guineas in gold for you if you do as you are bid.   You know you were always reckoned the image of my father; and before he took ill, you were mistaken for him every day.'

' Anan,' said Mr. Cregan, now getting somewhat frightened.

' Well, what I want you to do is for to come over to the house and get into bed.'

' Not beside the corpse' said Mr. Cregan trembling ?

' By no means, but by yourself, and you're to pretend to be my father, and that you want to make your will before you die, and then I'll send for the neighbors and Billy Scanlin the schoolmaster, and you'll tell him what to write, leaving all the farm and every thing to me, you understand.   And as the neighbors will see ye, and hear your voice it will never be believed but it will be himself that did it.'

" The plan succeeded admirably.   Mr. Cregan, senior, got into the bed in due time, the neighbors and Billy Scanlin, the schoolmaster, were sent for, and the old gentleman commenced making his will, the room in which the occurrence took place being as much darkened as possible.   ' I bequeath to my son Peter,' said he, ' the whole of my two farms of Killmadooney and Knocksheboora, with the fallow meadows behind Lynches' house, the forge and the right of turf on the Dooran bog. I give him, and much good may it do him, Launty Casson's acre, and the Laury field, and the limekiln, and that reminds me that my mouth is somewhat dry, so let us have a taste of the jug.'

'Here the jug was handed to Mr. Cregan, and after he had wet his lips, the poor fellow continued.

'I leave him—that is Peter, I mean—the two potato gardens at Noolan's well, and it is a fine elegant crop grows there. And hold on, are the neighbors listening, is Peter Scantlan listening?

'Yes, sir; yes, father, we're all listening; chorused the audience.

'Well then, it is my last will and testament and may—give me the jug—there is poor Con Cregan, as honest and as hard a working man as ever lived, who has a heavy family on his hands. To him I bequeath the little plot, near the cross roads, on which his cottage stands, and to his heirs in *secula seculorum*. Ah! blessed be the saints after that, it makes one's heart light after he has done a good deed, and now I'll drink all the companies good health and many happy returns ——"

"What Mr. Cregan was going to add it is impossible to say, but at this point the son Peter, who was now terribly frightened at the lively tones the sick man began to assume, hustled all the people to another part of the house so that his father might die in peace.

When all had left, Peter slipped back to Cregan, senior, who at that instant was putting on his brogues.

'Con,' said he, 'ye did it all well, but shure that was a joke about the two acres and a half at the cross.'

9

'Of course it was, Peter,' said he, 'shure it was all a joke for the matter of that—won't I make the neighbors laugh heartily when I tell them all about it.'

'Shure you would not be mean enough to betray me?' said Peter, trembling with fright.

'Shure you would not be main enough to go against yir father's dying words' And here a sly laugh succeeded that was perfectly intelligible.

'Very well, Con,' said Peter, 'a bargain is a bargain. You are a deep fellow that is all.' And so the matter ended while Mr. Cregan became possessed of the property."

*　　　*　　　*　　　*　　　*

Such was the story as told by the novelist, and which Guy Averall, all devouring reader as he then was, swallowed with much satisfaction. Some persons may possibly object that if our friend were a real hero, as he pretends to be, his reading matter ought to have been more choice at this epoch, that young men of his age are expected to know something of the longs and the shorts in trimeter catalectic verse, and as to that particle $\overset{\text{''}}{\alpha}\nu$ it should not have been so much neglected. Perhaps not, for the said particle is a very important syllable in its way, still are there not enough young men in the world who make themselves familiar with its use, year after year, without dragging the principal personage of our story into the category?

II.

But reading Con Cregan was not the only enormity which Guy Averall committed at this time— still worse than that, he was guilty of violating the police regulations of Fort Columbus, and as a consequence was committed in due form to durance vile. And thereby hangs a tale. In the first place it may be stated our hero again fell in love. It was not a very deep fall, still it was a fall for all that—the object of his affections being neither more nor less than a certain Miss Kitty Traynor, niece of one of the musicians who made her home with her uncle and aunt in that series of decayed, one-story houses, appropriated to the use of enlisted men, and which is known as Rotten Row by the various residents of the Island. As to Miss Kitty, she was acknowledged to be the prettiest girl in the garrison ; she had black laughing eyes, and sweet cherry lips, and teeth that looked like so many pearls, with a figure as lithe and graceful as Hebe herself. Indeed, the only fault that could possibly be found with Miss Kitty was possibly this, that like a good many other persons belonging to her sex, the young lady was something of a coquette. Guy fell the victim of her sly glances the very first time he met her, and forthwith began playing the dearly devoted to this belle of Fort Columbus ; but before many evenings he made the awkward discovery that he had a rival in the person of a certain Private Lawless, a member of Company " E," who was then acknowledged to be the most handsome man of his rank, on the whole Island. The history of Lawless, at that time, was sufficiently well known. Like Averall himself he was a native of Ireland, had enlisted in the English Cavalry, remained a while there, deserted thence, and was now a member of the same Company in which Guy was serving. The latter considered him a man of exceedingly irregular habits, and somewhat unprincipled withal, but what of that—the fellow was good-looking; while the smiling face and black silken locks which he habitually wore, seemed to produce an effect on Miss Kitty that could not be resisted. Still the young lady did not discard Guy entirely, spite of that; indeed, she gave him a little encouragement now and then, as if to sustain his hopes, and on the whole held the balance of power pretty evenly between the two rivals. But at this particular juncture an untoward event took place as far as Guy's hopes were concerned, for his opponent was made a Corporal. The fact of the matter was that both the subalterns, while on drill, had frequently noticed the erect, soldier-like bearing of Lawless, and his " about face " and " carry arms " were so much superior to these evolutions when executed by other recruits, that they instantly determined to advance him. So away they both posted to the good Captain Daisy, and opened their case; and Captain Daisy, as in honor bound, was graciously pleased to receive their suggestion. " Well," said that functionary, speaking as usual through his nose, " if Lawless is a goot ban, and you really think he will discharge the duties required, I'll bake him Gorporal."

" He is one of the most intelligent and capable soldiers, I ever saw," said Taper, who acted as principal spokesman on the occasion.

" Very well, I'll bake him Gorporal. Mrs. Daisy what do you say to that? Don't you think it would be a goot idea to bake Lawless a Gorporal?"

" The dear, sweet child!" exclaimed Mrs. Daisy. " I'm very glad indeed to hear you suggest it. Why Lawless is the most polite soldier that ever I knew.

Indeed, it was only the other day, as I was entering the garrison when the child was on duty as sentinel. As soon as I came within the customary distance, he immediately brought his musket to a "present," and he remained in that position too, till I had returned the acknowledgement. Now any one who is so gallant and well behaved as Lawless evidently is, deserves promotion most certainly, in my opinion."

"I'll bake him, I'll bake him," exclaimed the eager Captain Daisy. And sure enough that very same evening an order was read on parade, which made the formal announcement that Private Patrick Lawless was hereby appointed a Corporal in Company "E," Twenty-sixth Artillery, and was to be obeyed and respected accordingly.

Now Guy Averall, although a good enough fellow in his way, was not a perfect paragon in all respects; and if the truth must be told, he felt a momentary annoyance at the promotion of Lawless, not on account of the advancement in itself, for that was a thing of minor importance, but for the advantage it might possibly give his rival in pressing his suit. But this feeling only lasted for a second; a moment's reflection, indeed, served to convince Guy that it was perfectly competent for the officers of his Company to promote any member of it that they chose; and if Miss Kitty Traynor was such an enthusiast about rank as to prefer one man, with a couple of worsted stripes, to another man without them, why that was her affair, not his. And the consequence was, that when Miss Kitty, a few days afterwards, met our adventurer, and told him in her usual laughing way, that she had got a new Corporal, just then for a beau ; and what was better, had almost made up her mind to stick by him too, our friend took the observation in the spirit in which it was given, and asked who the Corporal was.

" Why Corporal Lawless, of course," was the immediate answer.

" Oh pshaw," said Averall, " I can cut him out any day that I choose."

" No you cannot," was the rejoinder, "he is the best looking non-commissioned officer in the garrison."

" No matter for that, no matter for that," answered Averall, " I'll just draw off, and let him go ahead for a while, and then when he thinks everything secure, I'll come in once more and show him his real place."

The coast was now clear as far as Master Guy was concerned, and had that young gentleman kept aloof both from· Miss Kitty and her inamorato, he would have avoided all future difficulties. But this unluckily he did not do. One morning Guy was on the point of starting to New York, as a member of a boat's crew, when Lawless came up to him, and thrust a silver half-dollar into his pocket. " I want you to get something for me," said he. " I am very sick, and you are the only person in the garrison on whom I can depend in making the purchase."

" What is it you wish me to get for you ?" said Guy.

" Hold on, by the way," rejoined the other laughing, " I have a big story to tell you. I was over at Rotten Row last night, and saw Kitty Traynor there. She is a great flirt, but I am going to give her up this very night, and once I am out of the way, you will have nothing further to trouble you, and then you can have her all to yourself."

" Oh," said Guy, " as far as that is concerned I have made up my mind to abandon flirtation. I never was very successful in that way. Still, let me know what you want in New York, and I will get it for you if I can."

" I wish you to get me a bottle of whiskey. I tell you again, you are the only person in the garrison I would trust in such a thing as that."

" Won't I render myself liable to punishment by doing so ?" asked Guy.

"No, you won't," said the Corporal, " go about the thing quietly, just take the bottle and keep it well concealed in your coat. When you land on the Island come up to my room, hand the liquor to me, and the whole affair will be right."

Alas ! alas ! for Guy Averall on that fatal morning, he was foolish enough to oblige Lawless in the way he suggested. *Facilis descensus Averni,* says the poet when speaking of Hades ; and easy is it for the United States soldier, once he has taken the path of error, to go further and further astray. Hardly had Averall touched the wharf, on his return to Governor's Island, before he was arrested. In point of fact the renowned Heidenrick happened to be strolling around the landing at that instant, and noticing a somewhat suspicious looking protuberance under Guy's coat, he approached the latter, seized hold of the forbidden article, asked Guy what it was, and on the latter ejaculating the word "whiskey" he ordered the offender into the guard house. There lay poor Averall, in most doleful plight, regretting his want of resolution in not acting according to the card, and promising mentally all sorts of good behavior in the future. All this, however did not avail him—in the guard house he was allowed to stay, for Heidenrick, gallant soldier as he was, had carried off the bottle and exhibited it to the good Captain Daisy as proof positive of the fact that he, Heidenrick, had a watchful eye on the officers of the garrison, and that if he got a fair chance, he could capture more bottles of whiskey than all the other Sergeants of the Island put together. And thus the consequence was that in a few days a court martial was assembled; and, Averall, as a culprit, was brought before it.

Ah me! what a dread appearance a military tribunal presents, the first time an unhappy offender is brought before it. To see that glittering array of officers, with sashes around their waists and swords by their sides, all sitting in a circle around a table, on which are spread charges and specifications and law books without number. Guy appeared, heralded in by the Sergeant of the Guard, when the order convening the Court in the first instance was read. Then the prisoner was asked if he objected to any officer present, named in the detail, to which question he replied in the negative. The Court was then sworn, "in presence of the accused," the charges were read, and Guy Averall was asked to say whether he was guilty or not guilty.

"Guilty," said Guy.

"How do you plead to the specification which alleges that you, Private Averall, Company "E," Twenty-sixth Artillery, did introduce a quantity of intoxicating liquor into the garrison?"

"Guilty also," was the rejoinder.

"Have you anything to say in your defence?" asked Lieutenant Spruce, who was at the time acting as Recorder.

"Nothing whatever," was the reply.

"Have you any evidence to submit in regard to character?"

"If there is no objection, I should like to call on my Company Commander, Captain Daisy, who is present," said Guy.

Here Captain Daisy rose to his feet, and after giving his dear old nose a twist or two, with one hand, he was sworn.

"Do you know the accused?" said Spruce, who in his office as Recorder, put the necessary questions.

"Tow the accused!—yes I tow him as a member of my company."

"How long has he served in your company?"

"Don't tow exactly—maybe one or two months —cannot tell without looking at the morning report."

"Has he ever been in the guard house before?"

"Don't tow, but think not—good man—pulls in the boat's crew now and then, and has never given me any trouble, as far as I know."

"Then you think this is his first offence?"

"Think so, but am not sure—if he had been a pad man, I should have recollected him better. I think he has always done well."

Guy Averall, if the truth must be told, felt somewhat surprised that his own Captain had not a better recollection of him than was exhibited; the case, however, was here closed, and the Court being cleared for deliberation, our friend in due form was conducted to the guard house. There he remained for three or four days, and at the expiration of that time his sentence was read. He was marched up by a file of the Guard, in company with three or four other culprits, placed alongside the battalion, and with due formality received his doom. Blodgett, the irresistible, who still acted as Adjutant announced the sentence. It's terms were to forfeit to the United States, three dollars of his monthly pay for one month, and to be confined at hard labor in charge of the guard for a fortnight. This sentence was certainly no more than the offence deserved, but in consideration of the youth and inexperience of the prisoner, as well as the excellent character which was furnished him by his Captain, the main portion of it was afterwards remitted. And thus ended this little rencontre on the part of our hero. As to the gay and pleasant looking Lawless, he still continued his attentions to Miss Kitty Traynor, just as if nothing had happened; and as to Averall he made a solemn resolution that let him commit whatever follies he might in the future, from Corporal Lawless, and all men of his kind, he ever would keep himself apart. And to the credit of Guy be it said, this vow was fully kept.

III.

Now about this time there was another member of Company " E," who began to attract considerable attention, both on account of the position he then held, and of the career that was evidently open to

him as a soldier, a gentleman, and an official in the
American Army. This man's name was Ryan, a
countryman of Guy's, a broad-shouldered, swaggering, half ruffian-like looking fellow; who in consequence of his strength of arm, and depth of chest,
was selected as half orderly, and half working man,
to the good and amiable Mrs. Daisy. "I want a
strong ban to work a bangle," was the constant exclamation of the gallant Captain himself, every time
the Company was formed. So one morning after
the clothing of the recruits was reduced to proper
dimensions, Private Ryan was selected as a fitting
orderly, and directed to report to his commanding
officer. The duties of Ryan were of a somewhat
variegated nature. He had to milk a cow, to work a
mangle, to run errands to the Commissary, to pull
Mrs. Daisy in a boat, now and then, round the Island,
and perform other little offices of a kindred nature.
As to his meals, Private Ryan obtained them at
Headquarters; a circumstance sufficient to suggest
to the other members of the Company that their
quondam associate had abandoned his legitimate
sphere as a soldier, and was now transferred into the
useful, but at the same time not very exalted occupation of a " dog robber," the name by which a person in Ryan's position is commonly known. Still,
as far as that fact was concerned no one in the Company felt very sorry for it; indeed they were all
rather glad to be rid of the Tipperary man, for a
more brazen faced, open mouthed bully there probably never existed.

The first time that Guy Averall took particular
notice of the orderly, was in that recruiting depot in

Newark, where our friend became a soldier. He swaggered into that room which Captain Daisy occupied as an office, said he wished to enlist, and when ordered by Heidenrick to remove his cap, he jerked it off with a suppressed grin, just as if he enjoyed a little browbeating. After the ceremony was over, and he was duly sworn in as a soldier, he made an assault on poor Guy, for he came into the room where that somewhat disconsolate youth was sitting, and after setting his teeth he expressed the desire of having a "bloody Enniskillener" or two to eat, and then his growing appetite for such food would remain satisfied for the present. A couple of very quiet Germans, who were sitting together, looking over the poems of Schiller, were the next object of his compliments. But finally the bully caught a Tartar, in the person of the cook, Sullivan. Supper being served, Private Hogan and the cook had purchased a half pound of butter, as an agreeable addition to their meal, which consisted merely of the usual six ounces of dry bread that falls to the soldier's lot, and the ordinary pint of black coffee. No sooner did Ryan notice the butter than it immediately attracted his eye; and forthwith the bully expressed his intention of having a share of it.

"Aisy," exclaimed Sullivan," aisy if you plaise— don't be so rash. Supposin' you had said 'by yir laive' before takin' it. As the case stands, if you had axed me civally for a rub, I don't know but I might have obliged ye, but since you are so obstrepuous, I now say that the butter before me is mine, not yours, and as such I shall treat it till the last ounce of the article is demolished."

"Yours!" answered Ryan, "I know a confounded sight better. I heard you and the Company Clerk makin' up a plot to have something good for supper. That butter belongs to me, and to every man at the table. I suppose bekase you are an owl soldier, you think you can impose on us innocent recruits."

"Innocent or not," was the rejoinder, "it makes but little difference. The butter belongs to Hogan and me, and you for one, shall not touch it."

"Not touch it," said the other. "I'll let you see whether I will or not." And at this instant the friend of equal rights put out his hand, as though he would appropriate the article to himself.

This movement on the part of Ryan rather stimulated the ire of his opponent; who having paid his own money for the condiment, could not see why he was not entitled to possession of the same. Sullivan now felt that his rights as an individual were somewhat in jeopardy, and to be browbeat or overriden in the matter was opposed alike to his sense of justice, and to his personal taste. So to put a quietus on the attempt of the other, the cook jumped into a corner, seized hold of a big carving knife, swung it over his head, and then swore that if the other laid a finger on anything that did not belong to him, he would make him acquainted with cold steel, even if it cost him his life.

That threat proved a pacifier. In spite of his bluster there was a certain method in the madness of Private Ryan. He weighed the delight to be derived from appropriating an article that was not his own, especially when that article was an eatable, he counterbalanced the annoyance and possibly the harm

that might result if the knife wielded by Sullivan
should really make a hole in his side, and on a quiet
calculation of the possible chances in the case, he
resolved to forego the expected good for fear of the
anticipated evil. Had Sullivan appeared less resolute,
his course of procedure would undoubtedly have
been different; for butter, be it observed, is a very
agreeable article to have on a soldiers' supper-table,
especially if it costs you nothing. So all the patriot
could accomplish on the present occasion was to scold.

"Och, it is yourselves are a nice set of fellows,"
said he, as he planted his big hobnailed pumps on the
floor. "If this is the way you manage things in
Amerekay, I have my own opinion of life, liberty and
the parshoot of happiness. Nice liberty, eh! Bad
luck to me, but there is every bit as much oppression
here as in Oireland itself, with this difference, that
there you have no one but a rale owl-fashioned gintle-
man to ride over ye, and here you must submit to the
whim of every little Jack that you meet."

"I'll let that word go for once," exclaimed the
irate Sullivan, "but by the holy teapot, Ryan, if you
call me a Jack again, I'll knock every tooth in your
head down your ill-mannered throat."

"Oh, I see how it is," answered Ryan, "I must'nt
spaik. Land iv the brave and home iv the free, eh!
So it is, in me eye. Oh ye are all combined against
a poor dissolute stranger, and I must howl me tongue."

"Give the poor fellow a piece of butter and let
him go," shouted Hogan at this juncture by way of
banter.

"Not so much as the tenth part of an ounce,"
replied Sullivan, "but to show him that I am not

mane or stingy, I'll make a divide of all I have with the rest of the crowd."

And hereupon Sullivan proceeded round the table with the paper full of butter in one hand, and a knife in the other, and laid a dab of yellow grease on the plate of every single recruit in the room.

"Come boys," said he when this work of love was accomplished, "I want you all to ate and be merry. A soldiers' supper is not a very sumptuous one, but such as it is, let us enjoy it. As to that butter it is mine, and not Mr. Ryan's, and in bestowin' it I say here is life, liberty, and happiness to us all."

"Oh, I see what you are afther. I see what you are afther," exclaimed Ryan once more. "Strivin' to raise a prejudice against me. But no matter. I'll have butter meself one of these days, and you'll see with whom I will divide it. Long lane has no turn— did ye iver hear them words, Misther Sullivan. But no matter, I see I can't open me mouth here. Well there is no justice for Oireland, at all, at all. But I'll keep quiet, and we'll see how things will come out in the long run. That is all I have to say on the subject, friend Sullivan."

And with these words, and sundry mutterings to himself, Private Ryan finally left the supper table and sought his own room. This, then, was the man who was now selected as orderly to Mrs. Daisy, and whom that lady afterswards designed for still higher honors.

IV.

AFTER his release from the Guard House on Governor's Island, Guy Averall took to his studies once more, and in that haphazard discursive way, which was now habitual to him, he read quite a number of works of an imaginative and historical nature, such as are in common use among the rank and file of the Army. The "Knight of Gwynne," "Harry Lorrequer," "Tom Burke of Ours," and so forth came duly into requisition; all of which compositions proved to be both interesting and instructive. Meanwhile it must be noted that in another direction Guy Averall was constantly improving. That polished tone of manners which is only found in the highest and best circles of life, was set forth in proper form before his eyes, and as such was duly appreciated by him. It happened, for instance, one day that our friend was detailed, in the usual manner, as member of a boat's party; and while waiting very conscientiously for the return of the Officers at Castle Garden, the gallant Brigadier again hove in sight.

"Oh, Mr. Spruce, Mr. Spruce," said the lady on the approach of the officer, "I have a great project on hand. I intend in the course of a week or two, to put the Hospital on Governor's Island in proper order; and then issue invitations to some of the richest and most fashionable people in New York City. As soon as I get them on the Island, we can all have a delightful time. I fully intend that we shall dance the *Chapeau Bras*."

"The *Chapeau Bras*," repeated the officer somewhat puzzled, "I am sure I shall be delighted to participate in it. Meanwhile let me ask one question? Will you be kind enough to tell me what the dance, just named, really is?"

"My dear Mr. Spruce," was the rejoinder, "can

it be possible in this enlightened age and country, that you should remain ignorant of the real nature of the *Chapeau Bras*. The *Chapeau Bras*, let me inform you sir, is the most fashionable dance in Europe at the present time. Its origin is due to the Emperor Louis Napoleon, who introduced it in proper form into the Tuleries. Its leading characteristic is that each gentleman present, instead of leaving his hat in a certain apartment, carries it with him during the whole of the evening; and while in that condition goes through his evolutions on the floor. The whole thing is perfectly delightful, I assure you."

"It would afford me infinite pleasure to participate in anything which is brought out under such auspices," was the rejoinder.

"Then I shall appoint you master of ceremonies on the occasion," was the reply.

Thus ended the conversation for the present, and in due time both officers and lady returned to the Island. Shortly after, it must be noted, the most extensive preparations were inaugurated at Fort Columbus in view of the grand display which the good Mrs. Daisy had resolved to make. Invitations were issued in the name of Major Daisy and his excellent spouse to the families of the several officers, then stationed in the Harbor ; in which the words *on dansera* and *chapeau bras* appeared in a corner. Men in squads were sent down to the Hospital, so as to put it in proper order, festoons were made of cedar, laurel, and other evergreens ; cakes, ices and similar delicacies were engaged in large quantities in the city, while to crown all, those elegant young gentlemen, Messrs. Spruce and Taper, pledged their pay accounts

10

for a couple of months in advance, and then each ordered a suit from Ackerman, the military tailor, who keeps the well-known establishment on Broadway. Not that the suits now spoken of were to be military suits, —far from that—for Messrs. Spruce and Taper, in a spirit of innovation which was in itself, almost audacious, resolved to throw their regimentals aside and show themselves in the swallow tail coat and black trousers which properly belong to the civilian. These preliminary arrangements having been completed, there was nothing more to do but to wait with patience till the eventful evening arrived. Finally it came, and at the hour of nine o'clock on the twenty-sixth of November, eighteen hundred and blank, the triumph of Mrs. Daisy, wife of Captain and Brevet. Major Daisy of the United States Army, was complete, for in the presence of the whole garrison of Fort Columbus she inaugurated that highly aristocratic affair which is known in foreign countries, especially in France, by the name already mentioned. The whole thing was a tremendous success, so tremendous that the fame of it extends through the length and breadth of Governor's Island even to the present day, and men date events from Mrs. Daisy's ball in the same way that the Romans reckoned their time from the building of their city; or the people of Oriental countries from the flight of the prophet. The grand idea was to make the thing as much like the Imperial Court of France as possible. But lest we should appear to slight so important an event as the *chapeau bras* by a mere hint, let us say here, that those powers of persuasion with which Mrs. Daisy was endowed had all been exercised in a proper manner "on the best and dearest man that ever existed," so that as far as the preliminary arrangements are concerned, the Brigadier had every thing pretty much her own way. The floor of the dancing room was well waxed, the whitewashed walls of the building were ornamented with evergreens, the garrison flag gracefully draped at one end of the apartment, where a small platform had been erected, formed a gay canopy over the spot where the Brigadier intended standing to receive her guests. Chandeliers composed of bayonets belonging to the company were to light the room, emblems in the shape of that flower from which the lady derived her name were placed here and there throughout the apartment, while in order to impart an air *distingué* to the occasion, it was arranged that half a dozen soldiers, with Corporal Sullivan at their head, were to represent the "Garde Imperiale" of France, and to give Captain and Mrs. Daisy a "present arms" as they passed. Guy Averall, it may be noted, was a member of the aforesaid "Garde," on that eventful night, and when the word of command was given in proper form by Sullivan, he brought down his musket with a certain reverential awe, which certainly must have sent a thrill of delight through the heart of his patroness. "How are you all my dear children—that's very well—why Corporal how do you do? And Guy why you really are becoming a very fine soldier. Corporal don't keep the men very long at a present." And after giving the military acknowledgement to the salute, in a bold and warlike manner, the gallant Brigadier passed into the interior of the building.

But let us leave this outward show and proceed to the great centre of attraction, the dancing room itself. Here the commanding officer and his excellent wife received their guests—the former being dressed in *grande tenue* with his sword by his side and his hat stuck under his arm, while his beloved spouse was arrayed in a pale, peach blossom colored satin, very low in the neck, and very short in the sleeves, so as to reveal the imperial charms of the wearer to each and every beholder. After receiving her guests, with what delight did Mrs. Daisy seat herself upon that particular fauteuil which she had reserved for her own especial use, and gaze majestically on the scene before her! What satisfaction she felt on beholding the success of her undertaking, for every person around her had an undoubted French air, while all the gentlemen carried their hats under their arms just as if they were walking through the Tuileries. There was Taper, with his budding moustache, waxed from end to end, as if he were an incipient Napoleon, and wondering meanwhile if that Princess Louise, then before him, whose home is on Twenty Fifth avenue, has a sufficient quantity of "rocks." There is Spruce on the other hand, the ferocious little rascal, he does not care about "rocks" at all, he only meditates on "la gloire," for he innocently tells that young girl, leaning on his arm, that to die on a battle field is his only aim and desire, and provided he were sure of this boon, his heart would remain content forever. Some of the heavy fellows, the Engineers be it understood, contrive to say a word of compliment to Mrs. Daisy now and then; one of them indeed, who

has visited Paris the year previous, assures his hostess
that the Hospital as it now stands, although only an
ordinary two story brick building, reminds him very
much of the Tuileries, and that madam herself
would almost be mistaken for the Empress Eugenie.
But hark! the band strikes up; we have a march,
and a quadrille, and a waltz, and a polka, and during
all this time the hats of the gentlemen remain glued
to their arms, just as if they could not be given up
—indeed the only person who chooses to violate the
customary etiquette is the easy going Commandant
himself, for in spite of the frequent reminders of his
wife that this was a real chapeau bras, not a common
ball, the old fellow, after a time, saw proper to sling
the covering of his upper story into a corner, just
as if it were a pea wisp, and then vowed, in addition, that it was all nonsense for plain Americans
to assume those ridiculous French airs; that the
United States was as good a country, at any time,
as that ruled by any foreign Emperor, and if he
had any voice in the matter he would banish these
chapeau bras, and other exotic dances, away in an
instant, and in their place would substitute a good,
plain, old fashioned Virginia reel, such as he himself
had led off when he was twenty.

The supper was eaten, the dancing was over, and
the guests were going away, and as the Garde Imperiale presented Arms in the usual manner, Guy
Averall noticed a young lady, in company with the
Commandant, not richly attired like the Brigadier's
great friends from New York, it is true, but dressed
very becomingly in spite of all that, and with a face
such as a woman of good heart and high principle

alone could wear. The features were delicately chis-
elled, a certain breadth between the eye brows gave
an expression of intelligence and good sense which
was unmistakable; the figure, somewhat under the
usual size, was rounded so as to present a series of
graceful curves, while a prettily shaped foot and
hand gave indication of the pure blood that coursed
through that woman's veins. Guy glanced at the
stranger for a second or two in a true and unre·
served spirit of reverence, and after she had passed
out, he could not help asking the name of the visitor.

"Do you not know," said Hogan, who for once
did not choose to be irreverent, "that, sir, is the
Queen of the Island, at least so she is esteemed by
some of us rough soldiers. That lady, sir, I verily
believe, would rather find occupation in doing some
little unostentatious work of charity, even supposing
that the recipient were nothing but an ordinary
private in the Company, like you or me, than in
attending all the fool dances that ever were invented.
Her name is Miss Davis; her father, an old officer
in the Regiment, was killed during the Mexican war,
and his only child has lived ever since with her uncle
on the mothers side, Captain Daisy. That relative,
I really believe, is disposed to be as kind as his general indolence will permit; as to his wife, she certainly,
at the very least, is patronizing. However as far as
that point is concerned, her good offices are not lost;
for Miss Davis relieves her aunt of most of those
household cares which the other is too "aristocratic"
to assume. She takes almost entire charge of that
cub of a boy, belonging to the Brigadier, doing her
utmost to instil into his head a little elementary

French and music. The girl earns her own living, I
assure you."

"That is news to me," said Gay. "I was not
aware that Mrs. Daisy had any family but herself
and Tom."

"Faith she has. The sprig is twelve years old,
more or less; and as thoroughly spoiled a brat as
you can find in the country. But don't you know
Hector?"

V.

La jeunesse est un ivresse continuelle says Roche-
foucould, and in illustration of this maxim, as well as
in evidence of her gaity of heart, it may be noted
that after the customary acknowledgments were paid,
and Mrs. Daisy had sketched landscapes and examined oysters and other marine curiosities for a
while, she finally made up her mind to give another
chapeau bras. This announcement, innocent although
it may seem, was not received with much favor by
the men of Company " E," who had already enough
of hospital scrubbing and decorating to satisfy them.
But what of that—a woman like Mrs. Daisy is a sort
of avalanche, and once she is set in motion, there is
no other alternative but to let her have her own way.
So as a natural result the floors of the Hospital were
waxed once more ; and one or two sick men, who
happened to be there, were hoisted like so much
lumber into the garret. It was in consequence of
this latter act, that the bard Hogan resolved on a
soldier's revenge—to get drunk. For this act of his,
reprehensible though it was, the clerk had every
reasonable excuse. The muster rolls, for instance,

were all completed; the Company returns had been properly signed; the usual official letters to the Adjutant-General, the Quartermaster-General and the other authorities in Washington had all passed from his hands; his mind, in fact, was free as far as his own immediate duties were concerned, so by way of indignation, if not of jollification, Private Hogan as before intimated, resolved to rejuvenate himself. Not that Hogan by any means was a habitual toper—far from that—he loved his wine, of course, in the way that an Irishman naturally does; still, if his official duties required him to sit up to twelve at night, during half the year, he never would have abandoned his place till every scrap of paper under his charge was properly disposed of; and the last return under his cognizance was signed and sent to its ultimate destination. But these duties once completed, a certain latitude had to be allowed. Shortly after tattoo therefore, on the night that Hogan was informed of Mrs. Daisy's intentions, the clerk very quietly sought the shades of Rotten Row, and going into the quarters occupied by one of the laundresses in that classic vicinity, he procured a bottle. From this he took a couple of good pulls, just to see how the liquor would taste, and feeling somewhat refreshed by the draught, he thought he would pay a visit to his friends in the Fort. He accordingly started off, and before many minutes he was standing by the side of that bunk which contained the sleeping form of Guy Averall.

"Here young fellow," said he, "wake up and take some comfort. Best whiskey that is to be found on Governor's Island."

"What do you want?" said Guy, raising his head from under the blanket.

"Don't make any noise, confound it, or old Heidenrick will discover us. Here is something that will do you good."

"What is it?" asked Guy.

"Here take hold of it, and don't ask any questions. I have always had a liking for you. You are every whit as good a man, at the bottom, as Heidenrick or Lawless or any one else."

"What do you want though?" said Guy.

"Why, I say you're as good a man as any one of them, even supposing you have been a few days in the guardhouse. Come take a swig of this, and be a soldier at once."

At this instant Guy Averall from the sheer desire of getting rid of his troublesome friend, put out his hand and took the bottle that was offered, but hardly had he tasted its contents, than he spat out all over the floor, just as if he had been imbibing so much fire. Of all the diabolical compounds in existence this seemed to be the very worst, for it almost suffocated the young soldier!

"There now," said the bard, "you are all right— I wanted to show you that you have one or two friends in the Company, at any rate, even supposing that you and I differ somewhat on this or that controverted point. You are as good a man as Heidenrick, I say, even supposing you have not so much rank."

"You had better keep quiet," said Guy, who in return for the bards civility thought it only becoming and proper in him to afford the latter a bit of seasonable advice.

"Hold your whist," rejoined the other. "I know how to behave myself as well as any other person in this place. I wasn't born—hic—in a cave exactly, even supposin' that my tongue is inflicted with a small bit of the brogue. I endeavor to behave myself discreetly—hic—so that even Sergeant Heidenrick himself cannot find much fault with me, unless indeed he happens to be uncommonly severe."

Hogan's behavior was in general terms unexceptionable, as every candid person will admit, but at this particular instant the obnoxious Sergeant himself appeared, armed with a tallow candle in his hand, so as to institute a proper search as to the cause of the disturbance. At the same time it may be noted that Hogan having taken a few additional mouthfulls from the bottle, now began to feel decidedly exalted, while at the same time this unaccommodating hiccup became worse and worse each instant, so as materially to affect his enunciations as he spoke.

"Here comes Di-og—hic—Diogenes in search of an honest man; but being a simple Private he can hardly select me. However I'll stand the glare as well as I can."

"For what are you up here, at dis ere hour of the night you veller, Hogan, I says," exclaimed the Sergeant.

At this moment the bard began to nod his head in a way that was very significant, for in truth the last pull he took from the bottle, now began to produce a miraculous effect. He pointed to Guy, and then muttered, in a sort of solemn undertone, that he was simply speaking to one of his friends.

"Speaking—for what you speaks at all at this hour of the night—you go to ped."

"I'm keeping good company," replied the bard, "the boy is not bad—hic. *Est bonus, ut melior vir non—hic—*"

"Vat's that you say?" exclaimed Heidenrick.

"*Est bonus, ut melior vir non alius—*hic—"

"You quit talking your wild Irish, and go to ped."

"The boy's not bad—hic—*formosa facies muta commendatio—*hic—well no matter I know the rest, but let it go—hic. The boy Averall is not bad."

"You go to ped at once, or I'll put you in the guard house."

"Oh, guard house—hic—guard house be hanged. Well by the hole of my coat, Governor's Island is a funny place—full of the high falutin', is it not? I've been to Rotten Row this evening, I have, and of all the places for bad whiskey, I say that Rotten Row——"

"Donner und blitzen—you shut up or I'll knock your head off. Go to ped."

Here Guy spoke up, and advised his friend for the sake of peace to lie down, but Hogan having the spirit of opposition roused in him, partially through the effects of the whiskey, and partially by the words of the Sergeant, did not care apparently whether he went to the guard house or not.

"Sergeant Heidenrick," said he, "do you know what—a few days ago—hic—I saw an extract from an old book, which with your kind permission I should like to relate."

"Tont vant to hear anything of your relate. You shut up."

"Sergeant Heidenrick, did you ever carry round a monkey and organ in the course of your life?"

"Dunner und blitzen vats that you have to say?"

"The story I have to tell is from an old book, whose name I need not mention. It is about an elephant and a hog."

"I tont vant to hear anythings about elephants or hogs. You take off your clothes and lie down."

"You need not apply the thing to yourself unless you are particularly anxious to do so. The story is to this effect, that Noah when in the ark, being in want of a scavenger, stroked down the back of the elephant, and the elephant in due time brought forth a pig, so between this pig and another animal in the human form, with three stripes on his jacket, we have been able to make away with all the dirty garbage that is to be found, inside or out, far or near, in a company of Artillery, even to the present day."

This humorous recital, picked up by Mr. Hogan in his miscellaneous reading, was rather too much for the first Sergeant. To have Hogan drunk was certainly bad enough, but to be compared to an animal of the genus *porcus*, was really more than the official could stand. His command in consequence was both quick and sharp. "Dat vill do—I've heard your story—you walk." Hogan seemed to understand intuitively that the Sergeant now really meant business, for he gathered up his blanket without saying another word, and then trudged off to the guard house without delay.

In due time a Court was assembled for his trial, and the bard was arraigned under the usual charge: " Conduct to the prejudice of good order and military discipline," the specification setting forth, in the first place, that the offender was drunk and disorderly in his quarters; and secondly, that he had compared Sergeant Ernest Heidenrick to a hog. To all these indictments the bard chose to plead "guilty"; a confession which the Court saw fit to approve. At the end of a few days the sentence was read, "to forfeit to the United States, six dollars of his monthly pay for one month; and to be confined at hard labor, in charge of the guard, for the period of ten days." Hogan had the privilege of telling his little legend about Noah and the ark, but as a necessary consequence he paid the corresponding equivalent.

During the period of his confinement, the bard had an opportunity of composing an imitation of one of the best known lyrics in the language, which ran in something approaching the following:—

1

There came to the guard house an Exile of Erin,
  The mud on his shoe tops lay heavy and thick,.
For his bitters he sighed, as the morning was wearing,
  For the truth was the man was most terribly sick.
    The evening before all was free and delightful,
    But the close of a 'bender' it always is frightful,
    The soldier is thrust, in a way low and spiteful,
      To the depths of some cell by severe martial law.

2

Sad is my fate, said this child of affliction,
  How I envy the life of the Tom cat so gay!
By moonlight he crawls over housetops and fences,
  In lover-like courtship the time glides away.
    But oh! if by night I should seek the low bower
    Where the bottle's replenished, I'm doomed from that hour,
    I never am freed from the shackles of power,
      Till tried and convicted by stern martial law.

3

Sweet Rotten Row ! in the midst of my wailings,
  Oft to your shades does my mind take its flight,
Still do I dream on your backyards and palings,
  Your clothes lines and wash tubs are still in my sight.
    Oh cruel fate ! how I silently ponder,
    On that dear chosen spot, where I nightly did wander,
    And still of my jorum grew fonder and fonder,
      Till trapped and imprisoned by stern martial law.

4

Friends and companions that with me have sported
  Where, may I ask are you now one and all,
Ye that have with me so often consorted,
  Your joyous features I here will recall.
    One o'er his tactics is silently poring,
    One on his guard bunk is quietly snoring,
    One *plenus veteris bacchi* is roaring,
      While I am imprisoned by stern martial law.

5

But all these sad recollections suppressing,
  One joyous thought my lone bosom may fill,
Though the time lags, yet the month is progressing,
  Nearer and nearer to pay day I'm still.
    When that time comes, with my cash in my pocket,
    (Some sure is mine, though courts martial may dock it),
    I to New York would then speed like a rocket,
      And sink for a day there, this stern martial law.

VI.

During the time that the bard was in confinement, a dastardly attempt was made on the person
of a plain, hard working girl, a resident of Rotten
Row, whose character, as far as any one knew, had
always been unexceptionable. This affair caused a
good deal of indignation among all classes; for soldiers, although prone occasionally to minor misde-
meanors, are very rarely downright ruffians, and are
every whit as likely to condemn an act of this kind

as the most staid and sedate person in the community. Lawless, in particular, was very indignant on
this theme ; he was acting as Corporal of the Guard
on the night that the attempt was made, and when
informed of the real occasion of the fracas, he
rushed over to Rotten Row in an instant, inquired
of the sentinel whose house was attacked, and then
vowed if he had his way, and could discover who
the transgressor was, he would pinion him with his
.bayonet, before the villain had time to draw another
breath. After such earnest protestations as these,
no one, of course, could suspect the handsome Corporal Lawless of having a finger in the pie ! But
all attempts to discover the malefactor were in vain,
the utmost that was known was simply this, that
Corporal Lawless was standing outside the guard
house, according to his account, at about half past
eleven at night, when he heard a screech given apparently by a woman, and immediately afterwards
recognized the call of the sentinel, at post No. 4,
that without even waiting for his musket, he ran in
the direction of the voice, and was told by the sentinel, after challenging, where the cry had originated,
and on entering the quarters indicated, the aggressor
had evidently fled. This was about all the information that could be elicited on the subject, during the
investigation which took place at Head Quarters
next morning—the night was dark, and beyond the
fact that the person who had entered Mrs. Levigart's
house was a soldier in uniform, it did not seem that
anything more could be discovered. So after a
while the affair blew over, and the peace and quiét-
ness of Governor's Island was not disturbed again,

in this way, as long as Guy Averall remained on it.

During the commotion occasioned by this affair a rumor was circulated around Fort Columbus that the Indians in Florida were committing the most unruly depredations—stealing cattle, burning houses, and so forth—and that there was a strong probability that the Twenty sixth Artillery would be sent to that part of the world, as a police force for the occasion. This news, on the whole, was not unpleasant to the various residents of the Island. Hogan had been released from the guard house, and felt free to go wherever he was bid; Messrs. Spruce and Taper both wished to dye their maiden swords in blood; while as far as Guy Averall was concerned, he had already seen a sufficient amount of garrison service, and therefore longed for the more active duties of the field. The same round of guard meetings, and inspections and boat parties, and garrison Courts Martial had been observed at Fort Columbus, ever since he arrived there, so that the prospect of a little campaigning had something absolutely exciting in it; and hence it was that most of the soldiers began to look forward to the expected transfer with a good deal of pleasurable anticipation. Florida, the land of the palmetto and the mangrove; the home of the Seminole and the alligator; the place where those early Spanish adventurers sought for that perennial spring, which was to impart the vigor of youth to every one who bathed in its waters—even in the very name of the state there was something enchanting! Guy accordingly began to collect all the miscellaneous information he could gather respecting this particular part of the earth's surface, and taking up an old history of the state, which was lying in the Orderly room, he soon became cognizant of the fact that Florida was first seen by Ponce de Leon, who landed near St. Augustine in the year 1513. and that the country received its name, either on account of the beauty of its vegetation, or because of its being discovered on St. Flores day. In 1539, according to the same authority, Fernando de Soto explored Florida, and after passing through a series of romantic adventures he appears to have died on the banks of the Mississippi in the year 1542. In the middle of the sixteenth century, many Huguenots visited the country, but only to experience greater evils than they had endured at home. In 1564 they were attacked by the Spaniards, and many of them were hung on the trees with the inscription that they were destroyed, "not as Frenchmen but as heretics," an act which serves to indicate the civility and good manners that existed during these times; and which was requited soon after by the Huguenots attacking the Spanish fort, and hanging up its garrison with the inscription that "they were hung up, not as Spaniards but as cutthroats," a Roland for the Oliver formerly bestowed. Florida remained in the possession of Spain till the year 1819 when it was ceded to the United States, and formally surrendered in the year 1821. In 1835 the war with the Seminole Indians broke out, the occasion being their removal to the country west of the Mississippi. Three years previous, a treaty had been signed by some of the chiefs at a place called Payne's Landing, in which they agreed to relinquish their claim to the land in

11

the State, and to emigrate to the Indian territory. On presenting this treaty, however, to the Indians at a subsequent period, many of them declared against being bound by it, and as an immediate result, one of their chiefs, Osceola, was put in irons, by the United States Commissioner, General Thompson, for alleged abusive language. In a few days after, Osceola was released, but this did not prevent an attack on Thompson, who was murdered at the seat of the Indian Agency, Fort King. Troops were now marched into the country, and on the 24th of December occurred the well-known battle between the command of Major Dade and the Indians, in which the whole of the former were cut off, with the exception of three men. Subsequently several officers commanded in Florida; Clinch, Gaines, Scott and others; but in 1837, while holding a conference, under a flag of truce, with General Jesup, Osceola was treacherously seized, with a number of his followers, and kept at Fort Moultrie till the time of his death, which occurred about six months afterwards. The war lingered on for four or five years after this, costing meanwhile a good many dollars in money, and the lives and the health of a good many officers and soldiers; but it finally was settled by a compromise in which part of the Indians were permitted to live in the southern part of the peninsula; and the remainder of them consented to emigrate to the land set apart for their use, west of the Mississippi.

Such was the information that Guy Averall, at this particular time, was able to collect, respecting that portion of the aborigines who inhabit what some are pleased to characterize as one of the most beautiful and interesting States in the American Union.

VII.

REPORTS still continuing of further depredations in Florida, it was at length announced, in official orders, that the Twenty-sixth Artillery should proceed at once to the sunny south; and take post in various stations in that part of the country. This news, although fully anticipated, was the occasion of some little flurry at Governor's Island; for in the first place Messrs. Spruce and Taper had to start over to New York, to make their adieus to those two "lovely girls" on whose merits they had been expatiating for the last twelve months; while Blodgett, the irresistible, although willing to serve his country like a man, just wanted "by Jupiter" a day or two in addition so as to put the finishing touch to some wonderful machine on which he had been spending his best efforts for the last couple of months. Corporal Lawless too—he had his affaire d' amour; for when off duty he was constant in his devotions to Miss Kitty Traynor, and was even reported as having pressed his suit so far as to ask that somewhat inconstant belle, to accompany him to Florida, as his wife. But the girl, spite of her apparent thoughtlessness, seemed to understand the non-commissioned officer pretty thoroughly. "Indeed Corporal Lawless," said she, "you surely don't want me to make a ballyhaise of myself, and have all the garrison talkin' of me. I'll never marry a man unless he is willing to court me, at the least, for two or three years. Just go down to Florida, and remain there, and try and do your duty as a soldier, and if I hear a good account of you when the Company comes back, perhaps then I may take your case into consideration."

"Do you not wish me to write to you?" was the somewhat cautious retort on the part of the non-commissioned officer.

"Write to me! now what is the use of talking about writing to one of your plain spoken, camping women, as a friend of mine, high in authority, once chose to call me. No, no, Corporal Lawless, we must forego this thing of writing for the present. Things that are put down on paper, you know, are apt to stick. Just behave yourself properly, and try and do your duty in Florida, as I told you before, and if you come back to Fort Columbus with a good character, you certainly will have an opportunity of speaking to Kitty Traynor." And unsatisfactory though it was, the gallant Corporal was obliged to remain content with the foregoing very indefinite answer.

These manifold preparations being all completed, trunks packed, bills paid, friends blessed, and extra baggage sold, the twelfth of February, eighteen hundred and blank, was finally selected as the day on which the troops were to take their departure for the land of the Seminole. On the afternoon of that date, therefore, the good ship Peerless, of the New Orleans Packet Line, appeared opposite the wharf at Governor's Island, in her quality of transport. A judicious care had been exercised by the Quarter-master's Department in selecting the vessel, and when the troops went on board, they found every possible accommodation for their comfort. Some of the older soldiers saw fit to thank the proper staff officers for this kindness, and only wished that a like solicitude would be exhibited in providing a good, clean vessel for voyaging at sea, on all future occasions, for some of the rotten old hulks, that occasionally serve as transports to United States troops, are a disgrace to the country, and have cost the lives of a good many officers and men. On going on board the Peerless, it was discovered that a particular set of bunks were assigned to the use of Company " E "; Guy therefore and his friend, the Scotchman, selected one of these ; put their knapsacks in it, and then going on the upper deck, they took their seats on the forecastle and indulged for some time in that careless chit-chat which constitutes the usual style of conversation among persons of even greater weight and importance than those who, in the words of Falstaff, serve as mere " food for powder."

Every person being on board ; officers, men and all, the Captain of the Peerless gave orders to heave anchor, when soldiers and sailors alike stationed themselves round the Captain, took hold of its bars, and circling round and round, the heavy anchor was finally dragged up. During this process one of the tars chanted an ode, written by some American Dibdin, the only verse of which preserved, at present, is the following :—

> The Peerless is a saucy boat,
> Heave-he, heave-ho.
> And a bully crew's on her afloat,
> Heave-he, heave-ho.

So here's farewell, my own love true,
Heave-he, heave-ho.
Before me speeds the water blue,
Heave-he, heave-ho.

These lines, prosaic though they may seem, produced a really capital effect, when chanted by the
sailors, one of whom gave the words themselves, in
a clear, manly voice, and the others, after heaving on
the bars, joined in the chorus. After a while, the
anchor itself came up, and was secured in its proper
place by a tackle; the little tug that had been puffing and fretting alongside the Peerless took her in
tow; a few sails were set, and the vessel slowly proceeded down the harbor. Governor's Island, with
its guns and red castle slowly receded from view;
the Narrows finally were reached; Fort Hamilton,
Staten Island and a lightship were all passed; and
before long the Peerless and her pilot were well
out on the broad ocean. In the long run the pilot
himself was taken off, by means of a boat; and a
guard and sentinels, having been stationed in various
parts of the vessel, the usual routine of life at sea
now began. Some of the men got sick, in the course
of a few hours, and crawled into their bunks; others
remained manfully at the forecastle, as if determined
to brave that unenviable malady to which "land
lubbers" are pretty sure to be subject. In the end,
a considerable proportion of these succumbed to sea
sickness; while the remainder, deeming it useless to
sit up much longer, retired to their bunks, so that by
the time "four bells" were sounded, at night, nothing was stirring save the officer in charge of the
watch, who kept pacing the quarter deck, and the

sentinels who were stationed in appropriate places in the vessel, both above and below.

> White is the glassy deck, without a stain
>   Where on his watch, the staid Lieutenant walks ;
> Look on that part which sacred doth remain
>   For the lone chieftain, who majestic stalks,
> Silent and feared by all—not oft he talks
>   With aught beneath him, if he would preserve
> That strict restraint, which broken over balks
>   Conquest and Fame : but *Yankees* rarely swerve
>   From law however stern, that tends their strength to nerve.

And so Guy Averall is on a vessel bound to Florida, in order to fight the Indians! Query, is it not possible to manage these same Indians, without fighting them eternally?

VIII.

BUT before going any further we wish to correct a slight mistake. It has previously been stated that all the members of Company " E," both officers and men, were on board the Peerless when she sailed. In the strict sense of the word, however, this is not true ; since the former orderly at Headquarters, Private Timothy Ryan, was absent, he being at that time in New York, a prisoner in the hands of the civil authority. The state of the case was this. A few nights previous, that gentleman had been prowling round the lower extremities of the city, in a lively manner, when wishing to regain his quarters, as quietly as possible, he offered a boatman a stipulated sum, provided he were willing to bring him back to Governor's Island. According to the code of honor, however, which that patriot had adopted, there was no great need in fulfilling his part of the obligation, once the service was performed; so instead of paying the money as agreed, Ryan turned on the boatman and gave him a most unmerciful beating. The latter, nevertheless, was determined to seek satisfaction in his own way; so without more ado, he went to the office of the District Attorney, procured a warrant for the arrest of the offender, and sent a deputy marshal over to Governor's Island to execute it, Just as Guy's company was embarking on the transport, this official handed the warrant to the officer in command, who was obliged, as a matter of necessity, to acquiesce in it. So away went the Marshal, and away went the prisoner to New York city; and if the truth must be told, there were not many men in the Company who seemed very sorry to lose him. "I wish him no harm," said Sullivan, who probably still recollected the encounter in the recruiting depot at Newark, "but I do not like Ryan's ways, and I sincerely hope I never may see the gentleman again." And well would it have been for poor Sullivan if this desire had been gratified, but the fates willed it otherwise. Yet notwithstanding this general indifference it is but fair to say that the prisoner had at least one friend in the Company, for the excellent Mrs. Daisy, who was standing on the wharf, at the time of the arrest, saw fit to exhibit those sympathetic feelings which she, as a kind-hearted lady, had always at command.

Oh the child! the dear child! mine own good orderly " said that truly excellent woman, as she applied the tip of her handkerchief to her eye for an instant, "my poor heart aches to see him go away under charge of that cruel monster of a law officer. I always respected poor Ryan as one of the best men in the Company, and it really is a great shame that a United States Soldier, belonging to my husband's command, should be subjected to such an indignity."

" Don't mind it, don't mind it," said the gallant Heidenrick, who seeing the distress of Mrs. Daisy, thought it proper and right to offer a word of consolation. " De madam must know that Ryan was at times a little pit troublesome ; and now that he is gone, I'll say the Company wont miss him one pit. Still, if the lady cries, I cries too, for I cannot bear to see distress on the part of any one who is related to mine goot old commanding officer." And hereupon the virtuous Teuton, put his hand in his pocket, pulled out a dirty red handkerchief, and applied it to his eye, in sympathetic accord with a similar motion on the part of the Captain's wife.

At this instant a rather irreverent titter was heard among the crowd of soldiers, assembled on deck ; and it was observed in particular, that Hogan beat a somewhat rapid retreat to the other side of the ship.

"Come, Hogan," said some one present, " it wont do to laugh in that way, or you'll have the Sergeant among us, and then you know your fate."

" Yes, but I cannot help it," was the answer. "Such loyalty as is exhibited on the part of old Heidenrick. Oh ! Richard, oh ! mon roi ! Well, by the holy teapot, this will do as an incident in my chapter on beans." And here the bard, who had a keen eye for whatever was ridiculous, saw fit to indulge in a most immoderate fit of laughter.

"Don't make so much noise, or we all will be in the guard house," was the next exclamation.

"Yes, but such love and affection as I see every day around me, how can I resist it? Never did I see Platonic principle properly exemplified till I came to this place. But I'm not a Plato—I'm ordinary flesh and blood, and how can I control my risibilities. But who have we here—the Steward, Petersen, with his box under his arm, running at full speed. I'll venture to bet, though, that he cannot pass the Brigadier, without subjecting himself to a cross examination.

Private Hogan spoke with full knowledge of the subject, for in spite of the pretensions to the contrary there was something positively ridiculous in the curiosity of Mrs. Daisy—she always contrived to ferret out the most trifling circumstances that happened in any place where she happened to be. To think of a soldier like Peterson attempting to pass the author of the chapeau bras, with a box under his arm, without the other prying into its contents, was a sheer impossibility. No sooner had the Steward come within hailing distance, than the Brigadier immediately commenced her attack.

"Oh Petersen, how well you look this morning—going down to Florida, with the other soldiers, so as to fight the battles of your country. That is a good child, Petersen, I'm sure the Major will be proud of you. What have you got in that box, may I ask?"

"Curiosities, ma'm," replied Petersen with naive

simplicity, while at the same time he made an ineffectual attempt to get away.

"Curiosities! why Petersen there is nothing in the world on which I doat so much as curiosities. What *are* your curiosities, may I ask?

"Skulls if you please ma'am—human skulls, at that. Have four or five of them here. Can examine them whenever you chosse."

"Oh the dear good skulls, I do love them so very much!" was the rejoinder. "But you need not mind, Petersen, you need not mind opening the box, my curiosity for the present is gratified. Generally speaking I have the greatest possible desire to examine scientific subjects, skulls included, but for the present I will forego that pleasure."

And with these words the phrenologist was allowed to pass, while Mrs. Daisy casting her eyes, now and then, on Ryan, saw that worthy fast disappearing in a boat; or anon she turned them towards the afterpart of that vessel, where sat the bodily image of Captain and Brevet-Major Thomas Daisy of the Regular Army, "the best and dearest man that ever existed."

I.

BEFORE long the usual routine of guard mounting, washing of decks, drawing of rations and so forth was established on board the Peerless; and then in default of anything more exacting, the Clerk Hogan contrived to start a manuscript newspaper, in which the trifling events of the voyage were recorded. For instance, it was announced, as a very propitious event, that the coffee furnished the command, the day previous, was of very excellent quality, and that a certain member of Company " E," Twenty-Sixth Artillery, was seen making love to a big cucumber, such as are usually served out to troops of the United States when on board a government transport. Then followed a short dissertation on the cucumber as an esculent, in which it was noted among other things that the Hebrews long ago, when in the desert, longed for it; that Aristophanes mentions it among the multifarious good things, such as apples, pomegranates, garlic and little cloaks for slaves; that Theophrastus has fully described it in his treatise on plants; that Hippocrates recommended it, and Sergeant Heidenrick ate it, and therefore the soldiers of the Twenty-Sixth Artillery had no other alternative than to follow these illustrious examples. Next the song, " as slow our ship its foamy track " was furnished with a new dress to suit the circumstances of the voyage ; while in the following paragraph a very touching inquiry was made respecting the health of some unlucky wight on board, who still suffered from the effects of *mal de mer*. Of course that old joke about the string and the piece of fat pork could not be omitted, for this was recommended as a sovereign remedy to all persons who felt qualmish on board. But the masterpiece appeared to be a transcript of the book of Proverbs, in which "Hogan, the wise, now serving in his third enlistment," laid down sundry rules for the guidance of the young recruit, when doing duty in the Twenty-Sixth Artillery. A very agreeable pastime was furnished by the Germans on board, who usually assembled in the forecastle in the morning ; and there gave some song that spoke of home and friends and their own dear fatherland, their voices rising together, in unison, with very happy effect. But one amusement, story telling, must not be forgotten, and in this connection our friend Corporal Sullivan, certainly bore away the pa'm., for the Corporal, spite of the fact that he had been carrying a musket in the United States service for the space of some five or six years, still retained no inconsiderable portion of Irish credulity about him, and as to this question of ghosts and fairies and other weird spirits, he had not quite made up his mind as to whether they really existed or not. One of his recitals, given on board the Peerless, may not be out of place in this connection, as it will serve to illustrate the Corporal's conception of a really good narrative, such as a person in his situation may naturally recount. The story, an old one by the way, has on more than one occasion been given in print, but as it has the merit of being a genuine legend, not a manufactured one, and was frequently repeated by the Corporal, we here take the liberty to introduce it, especially as it contributed somewhat to the amusement of Guy Averall at the time. The tale gives the history of three men, Hudden and Dudden and Donald O'Leary, and has a moral obvious enough to those who read.

*   *   *   *

Hudden and Dudden and Donald O'Leary were three neighbors, who lived in the townland of Ballymagad. There they had each a small farm, which according to the custom of the country they tilled with an ox, that animal indeed constituting the principal article of live stock which either of them possessed. But Hudden and Dudden, being of an envious nature, got together and laid down a plan to kill Donald's ox, hoping by that means to embarrass him so much that they might eventually get his farm, and then divide it, in equal portions, among themselves. So one night they came to Donald's house, poisoned the ox, and then told the people all around that the animal had died of sickness.

When Donald got up in the morning and went to his outhouse, he there saw the condition of the poor animal, and immediately suspected who were the real culprits, even in spite of his neighbors protestations. "No matter," said he to himself, "they have killed my ox, that I know, but they have not deprived him of his skin, so I'll take it off, bring it to the market and sell it." Donald accordingly took his knife, skinned the ox, and away he started with the hide slung over his shoulders.

As he went along, up came a magpie and lit upon the hide, and immediately commenced picking at such little pieces of meat as were attached to the skin. Donald, after a while, happened to look behind him, and saw the bird, so without more ado, he stretched out his hand, took the magpie, and put it into his pocket.

Now this magpie, it may be remarked, was a very singular creature. It had travelled a great deal in its early youth, and among other places had visited the land of Cream of Tartar.

"Crim Tartary, you probably mean," said Hogan by way of suggestion.

"It is all the same in Frinch," replied the gallant Corporal with a wave of his hand which was truly magnificent. "The magpie had visited the land of Cream of Tartar, in his early youth, and while there had been taught Latin. So after a while it began chattering in Donald's pocket; asking, no doubt, to be set free, but in the long run it got tired of complaining, and went to sleep, in which condition it remained till after Donald entered the market.

In due time Donald sold the hide, took the money he had received for the same, counted it carefully, and feeling somewhat tired he went over to a tapster, and asked for a dram of his best. The tapster accordingly went to a keg, and commenced filling a gill, when at that instant the bird awoke from his doze and began to speak. The tapster was astonished, and accordingly asked Donald what sort of an animal that was which he carried along with him?

"It is a bird," said Donald.

"What kind of a bird may I ask?" inquired the other.

Now Donald in spite of his misfortunes was somewhat of a wag, and when an impertinent question was put to him he did not hesitate to give a corresponding answer. So without thinking of the consequences that might ensue, he informed the tapster that the bird in question was one of the most valuable animals that man ever possessed, for it invariably told him all sorts of secrets.

"He should not have prevaricated though," said Hogan who for the nonce seemed to adopt the character of censor. "Only stock speculators and newspaper men are guilty of such enormities as that."

"I can't answer for his conduct," rejoined Sullivan. "I simply tell the tale as it was told to me, so let me go on with my history."

"A bird that tells you all sorts of secrets!" ejaculated the vender of John Barlycorn. "And what secret, pray, does he impart to you now?"

"Why he says," was the answer, "that you have liquor, a great deal better than that you now sell, in your cellar."

"Dear me," replied the tapster, "how in the world can a magpie know so much. Why I'd give almost all I have in the world to possess such a bird."

"Could not sell him at any price," said Donald who still fibbed like a fox.

"Could not sell him," repeated the tapster, "why if you choose I am willing to give you my hat full of gold."

"Done, it is a bargain," was the answer. So Donald took the gold, put it in his pocket, and home he started.

Just as he was within sight of his own house, who should he meet but Hudden and Dudden walking towards him. "You are a couple of nice fellows," said Donald, "sharp as steel traps, I suppose. You thought you had done me a great injury by killing my ox ; but it was the luckiest accident that could possibly have happened. You were not aware of the demand for oxhides that exists at present in town. Everybody is crazy over them ; you can get almost any price for one of them that you please. I sold my hide early in the morning for a hat full of gold, and if I had held on for a while, and not parted with it so readily I might have doubled the price. Look, look, here are some of the shiners." And with these words Donald pulled out a handful of guineas, and exhibited them to his astonished neighbors.

"A hatfull of gold for an oxhide!" replied Hudden and Dudden. "If that be so, we will kill our oxen, without delay, and get a couple of hatfulls also." So both the fellows started off to their farms and slaughtered their beeves; but when they brought their hides to the market they soon discovered that oxskins would not command more than the usual price, and that meanwhile they had destroyed their chief dependence for cultivating their own soil. So back they came to their homes, vowing all sorts of vengeance on their more fortunate neighbor.

Their next plot was even more diabolical than their former one. In the first instance they had simply killed their neighbor's steer ; in the second they determined to make an assault on the life of Donald himself. But Donald already suspected their designs, and resolved to circumvent them if possible.

12

Now about this time Donald's aunt, who kept house for him, and who by the way was not a particularly agreeable old woman, took it into her head to die. Donald of course was very sorry for this, and in order to honor the remains in a proper manner, he took them up very carefully, and put them in the best room in the house. He then procured a sheet, wrapped it round his own shoulders, and sat down before the fire for comfort.

He had not been long in that position before Hudden and Dudden approached the house, under cover of the night, with the full intention of murdering him. They accordingly burst in through the window of that room where Donald's aunt lay stretched; but seeing the old woman, in the first instance, lying dead, and catching a glimpse of Donald, soon after, enveloped in a sheet; they immediately thought that the latter object was the old lady's ghost. So away they took to their heels, leaving Donald in possession of his own premises.

Next morning he determined to bury his aunt, and having no one to assist him, he took up the old woman on his shoulder, and thus started for the grave yard. Feeling somewhat tired after a while, he deposited the corpse by the side of the road, propping it up by means of a staff, so that it remained entirely erect. Donald then went to a house near by, to procure a cup, in order that he might obtain a drink of water. Now inside that house was an old miser, who spent most of his time counting his money, and in wishing that some rich lady or other would marry him. The old fellow being a great curmudgeon, received our friend very bluntly. " I can't lend you a cup or anything else," said he to Donald, after the latter had made his request for the use of that article.

"Can't lend me a cup!" replied Donald. "I'm sorry for you then, for you hardly know what you have missed. Do you see that old woman yonder, standing by the side of the well?"

"I do," replied the miser.

"You do, and yet you would wantonly disoblige her nephew. That woman let me say, sir, is the most extraordinary person in the kingdoms, for although a female, she can keep her tongue quiet from year's end to year's end, and as far as money is concerned, she would not sell herself, to any man living, for all the coin in the world."

"If she is so rich," said the miser, "I must go over and address her, for I have been hunting such a woman as she for a wife this many a day."

As soon as the old miser could secure his hat, he started off in order to pay his respects, and induce Donald's aunt to enter his house. He accordingly addressed her two or three times without receiving any answer, and at length, being somewhat worried with the dame's apparent want of attention, he applied his hand to his side, and gave her a shake. But before he had time to bless himself the corpse fell over and tumbled into the water.

"Heigh ho!" said Donald, who although a true born native of the Isle of Saints, could, now and then invent tales like a Chinaman. "Heigh-ho—a nice state of affairs we have here! Knocked my aunt into the well, and in all probability drowned her too! Oh! by all that is handsome, the woman is as dead as a door nail."

"Is that really so?" exclaimed the miser.

"Yes," was the answer, "and I dare say before long we will have a coroner's jury in this place; and they will sit in judgment on that corpse, and they will say that you yourself were the wilful cause of her decease, and they will recommend you to be hanged, and when you are going to the gallows tree top, you will feel both sorry and indignant with yourself, because you did not exercise some little care when applying your hand to that venerable dame, instead of thrusting her, like a dead rat, into the water."

By this time the miser began to be terribly frightened, and said he would give anything to compromise the matter, even to a hat full of gold, rather than run the chance of being hung.

"It is a bargain," said Donald. "I'll not be too hard on you, I'll take the hatful. Just help me to dig a grave and bury the old woman in decency, and then we can settle all the rest." The miser was only too glad to accept a settlement of any kind, so he assisted Donald to bury his aunt, and afterwards paid the cash, according to the agreement.

Donald now started home with his hat full of money as usual, when on approaching his farm, he met his old friends Hudden and Dudden. "You are a nice pair of fellows," said he once more, "you intended, I suppose, to kill one of your offensive neighbors, but instead of that you only frightened to death my poor old housekeeper. And as luck would have it I have received a proper reward for her venerable remains. See here, I have the full of my hat of gold! You never heard, I dare say, of the wonderful demand for old wives bones that exists at present in all parts of the country."

"Dear me," said they, "that is strange—why what in the world could any person require with old wives bones in this intelligent age and nation?"

"Why to make them into gunpowder," was the immediate answer,

"Well if that be so," said Hudden and Dudden "we will both go, and each kill one of our aunts, and see if we cannot obtain a couple of hatfulls of gold likewise." They accordingly perpetrated the deed, just as they had said, slung the remains over their shoulders, started into town and began shouting at the top of their voices "who will buy old wives for gunpowder! who will buy old wives for gunpowder!" But all the boys of the place, instead of buying the wives from them as they had anticipated, gathered together in a crowd, and commenced pelting them with stones till they drove them out of the place. Hudden and Dudden therefore left the village, in a terrible fit of disgust, went home, and vowed all sorts of vengeance on their more fortunate neighbor.

The day following the two worthies met, so they then and there contrived another plot, namely, that they would both go, seize hold of Donald, carry him off, and drown him. This design, before long, they put in execution. They got a big sack, put it over Donald's head, thrust him into it, tied it fast, and then carried both it and its contents towards a river that ran at some distance from their house. They had not gone far when they met a hound running after a fox, and as the fox seemed to be pretty well exhausted, they thought they would enjoy the sport. So away they started for some distance, thinking they would see the termination of the chase. Meanwhile Donald, being left on the road, tied up in a sack, began to sing. Soon a drover came along with a herd of cattle, and as the man came near to Donald, he stopped and asked him what he was singing about ?

" I !" said Donald, speaking from the inside of the sack, " Do you really wish to know ? I am singing because I am going straight to the Kingdom of Heaven. I am sure any person ought to feel well satisfied on account of leaving this wicked, envious world, and having all the blessed joys of Paradise before him."

" Going to Paradise !" exclaimed the drover. "And are you really sure you are going to that blessed place ?"

" Certain of it," responded Donald, "it is on account of that certainty I am now enjoying myself here."

" If you really are certain of your destination," said the drover, " I willingly would exchange with you, for the more I see of this wicked world, the more disgusted am I with its deceit, pretension and selfishness."

" If you wish to exchange places with me," answered Donald, " I am willing to do so provided you allow me that drove of cattle, now under your care, by way of bounty in the transfer."

" A bargain," exclaimed the drover. So, in an instant the sack was opened, Donald came out, the drover took his place, and Donald taking possession of the cattle, brought them home, and drove them to pasture on his farm.

Meanwhile, as soon as Hudden and Dudden had satisfied themselves by chasing the fox, they both came back, took the sack in their arms, and deposited it and its contents in the river. Great however was their surprise when they came home, to see the farm of Donald filled with the choicest cows, and the man whom they had supposed to be drowned, sitting quite contentedly at his own door !

"You are a nice pair of fellows," shouted Donald once more. "You thought, forsooth, you would ruin me by carrying me off to the river, and attempting to drown me in it. Instead of all that, however, it was the most fortunate circumstance that could possibly have happened. Such droves and herds of cattle as there are grazing down under the water ! Why, if I had proper assistance I could have secured not only the paltry collection of animals now before me, but a herd ten times as great. I never saw such splendid longhorns as there are down at the bottom of that river. It would do any person good to look at them."

"If that is so," said they, "we too would like to secure a portion of them ourselves. Are you willing to show us the way ?"

"I am," said Donald, "on two conditions. First that you will let me alone in the future ; and second, that you will give me a third of the cattle you may secure in that place."

"Agreed," said they, as if anxious to make a big haul.

Away they started, while Donald was careful to

lead his persecutors to the broadest and deepest part of the river. "That is the place," said he, "where the cattle are grazing—all you have to do is to follow my movements. I'll just step back, a few yards, so as to make a good jump; and as soon as I disappear under the water you can follow me. If we do not soon afterwards secure some of the finest beeves in existence, why then you need never address me afterwards as Donald O'Leary.

"Hold on," said they, "since you have shown us the way we have no further need of your assistance. We are both healthy and strong, and can secure the cattle for ourselves."

Led away by their greed in this manner, they now thrust Donald aside, and first one jumped into the river, and soon he was followed by the other. Two little whirlpools, in the water, marked the spot where each went down, so that was the end of Hudden and Dudden.

*   *   *   *

Such was Corporal Sullivan's recital, the story being enlivened by many interpolations which we have not seen fit to reproduce. After all was over, the clerk Hogan remarked: "A very good story, Corporal, a very good story indeed—that is to tell to a crowd of soldiers, although it would hardly answer to print in a child's magazine."

"I know nothing about children's magazines," was the answer. "I have told the history as it was told to me, and have no further care in the matter. I wonder though, if such adventures as these did really ever happen?"

"Of course they did," was the reply on the part

of the bard, who never vouchsafed a single smile. "There · is a certain air of probability about the the thing, which gives it all the appearance of a real transaction."

"There were many strange things that happened in those old ancient times," said the philosophic Sullivan, with a sigh, "although I very much doubt the reality of all that is said concerning Hudden and Dudden."

"Why so?" asked Hogan.

"Hold your whist, man," was the rejoinder, "for in the first place how could a lot of live cattle live under the water ; and again how could a common magpie learn such an elegantly written language as the Latin."

II.

THE voyage to Florida was, on the whole, a pleasant one, with little variety in it beyond the change from a cold, to a more genial climate. Occasionally, during the passage, might be seen that most majestic object at sea, a ship in full sail, appearing at one time as an indistinct patch on the horizon, and later, as the many winged cruiser of the deep that she really is. Sometimes a column of water, ascending into the air, indicated the spot where a porpoise was blowing ; or anon, in the immediate vicinity of the Peerless, a gay colored "Portuguese man-of-war," the *Physalia arethusa* of naturalists, might be observed, drifting over the surface of the blue sea, and challenging many an inquiry, as to its place of departure, and ultimate destination. On the fifth or sixth day after leaving New York, that singular curiosity, the "Hole in the Wall" became visible; the "Hole" being neither more nor less than a perforation through one of the smaller islands belonging to the Bahamas, occasioned, no doubt, by the action of the sea on the soft rock of which the group is composed. Then the southern extremity of Florida was passed, a light-house, here and there rising apparently out of the water, marked the general direction of the long line of reefs which extended for fully a hundred miles into the Gulf of Mexico. At Tortugas, the extreme point of this reef, the vessel stopped for several hours, in order to discharge some stores intended for the use of the Engineers at work on the fort just commenced at that place. Here a couple of residents belonging to the island came on board, and offered for sale some of the coral that is found at this place, along with several samples of the sea-shells and other curiosities which abound in the vicinity. The general appearance of these islands was not inviting, indeed they are nothing but a collection of low beaches of sand, standing in the midst of the ocean, and covered in some places with a collection of bushes, and a few mangrove trees, here and there on them. The phrenologist, Petersen, however, being a scientific man, chose to consider the Tortugas as very interesting spot, and mentioned among other things that the growth of coral, as observed in these places, had furnished pretty accurate data for estimating the age of the adjacent coast of Florida, a portion of the country of a very recent origin, in a geological sense, but which, according to scientific evidence, must nevertheless, have been ever so many hundreds of thousands of years in forming.

After disposing of her freight at Tortugas, the Peerless finally cleared for Tampa Bay, distant one
hundred and fifty or two hundred miles from the
spot where they now were, and on the twelfth day
after leaving New York, she eventually reached her
destination. With some feelings of interest and curiosity, such soldiers as had not yet visited the South,
now examined the outline of the country, which was
to be, for several months, the scene of their future
service. It presented the features usually found in
the Gulf coast; a low beach of white sand, just
above the line of the water, a blue sky and blue
waves, with interminable forests of the dark colored
pitch pine of the South in the distance. On account
of the shallowness of the water, the vessel could not
approach any nearer the town than the outside bay.
From this point a boat was dispatched to Tampa,
with intelligence that the Twenty-sixth Artillery had
arrived; and accordingly in the course of a few hours
a lighter appeared to convey the troops on shore. All
got on board, and the sails were hoisted; before long,
however, the wind died away and the schooner remained on the water "as idle as a painted ship upon
a painted ocean." This was vexatious, for officers
and men were alike tired of their long imprisonment,
and heartily longed to set their foot on terra firma
once more. In the end, however, a kedge anchor
was dropped in a boat, carried some distance ahead
and then let go; when Guy, with some other soldiers
were sent to haul it in, so that by dint of lifting and
hauling, and again lifting and hauling the command
finally reached the shore. The troops were then
marched from the wharf to their barracks, a set of

low buildings one story in height with a piazza in front
and rear. Here the men were dismissed, and immediately the work of setting their house in order
commenced, muskets were cleaned, rooms swept,
wood procured for cooking, and provisions drawn
from the Commissary. The quarters occupied by the
officers had also to be "emptied, swept and garnished,"
and for this a number of men were specially sent.
The older soldiers, who had been in Florida before,
went through these preparations in a half mechanical
sort of a way, as if they had long been acustomed to
the various incidents of campaigning. As to the
younger ones, they could not resist the temptation
as soon as their quarters were cleaned, of sallying
out, so as to institute an examination into the sur-
roundings of the place. No life-giving fountains,
such as were dreamed of by the early discoverers in
Florida were visible—these had all dried up—but to
the right, left, and front, as far as the neighborhood
was examined, a weary waste of indifferent sandy
soil was visible, although in one group, inside the
garrison grounds, were a number of those live oaks
which are peculiar to the Southern States, and which
were covered over with a drapery of that grey Spanish
moss, characteristic of that part of the country,
hanging from the branches of the trees in long
bearded-looking festoons. The latitude of the place,
or if we choose to change the phrase, the mildness of
the climate, was sufficiently indicated by the collection of semi-tropical plants and fruit trees which
were congregated around the officers' quarters. The
orange, lime, lemon, cape jessamine, banana, guava,
crape myrtle and several varieties of camellias were

found here, or else around some of the better class of houses in the adjoining village. But the thing which chiefly interested Guy at that epoch were some specimens of the country people that he saw approaching the barracks, long, tall, gaunt, sallow-looking fellows these Florida "crackers" were; without shoes on their feet, at this time, but with immense broad brimmed straw hats on their heads, as a sort of equivalent for the former deficiency. They are the same people, in fact, whom Edmund Kirk, in his book, "Among the Pines" has described with so much accuracy. Talk of intelligent and enlightened citizens, as people frequently do in America! There never was a more inappropriate term given to any set of human beings, unless indeed it were applied by way of irony. And yet these men could talk very dogmatically about their constitutional rights, as citizens; and argue at the same time that a white person, in the Southern States, had a perfect right to buy and sell a negro! As to that unfortunate class a number of them were seen, assembled under a shed, engaged in piling up a quantity of corn, which was intended for the use of the quartermaster of the Post. Some of the "darkies," it was observed, had profiles which strongly suggested the probability of the Darwinian hypothesis; one or two, however, had countenances which might have done credit to many a European. Guy spoke to one of these Africans, whose face seemed to indicate more than average intelligence, and learned from him that he was born in Maryland, was subsequently brought into Virginia, where he married, was afterward separated from his wife, and then sold to a planter in Florida, who had now hired him out for the sum of twelve dollars a month to the United States government. There was no use of denying the fact, the man spoke with evident feeling and şense, and Guy certainly thought it curious that a country which boasted of its freedom, the person before him should be bought and sold like a chattel.

But—

> Vice is a monster of so frightful mien,
> That to be hated, needs but to be seen ;
> But seen too oft, familiar with her face
> We first endure, then pity, then embrace.

And in this connection, it may be observed, that some of the greatest admirers of slavery in days gone by, were to be found among those who were brought up under far different auspices. The fate of the negro has been a singular one in America ; at one time shamefully oppressed; at another successively elevated, he has never had exact justice done him by either his friends or his enemies. What the colored man really wants, at present, in America, is protection for life and property according to law, as he would have in any civilized country in the world with the opportunity of bettering his condition, just as we afford the same chance to every white emigrant who comes to our shores. And if any certain African shows himself to be a capable and honest person for a public position, for heaven's sake do not let the color of his skin be an obstacle in attaining it. But on the other hand do not let so-called " political necessities," serve as an excuse for thrusting him into a place for which he has no possible qualification ; do not let the fact that all men are entitled to protection as citizens of the same country be confounded with the equally important fact that the art of government is in reality one of the most difficult of arts; and spite of the universal suffrage which at present obtains support, that no person should be allowed to dabble in politics, unless he has some previous training, either by education, habits of life or a converse with universal principles.

III.

THE day after the arrival of the Twenty-sixth Artillery at Tampa, a part of Guy's company was sent out, as an escort, to a train of wagons about to proceed into the interior of the country ; and of this detachment Blodgett the irresistible was given command.   The remaining portion of Company "E" was ordered to unload a government transport, the Fashion, then running between the coast of Florida and New Orleans ; and as Guy Averall had already established a reputation for good natural bodily strength he was elected for the latter duty. The boat was loaded with hay, oats, and such commissary stores as are required for the use of troops, so that while occupied in the way he now was, our friend had a very good opportunity of developing his muscular ability by rolling up barrels of pork, lifting up bales of hay, slinging bags of grain over his shoulders, and amusing himself generally in these and various other interesting ways. Some persons, spending their lives in academies and schools and other high places of learning, may object that the occupation of Averall, at this time, was neither statesmanlike nor intellectual.   Alas ! is it not true, that the world, at present, is devoured with too much intellect ; and for the hard manual labor of life no one is left to perform its functions.

In the labor of love in which Guy was at present engaged, he found a chum and associate, Paddy Oakley by name, who deserves in this connection, a passing notice. Patrick was by nature one of the most stupid men that probably ever lived; big, broad, fat, and lazy; he was the occasion of a few laughs, and a good many scoldings, but seemed as insensible to the one as the other. If Patrick was lifting a bundle of provisions or rolling a bale of hay with Guy, and the thing seemed too heavy, the fellow would instantly let it go with a "be gorra, that thing is too much for me," and then the whole weight would come on Averall. On one occasion a barrel having slipped out of his hand, and fallen on Guy's toes, the latter was tempted to give his friend Patrick a smart cuff, by way of requital, but the other took the affront so good naturedly that from that day henceforth, Guy could never lay a finger on the offender. For all this Private Oakley paid him in full, for many and frequent were the burdens that Guy was compelled to bear. On only one emergency could Oakley be relied on for doing his duty—that was to say when dinner was served ; for Paddy was always blessed with a generous appetite. On these occasions Hogan seemed to take peculiar delight in teasing him ; for if Paddy seemed to be particularly engaged with the victuals before him, some nonsensical question was sure to be propounded as a means of interrupting the Irishman's satisfaction, and then the scowl that passed over Oakley's face gave sufficient evidence of the indignation which was felt by that worthy individual.

Before his advent at Tampa Bay, it is related, that Oakley on one occasion had an opportunity of bettering his condition, for the Doctor on Governor's Island, being in want of a cook, saw fit to apply to Sergeant Heidenrick, who promised to send a " good, useful, intelligent man" to wait upon that functionary. Paddy's appearance when he reported to the Doctor was somewhat against him, so the latter thought it proper and right to institute some inquiry as to the attainments of his servant. "Have you ever cooked before, was the question ?"

" Best cook in the Company, sir," said Oakley with that modest assurance so acceptable in one of his race.

" Very well that will do. I have ordered some lettuce, to-days, from New York. Be careful how you prepare it for table, for at this season of the year I consider it a very great delicacy."

Oakley promised to obey, and in due time placed a covered dish on the table. The Doctor, on sitting down, saw proper to ask for his favorite vegetable, when Oakley without moving another muscle, pointed like a finger post to a particular spot on the board. The Surgeon in his anxiety removed the cover, and there to be sure, was the lettuce, *well boiled*, with a big piece of pork stuck in its midst by way of seasoning. It is needless to say that after this proof of his skill, the Doctor saw fit to dispense with the services of his subordinate.

Paddy's end was, on the whole, a tragical one,

13

and his fate ought to serve as a warning to all fat recruits when stationed in such a place as Florida. One day, when engaged in his usual labors at the wharf, an officer appeared, bound for New Orleans; but who, in the hurry of departure, seemed apparently to have forgotten his baggage. " I want some of you men," said an old irascible martinet, Major Jewett by name, who was standing at the time on board the Fashion. " I want some of you men to run up to Lieutenant Brown's quarters, and bring down his carpet-bag." No one appeared immediately to attend to the summons, so in the end Oakley was singled out, and told to start for the missing article without delay.

" Run, sir, run," shouted old Jewett, "and don't keep the boat waiting here all morning. If you don't move those big, lazy legs of yours, sir, I'll let you feel the weight of this stick before you are many minutes older."

The threat thus enunciated proved sufficient to stir up Paddy. Away he went on what is known as a jog trot, and after a reasonable delay he reappeared with an old grain-bag, suspended between his thumb and forefinger.

What is that you have got, you thundering scoundrel ?" again shouted Jewett at the top of his voice.

" The bag sir—the Liftinant's bag, just as you told me," responded Paddy, to whose mind a bag for clothing and a sack for grain were evidently one and the same article.

" You thundering rascal, go back," roared out the Major. "Ask my servant for Lieutenant Brown's carpet-bag, and hurry back, or I'll break every bone in your body."

Oakley once more hurried off, and in due time appeared with the intended article in his hand— doubtless the servant at Major Jewett's quarters had handed it to him, and thus prevented any further mistakes. But the race and the excitement, and the scolding of the irritable old Major on that eventful day, proved too much for poor Patrick. "Oakley," said Hogan, as he surveyed his comrade with a half-comical smile, "I have seen you do a thing to-day that I never supposed you capable of accomplishing, that is *to run*, but mark my words, that race for the carpet-sack will yet be the cause of your death." These words, although uttered in jest, proved prophetical, for the very next day Oakley complained of a headache and went to the Hospital. The headache finally developed into a fever, and in spite of all the care of a nurse and the skill of a physician, the poor fellow got worse and worse, till in the long run he was forced to succumb. He died in the Hospital, was carried out of it and buried in the little graveyard belonging to the Military Post at Tampa. So that was the end of Private Patrick Oakley.

IV.

In the same graveyard, at a short distance from the spot where the worthy Irishman is interred, is a plain slab, on which appears the following inscription:

✝

SACRED

TO THE MEMORY

OF

LIEUT. LUCIUS O'BRIEN,

of the 8th Reg't, U. S. Inf'y,

who died at Tampa Bay, Fla.,

7th Jan'y, 1841,

aged 37 years.

—o—

Requiescat in pace.

Erected by his brother officers.

This simple monument deserves more than a passing notice, for under it lies buried the author of that song, which appeals so kindly to the American soldier's heart:

> Come fill your glasses, fellows, and stand up in a row,
> To singing sentimentally, we're going for to go,
> In the Army there's sobriety, promotion's very slow,
> So we'll join in reminiscences of Benny Haven's oh!
>   Oh Benny Haven's oh! Oh Benny Haven's oh!
>   So we'll join in reminescences of Benny Haven's oh!

O'Brien, a native of Baltimore, was educated as a Surgeon, and served in that capacity in the Army for some time, but, afterwards resigned, and was subsequently appointed a Lieutenant in that Regiment where he died. Tradition informs us that while sharing a soldier's weakness, he was a great favorite in his Regiment, and as a consequence a supplementary stanza of the song is dedicated to his memory.

From the courts of death and danger, from Tampa's deadly shore,
Comes up a wail of manly grief, O'Brien is no more !
In the land of sun and flowers, his head is pillowed low,
No more he'll sing " petite coquille " or " Benny Haven's oh !"

Well, peace to his ashes ! there have been greater names and persons of more exalted rank in the service, but none appeals more tenderly to the feelings of the Army, than does the author of Benny Haven's.

In some four or five weeks after the arrival of the Twenty-Sixth Artillery in Florida, that excellent gentleman and scholar, Private Timothy Ryan, made his appearance, and as some compensation for the indignities he had suffered while under the civil authorities in New York, he was promoted to the position of Corporal. To the good Mrs. Daisy was given the credit of this movement, but be the fact as it may, the Corporal assumed his new fledged honor with sufficient ostentation ; indeed he contrived to pick up a quarrel with Averall the very morning after he put on his stripes, the question in dispute being the right of ownership in a set of belts, which Guy had cleaned and pipeclayed with the utmost care. After a few thrusts and parries on either side, by way of logical discussion, the Corporal saw fit to adopt the knock-down argument—that is to say he briefly informed his opponent that if he did not cease talk-

ing and "spaikin" in the way he was now doing, he
the Corporal, would be obliged to "level him." As
Guy did not consider the matter at issue of sufficient
importance to bring before his commanding officer,
he was obliged to surrender the set of equipments
which he thought were undoubtedly his own ; and,
in order to avoid any further difficulty with a man
whom he inwardly despised, he ceased all attempts at
argument, and quietly subsided. But Averall, as the
event proved, was not entirely without friends, for
Hogan immediately took up his case, and with some
of that light banter, of which he was master, soon
contrived to turn the tables on the non-commissioned
officer. "What a wild-mannered youth you are
Corporal, and what a placid method you have of
enforcing your rights. How many miles of bog are
there between your family estate, and the nearest
horse fair in Ireland?" A few thrusts like this produced the desired effect, and off the Corporal started
at a tangent. "Oh I see very well how you are all
here—in a regular combination to abuse and browbeat every poor dissolute stranger who does not happen to plaise you. The sorra such a Company as
this in the United States service." But as Ryan's
protestations were not accompanied with any overt
act, he was allowed to talk for a while, and then
ceased grumbling.

After some time, the detatchment of men under
the command of Lieutenant Blodgett having returned
to Fort Brooke, it was determined to send three
companies of the Regiment down the coast to the
Caloosahatchie River, so as to establish a new post
in the Indian country. Orders to that effect were

accordingly issued ; and the troops designated were directed to take passage on the Fashion, and proceed to the southern part of the peninsular. The old scene of shifting quarters was now repeated, blankets were folded, knapsacks packed, and a supply of fat pork and biscuit was thrust into each man's knapsack. Finally the command was on the way to its ultimate destination.

The coast of Florida, south of Tampa Bay, presents the same general outline as that portion already described. The climate still seemed genial ; the sky and water were still blue, the land flat, the lead was kept constantly going from the bow of the boat lest she should run aground. Sometimes, towards the shore, a few turkey buzzards could be seen, circling around and around in the air, or perhaps keeping watch and ward over a fallen carcass from the top branches of an old blasted pine. Sometimes the sea seemed full of medusæ, which kept moving backward and forward through the water with the curious convulsive motion characteristic of that group of animals ; anon the boat passed over a bottom covered apparently with sponges, for in this particular part of the Gulf of Mexico our chief supply of these animals is obtained. Here and there, when the waters appeared brackish, could be seen a long lifeless looking object, stretched on the shore ; this was an alligator, taking his ease, in the sun, unconscious apparently of every thing that was going on around him. Finally the site of the new post was reached, the troops went ashore, hunted up a spring of somewhat indifferent water that was known to exist in the vicinity ; cleared a spot of ground a few rods in extent, landed some supplies, and then slept on their arms during the night. Next morning, work was resumed, a further piece of ground was cleared of its undergrowth of stunted palmetto and cacti, the remaining part of the stores belonging to the command were landed, and after this was effected, the Fashion again took her departure for New Orleans. A tent for the officers was now put up, and the men, after their days' work was over, amused themselves in various ways, telling stories, singing songs, and manufacturing witticisms chiefly of a broadly comic nature, till the call for tattoo was beaten. A guard had meanwhile been selected and a cordon of sentinels was established at some distance from the camp, with orders to be particularly vigilant during the night, lest the Redskins should attack the command. Indians, however, rarely attack when troops are vigilant, and in the present instance every thing remained quiet on the Caloosahatchie till morning.

For the next three months the command was about equally divided—one half of it was regularly employed on Guard duty, and to the remainder was assigned the erection of such buildings as are necessary to constitute a military post. Logs had to be cut, shingles made, and houses put up, while the ground, for a certain distance around the camp, was cleared of the usual growth of chapparal. As to the rest, the situation of the soldiers at Fort Myers, in many respects, was not an unpleasant one, for the weather during the winter months, except when a "norther" set in, was remarkably fine ; while game was plentiful in the woods, and the fish in the river was also quite abundant. The great drawback to the place was the want of good water, and as the season advanced, the sand-fleas and mosquitoes became almost unendurable.

V.

BOOKS at this time, of course, were out of the question ; but as an offset, it may be mentioned that during that period, Averall's friend, Moldwell, took considerable interest in him ; and in their rambles here and there, when not employed in any particular duty, our young friend received a good many very valuable hints from the Scot. The history of Moldwell may be briefly told. When young he had followed the occupation of weaver in Glasgow, but in a season of commercial distress he had enlisted as a soldier in the English Army, served some time in India, and afterwards emigrated to the United States. Here he had put in three successive enlistments, of five years each, and although now close on the age of fifty, he still seemed willing to devote himself as food for powder. But the creditable thing about Moldwell was this, that whatever leisure time he had was devoted to mental improvement; and hence he furnished an excellent example of the well conducted soldier, such as we occasionally find among the enlisted men of the Army. And let no one say that the account which we give of the Scot is an exaggerated one ; for knowledge, in this age of the world, cannot by any possibility be a sealed book. Indeed, as far as mental discipline is concerned, Private Moldwell had all the characteristics that a liberal training could give. Seated in his barrack room, a book was constantly in his hand, and in this way he

had gained a very capable knowledge of the literature
of his own country. Such compositions as the Paradise Lost of Milton, the poems of his countryman,
Burns, or that marvellous concentration of wit, wisdom, and sense, the Essays of Bacon, were all
dilligently studied by him, and as a consequence his
mind and heart was fully imbued with their ideas
and sentiments. With one foreign language, in addition, he was so familiar as to read it with tolerable
ease ; and was thus enabled to compare the habits of
thought most prevalent in another country with these
which were current in his own. Indeed the only
defect that was observable in Moldwell's character
was this, that he had not that enviable knack of
money-making, which is at present a prime requisite
in modern life ; and although the man could discuss
questions of morals and metaphysics at length, yet
in mere pecuniary matters, he was almost as unsophisticated as a child. Yes, and what was still worse,
there was not the slightest likelihood that, in this
direction, there would be any marked improvement
for the better.

One day, the two friends were rambling together
through the woods, when Guy Averall seemed somewhat inclined to indulge in pitiful complaints, " I
know," said he, " that in certain directions I am progressing, for in all the labors necessary to the public
service at Fort Myers, I bear an honorable, if not a
very distinguished part. I handle a musket, I now
and then pull an oar, I help to unload a steamboat,
engage in carrying logs, or perchance, undertake a
rough job of carpentry, in the way that any well-
disposed and able-bodied soldier is supposed to do.

All this, no doubt, is very well, and I am only glad that I am able to acquit myself so creditably. And yet, I candidly confess, I think I have some cause for discontent. There is that brute, Ryan, whom I inwardly despise, and whom I certainly think is inferior to me, in many respects, both as a man and a soldier. And yet for some reason or other he is selected as a functionary in the command to which I belong, and I must submit to him as if he were a demigod. I really believe it is a matter of principle with him to annoy me in every possible way; for if there is a dirty, disagreeable job of work to be performed round the quarters, I am sure to be the one that is selected for that purpose. How does it happen, in many cases, the greatest bullies and scoundrels in a company are chosen as non-commissioned officers in it? That is a point that I do not very well understand. There are Petersen, Hogan and some others —all of them respectable, well educated soldiers, and yet they have never been advanced beyond the grade of private, while Ryan, who can scarcely spell his name, is placed before them all. Oh! if our friend and protector, the gallant Brigadier, would only study the welfare of those 'dear children,' of whom she seems so very, very fond, how comfortable she might make us all! How easy it would be to keep those double fisted gentlemen in their proper place, that is to say as her body servants, while some worthy and respectable man, such as one of those whom I have named, would fill the place which they at present occupy."

These reflections, querulous though they may seem, were nevertheless perfectly natural to a young soldier, situated as Guy was, he was nevertheless disabused of these prepossessions to a very considerable extent by the Scotchman, who chose to act as mentor on the occasion. "My dear sir," responded Moldwell, after Guy had finished his story, "you form a very wrong conception of the position and occupation of the soldier in an army. A man does not join the service for the purpose of teaching geometry, or studying ethics, or attempting the quadrature of the circle, nor is he valued on account of possessing all these qualities. On the contrary, the understanding in our army is, that a good deal of severe laborious work must be done ; and some duty of a sufficiently unpleasant nature must be performed. With the troops on the frontier this is particularly the case ; for barracks must be built, roads must be made, and in many cases supply trains, and surveying parties must be guarded. Now in superintending such labor as this, it frequently happens that a man of inferior calibre, but with a certain amount of brute courage, is really a more effective person than one of more mental attainments. The consequence is, that in our army, at least, the man of education frequently remains a private ; or at best is transformed into a clerk at Regimental or Department Headquarters ; while some robustious periwig-pated fellow, such as some of our non-commissioned officers now are, enjoy such rank and position as the Army affords them."

"What you say," responded Guy, "in all probability is true, and yet this state of things does not render the service a very comfortable place for those who are very sensitive about their present dignity, when subjected to the dictates of men who in essential matters may be decidedly their inferiors."

" Then the remedy is," said Moldwell, " not to afford such persons the opportunity to bully or to sneer at you.   Nothing however is gained by attempting a discussion with a mere animal ; let him exhibit his ignorance and prejudice as he may, you should never make any effort to reason with him, or ten to one the thing will end in some attempt at violence on the part of your antagonist.   The best thing that can be done with such men as Lawless and Ryan is to obey them in official matters, and outside of that to let them severely alone.   Read Mrs. Barbauld's little essay on Inconsistent Expectations—it contains a whole world of wisdom, which is applicable to all conditions of men.   Even under all possible disadvantages, there any many things well worth your attention in the Army.   There are books to read, facts to be learned by observation, and that general communication with external nature to be kept up which every man who is not a mere clod, must have enjoyed and experienced.   In short, situated as we are, midst these pine woods and green palmetto trees in the Southern extremity of Florida, I cannot do better than repeat the advice once given by Polonius.

> Give thy thoughts no tongue,
> Nor any unproportion thought its act ;
> Be thou familiar, but by no means vulgar.
> The friends thou hast, and their adoption tried,
> Grapple them to thy soul with hooks of steel
> But do not dull thy palm with entertainment
> With each new hatched, unfledged comrade. Beware

Of entrance to a quarrel ; but being in
Bear it that the opposer may beware of them.
Neither a borrower nor a lender be ;
For a loan oft loses both itself and friend,
And borrowing dulls the edge of husbandry,
This above all —To thine own self be true,
And it must follow, as the night the day,
Thou canst not then be false to any man.

"A very pretty quotation truly," replied Guy, "but at present I'm so much disgusted with the service that I would prefer a clean discharge from it, to all the wise saws in existence. Still one thing I will never do. I will never desert my colors, even if every other soldier in the Company were a Ryan. But already I hear the beat of the drum, so let us return to our encampment."

VI.

A FEW days after, the two friends were enjoying a peripatetic ramble together, when the name of the American poet, Edgar A. Poe, was mentioned.

"An undoubted genius," said Guy, "that poem of the Raven, which I read when on Governor's Island, impresses itself indelibly on the memory. And yet, if I understand the case aright, Edgar A. Poe, who was sent in early life to the Military Academy at West Point, failed to graduate there ; indeed he was found " deficient," as the phrase goes, the first semi-annual examination to which he was subjected, and as a consequence was dismissed from the institution."

"True," said Moldwell in reply, " and yet of those who had Poe in charge, I doubt if there was one who could compose the Raven ; or produce anything approaching the grace evinced in the well-known lines :

> Helen they beauty is to me,
>> Like those Nicean barks of yore,
> That gently, o'er a perfumed sea,
>> The weary, way-worn traveller bore
>> To his own native shore.
>
> On desperate seas, long wont to roam
>> Thy hyacinth hair, thy classic face,
> Thy Naiad airs, have brought me home,
>> To the glory that was Greece,
>> And the grandeur that was Rome.
>
> Lo ! in yon brilliant window-niche,
>> How statue like, I see thee stand !
> The agate lamp within thy hand !
>> Ah, Psyche, from the regions which,
>> Are Holy Land !

It has been said of these verses that nothing could be more dainty, airy, amber-like than them ; in point of fact they are Horatian. We are told that these verses were written when Poe was only fourteen ; but we must either reject the statement, or reconcile ourselves to a miracle. In delicacy, exquisiteness and pathos the poem is unmatched by any of his later compositions. And yet, it seems from the fact of Poe's dismissal from the Academy, that he either could not, or would not master the very elementary matter, that is taught there during the first year of the student's course."

"And yet many an inferior person has accomplished this task," remarked Guy.

"All of which goes to show, in spite of some dicta to the contrary, that the poetic and technic powers are essentially different," responded Moldwell.   "The former may be the more brilliant quality ; but for very good reasons, the military authorities prefer the latter.   Poe could write verses whose finish is almost unapproachable, and yet he could not master the prescribed course at the Military Academy, and therefore he was very properly dismissed from it "

"An aberration of genius, an evident aberration of genius," exclaimed Guy.   "And yet this unfortunate aspirant for military honors afterwards composed the the Gold Bug, and the Murder in the Rue Morgue."

" He did," replied the other speaker, " nevertheless I must candidly acknowledge that on the whole the ultimate proficiencies of Poe as a literary man hardly corresponded with the expectations we naturally form from the ability he displayed in early life.   One thing we must never forget, that to be great in either art, literature or science, a capacity for labor is one of the essential requisites.   Shakspeare, Goethe and Voltaire ; Titian, Rubens and Michael Angelo ; Newton, Cuvier, and Herschel ; were all as much celebrated for their application to work as for their transcendent ability.   Now the objection to such men as Poe is this, that let their capacity be ever so great, they are by nature too dissipated and reckless to apply themselves steadily in any one direction. Poe's life was a singularly irregular one, his history being given in a biography to which I need not particularly advert.   He was born in Baltimore in the year 1811.   His father and mother died while he was a child, and the future writer was afterwards adopted by a Mr. Allan, a rich merchant who had no children of his own.   In 1816 the little Edgar came to England, with Mr. and Mrs. Allan, and was sent to school there. Some five or six years afterwards he returned to America, and attended an academy at Richmond ; from which he was, in due time, transferred to the University of Virginia. His talent from the first was conspicuous, but unhappily he developed along with it, and continued throughout life to exhibit a profligacy, almost without a parallel in the degradations of genius. Expelled from College on account of his whims, he returned to Mr. Allan, with whom he frequently quarreled on account of that gentleman's reluctance to become responsible for his debts. Quitting the home of his benefactor, he started for Greece, in foolish parody of Lord Byron, to take part in the war of Independence against the Turks. Greece he did not reach, but we find him turning up at St. Petersburgh, drunk and disorderly as usual, and becoming the tenant of a police cell. The minister of the United States interested himself to procure his release, and send him back to America. By the good Mr. Allan the returning prodigal was welcomed, and on his expressing a wish to follow the profession of arms, an appointment was secured for · him as a cadet. After his dismissal from West Point, he once more had recourse to Mr. Allen ; but rumor asserts that he forfeited the good will of his benefactor in a way which we hope, even for the sake of Poe's reputation, is not authentic. But this we know for certain, that Mr. Allan ejected Poe in a summary manner from his house, and would never afterwards hold any communication with him. Cast on his own resources, Poe now took the same step that you and I once did, that is to say he enlisted as a private

soldier, but some friends recognizing him in this
position, busied themselves to procure his discharge.
Shortly after this he began to contribute regularly to
the periodicals, for which he wrote in his drunken,
desultory way, poems, tales, criticisms and so forth.
His brilliant and known ability readily procured him
employment; and his frantic habits of dissipation,
on the other hand, insured his early and ignominious
dismissal.   He now married a cousin of his own, but
she shortly afterwards died, broken-hearted, it is
supposed by the course which her husband led.   A
feeble attempt at teetotalism which Poe ultimately
made was indirectly the cause of his death.   He
joined a temperance society, and was for some
months actually sober, but chancing to pass through
Baltimore, he was waylaid by some ancient cronies,
and on the morning afterwards he was found as usual,
lying in a gutter, from which he was carried afterwards to an hospital, where he died.   Such was the
end of this erratic nondescript."

"A somewhat strange story," remarked Guy, "As
far as I myself am concerned, I am thankful, nevertheless for one thing."

"What is that pray?" asked Moldwell.

"Why simply this," was the answer, "that even
admitting Mr. Spruce and Taper have their youthful follies; that United States officers as a general
thing are more regular in their habits than Edgar A.
Poe was.

"The mere fact that Lieutenants Spruce and
Taper are graduates of the Military Academy," responded Moldwell, "is of itself a sufficient guarantee
that they both are reasonably well conducted men;

for, let us criticize as we may, common honesty compels us to acknowledge that most of the West Point officers are of that class. And this in my opinion is the great recommendation of our national school. The course of instruction there may be somewhat narrow ; and a few of the graduates of West Point, I am sorry to say, do not seem to readily surmount the narrow notions which they there imbibe, but this we all must admit, that it is impossible to pass the scrutiny of the instructors there unless the graduate be possessed of fair technical abilities ; and is willing in addition to submit to the restraints of Army discipline. I only wish we had a military academy for the other side of the house."

" What do you mean ? " asked Guy.

" I mean for the ladies," responded Moldwell. " If we only had a Military Academy to bring these wives of Army officers under proper discipline. I think it would be much better for us all."

" You surely jest," said Guy.

" I don't jest at all," was the rejoinder. " I consider some of these feminine followers of Bellona, as simply horrid, and among the rest, I think our good friend Mrs. Daisy is one of the worst I ever met. Among other things the way she tyrannizes over that girl, Miss Davis, who is living with her, is simply atrocious. We all had a sample of the Brigadier's spirit, the very evening before she had that fool *Chapeau Bras* at the Hospital on Governor's Island. Every one was intent on making preparations for the event, and as the night was somewhat unpleasant, Mrs. Daisy chose to order out the cart and the Quartermaster's old horse, so as to reach the scene of her labors at the Hospital. Afterwards, while engaged in giving directions about decorating the room, the Brigadier was as lovely and amiable as usual ; but on a sudden she seemed to take offence at some trifling thing which Miss Eleanor had either said or done. Well, sir, do you know how she chose to show her lady-like temper ? Why simply by ordering back the vehicle in which she had come ! She got into the cart, rode back to her own quarters, directed the horse to be put up " lest the poor dear child should catch a cold," and as a consequence her niece had to trudge back to her quarters, though sleet and snow, without as much as an ordinary escort ! Is it a wonder, after such a transaction as this, that I should long for a Military Academy in order to discipline such personages as the Brigadier ? And am I not justified in making the prophecy that if Mrs. Daisy were sent to a feminine school, of the same kind that exists on the Hudson, before the first six months were over she would be expelled from the institution as an erratic and unruly character ?"

VII.

On another occasion, Averall and his associate were on their way to their tents, having already enjoyed a short ramble in the vicinity of the camp. Returning, they glanced for a moment at a small howitzer which had been planted in a particular position, as a protection against Indians. This piece of ordnance served as the occasion of a very acute discussion, for Guy in the first instance saw proper to remark, that he never passed by a gun of that character without thinking of the words of old General

Taylor at Buena Vista, " a little more grape, Captain Bragg," as an indication of the martial qualities of that hero.

" A significant expression truly," was the rejoinder, " and yet I doubt very much if it really ever were uttered."

" But the thing has been repeated from mouth to mouth all over the land," answered Averall. " No life of General Taylor that ever I saw omits the sentence."

" That may be so," was the reply, " still, as I said before, I see great reason to doubt if the speech were really ever utterred. With guns in the field, we have solid shot, whose character is denoted by its name ; we have shells, which are intended to be burst by an interior charge ; we have shrapnell, a shell filled with powder and bullets, and lastly we have canister formed by compressing a number of small iron balls in a tin case. As to grape, nine big bullets bound together by a ring and a screw, it is reserved entirely in our Service for guns in position. How then, in the name of common sense, could General Taylor order Captain Bragg to use grape in a place where no grape was to be had, and with a kind of gun which never employed it."

" I'm sure," said Guy, " I don't know—the thing I admit is something of a puzzle."

" The fact that a phrase is frequently repeated in this way," said the Scot, " is no proof whatever that it is true ; it merely shows that it is popular. In the case now before us the explanation is as follows : General Taylor was nominated as a candidate for the Presidency, a catch word was wanted that would appeal to the sentiments of the masses, everyone in America at that time felt jubilant over the results of the Mexican war, the phrase "a little more grape Captain Bragg" was invented as a formula well adapted to tickle the fancy; the thing took; the words spread; Captain Bragg and his grape was mentioned everywhere; and as a final result the good-natured, well-meaning, hard-fighting, honest old veteran, who is said to have employed these terms on the battle field, was triumphantly proclaimed the first magistrate of the country."

"If that be true," responded Guy, "I have nothing more to say. I only regret to find that you have destroyed the coherence of a very pretty little story, which we all loved to repeat."

"It is a pity to mention it," continued Moldwell, "yet nevertheless the fact remains true, that some of the most celebrated mots in existence, would hardly obtain credence if submitted to a critical test. Take for instance that attributed to the Duke of Welling- ton "up guards and at them," said to be delivered to a portion of the English troops by their com- mander on the field of Waterloo. Now this saying has passed from mouth to mouth as a veritable fact, and has been incorporated even into some respecta- ble histories, was nevertheless most stoutly denied by Wellington himself, on every possible occasion. So with the words "the guard dies but never surrend- ers." This phrase attributed to Cambourne was also vehemently repudiated by him. In fact we know that the saying was invented by Rougemont, a pro- lific author of mots, a couple of days after the battle."

"Well," said Guy, somewhat astonished, for in

truth the information thus given to him was quite new, "you almost destroy my credence in events whose authenticity, a short time ago, I almost imagined to be beyond the reach of controversy."

"I would not destroy your credence," was the reply, "but this I wish to point out that history, as it is called, is usually compounded of fact and fable; and any person would surely contribute to our intellectual progress who might compile a code of examination by which we can separate the one from the other. Indeed the times seem propitious for such an organon, since our trust even in lettered books is no longer so enduring as it once was. A few hints perchance may suffice. For instance, your own experience in the Army convinces you, that with some local differences of sentiment the natives of far distant countries are at bottom essentially the same. Now is it too much to extend this principle in another direction, and assume that the men who lived eighteen hundred or two thousand years ago, did not, in their natures, differ very greatly from us? This assumption is the leading characteristic of the critical spirit of which we all have heard so much of late. It presumes that the world of Numa or of Augustus is essentially the same world that now surrounds us, and then seeks to explain the current belief of past ages by an examination of the circumstances under which these beliefs may have been formed. For instance, if a city at any time becomes great and powerful, there is a strong disposition to deify its founders, and hence such persons as Theseus or Romulus are invested with the most extraordinary gifts. The lives of the saints may be laughed at, and yet to me they are full of instruction. They show me the opinions, the purposes and the prejudices of the men who wrote these lives ; the code of criticism that they employed, and how far a glorious ideality tempered the severity of their judgment. We may doubt if the good Saint Denis walked two full miles with his head under his arm, after that portion of the body had been cut off ; and question if Saint George of Cappadocia really slew the famous dragon at Beyrout with which he is credited. But never will we find fault with a meek grey-headed old cordelier if he really happens to believe these ancient verities."

"I think I understand your way of looking at things" said Guy.

"In reading history too," continued Moldwell, "we must take into account the prejudices and purposes of the author who composed the narrative ; for it is very rare, indeed, to find a historian who is strictly impartial. If one man wishes to extol monarchical principles, he gives us a history of Europe, in which everything in favor of republicanism is studiously suppressed ; if another has a liking for Napoleon the generous acts of his life are displayed to full advantage ; while his selfishness, his meanness, and his despotic will are passed over as leniently as possible. Macaulay gives us a huge whig essay, while writing his account ; and Hume, on the other hand, takes pleasure in portraying the fate of one of the Stuarts. Finally, it must not be forgotten that the elements of time and place are important ingredients in estimating the credibility of writers in an uncritical age ; for those who live near the period or locality they describe, are usually much more trustworthy than those who live far away from them. Livy tells us that wonderful story about Hannibal breaking rocks in the Alps by means of vinegar ; while Polybius, who lived much earlier, does not notice the circumstance. In the same way your countryman, Saint Patrick, writes a life of himself, which is as unostentatious and apparently as truthful as anything of the kind can possibly be. But when the Monk Colgan, who wrote in the seventeenth century, is required to submit his compilation, all the foolish old legends that could be collected about the patron Saint, previous to the time that Colgan composed his work, are thrust haphazard into the record."

SWEET WILLIAM.

I.

In about three months from the date of the establishment in Fort Myers, the term of enlistment in the case of Sergeant Ernest Heidenrick had expired; that official, therefore, received his discharge and went north, so that his connection with the Twenty-sixth Artillery was now severed. About the same time Captain Daisy was obliged to leave Florida; his health had indeed been suffering a good deal of late, the climate of Fort Myers was not a desirable one for an invalid; and hence he had been obliged to apply for a leave of absence. In consequence of this change, the command of Company "E" was now transferred to Lieutenant Spruce; while, as a result of Heidenrick's discharge, it became necessary to choose a 1st Sergeant, in order to properly administer the affairs of that organization. For this office the names of several soldiers were proposed, and Ryan in particular was strongly recommended on account of the bodily strength he was supposed to possess; an all important quality according to some authorities, in choosing the non-commissioned officers of a Company. But, in the long run, Corporal Lawless was selected as the proper man, because, in the first place, he was a good drill instructor, and secondly a handsome fellow, while one of the officers argued very astutely, that if a row arose after pay day, in consequence of a little·too much whiskey among the troops, and it became necessary to knock down a man or too, that Lawless could readily call in Ryan as his assistant, settle the case in a moment, and then each of these subordinates could return to their appropriate duties. This plan, which evinced considerable ingenuity, seemed to meet with un-qualified approval, so Lawless and Ryan were both made Sergeants, and to the former was assigned the charge of the Company. These appointments seemed to gratify those immediately benefited—indeed it was noted that Ryan and Lawless both sat down and played cards from retreat to reveille on the day when the announcement was made—yes, and what is better too, they kept up the same amusement, night after night, for a whole week in succession.

Now regarding this practice of playing cards, there is no use denying the fact, that American soldiers, now and then, do indulge in it occasionally; nay more than this, that at the bi-monthly pay day, in particular, it becomes a common if not a some-what expensive amusement. Among the games that may be mentioned, in the connection, are "euchre,". "forty-five," and "seven up;" but the palm after all seems to be given to that identical mode of hazard which Minister Schenck is said to have taught the young diplomats at the Court of Saint James—we mean the ancient and venerable game of "poker." And indeed it was both an amusing and cheerful sight. to see a number of soldiers, sitting round a blanket, spread in a tent, with their pile of quarters and half dollars before them, indulging in a fifty-cent "ante," going one or two dollars "better," or

perchance " doubling the stakes," and then " calling "
their opponent. Lawless and Ryan, as we said before,
both indulged in this game ; so did Sullivan, and the
bard Hogan ; but the latter, after a while, took offence
at something which was either done or said at one of
these meetings. He accordingly left the place in a
very abrupt manner, said he would have nothing to
do with Lawless any more, and which was rather
singular, he ever afterwards adhered to this resolution.
Some of the outsiders endeavored to allay this family
quarrel, by promising to propitiate the other powers,
if Hogan would only bestow his confidence, and
candidly tell what was the matter. But the bard was
by nature too polite and conscientious a man to
indulge in any underhand cavillings. He merely
said he had formed his opinion of one of the gentlemen, with whom he had sat down in a friendly
manner, but further than this he would not say anything against him. So the play went on—Sullivan,
Lawless, and Ryan with this or that other person
making up a game ; while Hogan for the future kept
aloof from all such proceedings. At length even
Sullivan got tired of this amusement ; for in the first
place he discovered he constantly lost money by the
operation, and in addition he thought he noticed
something very queer on the part of Lawless one
night, when the 1st Sergeant supposed there was no
one looking on him, and as a consequence the
Corporal finally came to the conclusion he could not
afford to sit down and play with any one who took
such an underhand advantage as Sergeant Lawless
evidently did. He therefore resigned his seat at the
gambling board, to some of the other gentlemen who

were to be found in the Company and who still seemed to take sufficient interest in this game of hazard to "double the stakes" "chip twenty-five cents," "call" an adversary or "go two dollars better."

In presenting the foregoing sketch of Messrs. Lawless and Ryan, short and imperfect though it be, we hope the reader will give us credit for being actuated by no mean or unworthy motive. In the first place we disclaim the fact that either of those gentlemen ever inflicted on us any real or personal injury. They never threatend to knock off our head for saying that they both were not the very greatest and most gentlemanly personages in the whole world, they never cheated us out of a dollar of money at "poker," "forty-five," "seven up," or any other game at cards; they never thrust us into the guard house in a violent and despotic manner for grumbling at any of their exactions; in short, they never injured us to the breadth of a hair in mind, body, or estate. We consequently have not the first particle of ill-feeling towards them, in any one way. Our duty, as recorder of this narrative, is simply to put into proper form such incidents as relate to the same. Had either of these non-commissioned officers been very different from the personages they really were, we willingly would have admitted the fact. Had they been highly accomplished and intellectual scholars, instead of the lively gentlemen that they appeared to be, the circumstances would be duly chronicled in this history. But to write an eulogy, under existing conditions, is impossible for us to do, and therefore we dismiss the whole matter with the foregoing notice.

During the spring of that year, two distinct expeditions were sent out from Fort Myers, for the purpose of finding the Indians, but both of these unfortunately met with little success. The first one consisted of about one hundred men, and was dispatched eastward, along the southern bank of the Caloosahatchie River, with directions to reach Lake Okee-chobee; and after examining the country there, to return by the opposite bank of the stream to the point of starting. In this affair, Guy Averall took part, marching with his lump of fat pork, and his four pounds of biscuit in his haversack, as manfully as the oldest soldier in the command. This expedition was absent five days, during which time it marched a distance of something over one hundred and twenty miles, but did not accomplish any thing definitely. Traces of Indians, no doubt, were to be seen here and there; but still no braves were captured, indeed a moment's reflection might be sufficient to convince any one that all these attempts must prove futile, for in such a country as Florida, covered over as it is with chapparal and hammocks, every Indian in it might conceal himself at the distance of a few hundred yards from the place actually occupied by the troops, and there remain undiscovered for an indefinite length of time. The next expedition was sent out in about a week after the return of the former one, and from the account given by the participants, it must have been a delightful one. The purpose, as given out, was to penetrate the country in the direction of the Everglades, capture the Indians there, and then return. But this too was unavailing.   The men sent out, marched a day, got into a country partially covered with water, waded through it, ate their hard biscuit and salt pork, while standing up, and having reached the spot where the post of Fort Simon Drum was afterwards established, they were actually obliged to erect temporary bunks, by means of boughs, cut from pines, in order to secure a place sufficiently dry for them to rest on during the night.   A large portion of the southern extremity of Florida, is in fact a mere swamp; covered with water to the depth of from one to six feet.   In the everglades this water serves to support a coarse species of reed-like grass, which grows to the height of several feet above its surface, and it was in this part of the country that General Harney, by means of flat-bottomed boats, attempted to capture the Indians toward the close of the first Florida war.   In the present case these repeated wanderings and counter marchings, on the part of the Twenty-sixth Artillery, began to be somewhat monotonous, and their uselessness having been again and again demonstrated, it was finally resolved to abandon them.   Why they should have been instituted, in the first instance, was a fitting theme for inquiry; as the case, however, now stood, the mountain would not come to Mahomet, so Mahomet was forced to go to the mountain; in plain terms, since the Indians could not be entrapped and brought into Fort Myers, it was necessary to have recourse to the charms of persuasion for that purpose.   At various times during the war in Florida, which ended in 1842, instalments of Seminoles had agreed to accept the terms offered by the United States government, and had emigrated to the Indian territory beyond the Mississippi.   To these accordingly, an agent was sent, asking that one or two Red men should return to Florida, to act as interpreters, and endeavor at the same time to persuade their relatives in that state, to follow the footsteps of those living under the protection of the general government in that section of country set part exclusively for the use of the Indians in the West.   This plan succeeded so far that a number of Seminoles were actually persuaded to come into Fort Myers, so as to hold a conference with the commanding officer of the Department, old General Twiggs, in relation to their wants and desires.   Guy Averall had already seen the interpreters on board the Fashion, as she steamed up to the wharf at Fort Myers, on her return from New Orleans, and doubted not but a conference would soon take place. The next morning these ambassadors started into the woods by themselves, and after the lapse of a week or therabouts they returned with the intelligence that the celebrated warrior, Bowlegs, accompanied by several other chiefs, would come into Fort Myers the following day.

In due time the Indians made their appearance, and certainly their first approach, as they strode into the post, one after another, was a remarkably imposing one.   Tall, straight, well shaped fellows, with graceful limbs, and a bearing that on the whole, was sufficiently dignified ;   there seemed to be nothing whatever of that squalid repulsiveness about them, which travellers assure us is commonly associated with the Red men of the plains.   On the forehead of each was a small silver plate, in the shape of a crescent, while above their head was a tuft of plumes from a species of eagle found in Florida. Leggins of deerskin and the customary blankets completed the outfit, and as they sat down, one after another, in front of the tent occupied by General Twiggs, a feeling of involuntary respect for them was awakened in the breast of every one present. Why should they be compelled, merely because their enemies, the whites, desired it, to abandon those woods and hammocks in which they and their fathers had hunted for ages, and then seek new homes for themselves in a country to which they were strangers? Would the palefaces themselves submit to be driven about like so many dumb cattle, at the will and beck of some fancied superior? But these feelings of reverence on the part of the enlisted men were unfortunately of short duration, for after a while the conference with General Twiggs broke up, and then the genuine character of the Indian appeared. In their "talk" with the officers, they had manifested a quiet dignity, but after this was over, a decided change took place. They invaded the tents of the officers and soldiers, they begged for whatever they could get; their chief, William, appropriated Guy Averall's shirt; and with this garment over his shoulders, and an old sword by his side, the fellow cut up the most curious antics. He marched, he strutted, he drew the weapon, he enunciated his word of command, he uttered all the persiflage of a mock emperor. None of the other Indians, except the chief, could speak English, and his regard for Guy was expressd in a somewhat singular manner. "If we go to war, me will kill you—shan't fall by the hand of any other brave—fine fellow like you should be killed by a brave warrior like me, not by an old woman like Tiger tail." Guy, of course, thanked William for this mark of his esteem; although when the former, by way of barter demanded back his shirt, Mr. Bowlegs expressed his desire to keep it, just as a mark of his love and affection—"never mind, when you come out to the Everglades again, me will fight and kill you, shan't fall by the hand of any other brave except myself, Tiger tail is nothing but an old woman, he not fit to kill you." Towards evening, the Indians by some means or other, obtained a supply of "fire-water," and then they assembled and gave one of their characteristic dances. A fire was lighted in the woods at sundown; the warriors, in various trappings, assembled around it, their hands were joined, a curious sort of see-saw chorus was struck up, they circled round and round the flame, gesticulating in the most extraordinary way, then on a sudden a whoop was given; a noise evidently intended as an imitation of a turkey gobbler, next followed, and lastly, each one present took a pull from that all potent spirit which seemed to infuse itself into the very life of the demons. A couple of black negro wenches, who accompanied the warriors as attendants, joined in these revels, and seemed to relish the exercise every bit as well as their sovereign lords and masters. Doubtless, they served an important purpose, for beside taking charge of such household cares as devolved on them, they had the foresight to hide the knives that were in possession of the warriors ere the fun commenced, Had this precaution not been adopted, some ugly results might possibly have happened.

At a subsequent visit to the Fort, the Indians brought in several of their children ; lads of from twelve to fourteen years of age, and the skill which these exhibited in the use of the bow and arrow was, in itself, something remarkable. Now and then these youngsters would follow a flock of young quail, that ran through the underbrush outside the Fort, fire an arrow at one, kill it and without stopping to pick up the bird, would proceed to the next one within reach, and after it was pinioned, a third and fourth victim would follow. After their arrows had all been exhausted, they would return, pick up the birds, and then attack another flock in the same manner as before. A silver coin suspended from a tree, at the distance of six or eight yards, was almost sure to be struck in the same manner. But the almost fiendish character of their sires, whenever they got excited, seemed to banish all the romance of the Indian character, and the promise of Mr. Bowlegs to kill Guy, in return for the use of his shirt, fully demolished any regard that young gentleman might otherwise have for the aboriginal inhabitants. Oh! James Fennimore Cooper, author of those Leatherstocking Tales, on which so many juvenile readers have doted, why didn't these not portray the Indian as he is, sneaking and dirty and merciless, instead of being the moral philosopher and expounder of the doings of the great Wahconda, that these would'st fain make us believe he is. Oh! famous Jean Jacques, thou that hast taken so much pains to extol the savage state, dids't thou ever see a real savage? You never did, for if you had, that discourse of thine, which attributes all possible virtue to the wild man, and all the meanness and deceptions of life to his tame brother, would never have been written.

The position of women among the Indian tribes, as is well-known, is not a very elevated one. A melancholy instance of this was once presented at a station where Guy Averall subsequently served, in which the daughter of a respectable citizen of London was the sufferer. The girl had actually eloped with a Chippewa Chief who happened to be on exhibition at the British metropolis. Her mind was apparently captivated by those stories which she heard of the prowess of the dusky warrior ; she fancied herself sitting as a queen, wielding royal sway over obedient subjects, honored and respected by all who surrounded her. Great indeed was her disappointment, when she awoke to the sad realities of the case ; to find herself thrust into a miserable hut, the companion of savages, whose habits were in every way unendurable. To submit to such a mode of life, year after year, was more than she could bear, she fled for protection to a good Catholic priest, who was then endeavoring to introduce the habits of civilized life into the tribe. By him she was placed in charge of the mission school, where she remained for a couple of years till she died. The amount of attention she might receive from those "buskined chiefs of swarthy lineament," as the poet Campbell chooses to call them, is indicated by the following harangue which was spoken by one of those identical braves.

"When the white man court," said the chief in his broken English, " he court maybe for a whole year—maybe for two year before he marry—maybe he gets a good wife—maybe not—maybe he works for him well—maybe he scolds all day. Still white man can do nothing—must keep his wife—never put him away once they are married. But with Indians things are different! When he sees squaw that works hard which he likes—he goes to him places his two fingers close beside each other—make two look like one—see him smile which is all one he says yes, so he takes him to live with him.' No danger that he be cross or scold now! Squaw knows too well what Indian does if he be cross! Throw him away and take another! Squaw loves to eat meat—no husband no meat. Squaw do anything to please husband. He do the same to please squaw—both be happy."

There is a common sense method in the sentiments thus advocated by the chief, which we would heartily recommend to that celebrated lecturer, Miss Annie C. Dickinson, and to all the other feminine advocates of social progress.

III.

But beside the two expeditions already mentioned, which left Fort Myers; another, in addition, was fitted out under command of Lieutenant Blodgett, who kept loudly swearing all the time that he, " by Jupiter," knew more of the woods in Florida than all the officers of the United States Army put together; and if that confounded nonsensical fool, old Twiggs, would only entrust him with supreme command, he would capture every Indian in the country in less than a fortnight. Much was expected from

Blodgett, on account of this braggadocio; but on the very day that this party set out, its commander got separated from his detachment, wandered through the woods, and was lost. A report was now circulated that the Lieutenant had fallen into the hands of the Indians who had probably scalped him, and as a consequence every officer in the Regiment felt predisposed to commiserate the unfortunate man's fate. "Well poor fellow," one would say, "he had his faults, just as we all have, still he had his redeeming qualities in spite of all that, and when I think of his untimely end, tied up to a tree, in all probability and tortured to death, I forget his ridiculous self-conceit, and every disagreeble quality that he had." But Blodgett, it seemed, had as many lives as a cat, for on the second night after his disappearance, as Averall was walking post, he thought he heard the voice of a man shouting on the opposite side of the river. Guy accordingly called for the Sergeant of the Guard, and after listening for a while they again thought the noise was repeated. The Sergeant now deemed it advisable to report the circumstance to the officer of the day, Lieutenant Taper, who after buckling on his sword, and listening for a while came to the conclusion he heard a man's voice also. A boat was accordingly sent over the river to the point from which the noise seemed to come; and there, wonderful to relate, the resolute son of Mars was discovered, sitting under the shade of a mangrove bush, his face haggard and dirty, his clothes torn into shreds by the palmettos among which he had been wandering, while his tout ensemble presented a picture of distress such as is seldom seen, even in a

Florida soldier. Still the Lieutenant to do him justice appeared as firm and resolute as ever. " Well, by Jupiter," said he as the crew made its apperance, with Taper in charge, " you fellows have been treating me in a handsome way."

"Treating you in a handsome way!" repeated Taper, " why what is the matter?"

"What is the matter!" exclaimed Blodgett. "Matter enough I assure you. Here I have been stationed, shouting to you for the last twenty-four hours, and not a single soul in the Fort seems to pay any attention to me. The deuce take it, if I ever, after such usage as this, will volunteer to hunt Indians in Florida." The officer was taken at his word, for he never afterwards was entrusted with the charge of another party. How it happened that he got separated from his command, crossed the river, and wandered down the opposite bank always remained a mystery, even in spite of his numerous explanations.

In the midst of these marchings and counter-marchings and wandering through the woods, the men, it must be noted, exhibited a very commendable spirit, most of them, indeed, seemed to rather enjoy this mode of existence. Among these in particular, the bard Hogan appeared on all occasions to be in the best of humor, for to him his present existence was so habitual as to be part almost of his nature. " Finest occupation that ever a young man followed," was his customary remark, " gives you an excellent opportunity of seeing the country and testing the virtues of beans. And if beans should happen to be absent, as is frequently the case with us, why a soldier is no soldier, unless he can live for three days and three nights on the smell of an oil rag." And when some one advocated the superior advantages of teaching Latin to a class of young gentlemen in New Jersey, rather than following his present occupation, the clerk immediately deprecated the ignoble idea, embraced in this remark ; and then, by way of illustrating this point, he favored his auditory with the following narrative :—

*   *   *   *   *

You must know, gentlemen, that according to Epictetus every subject has two handles, and that a soldier's life, in particular, resembles that of Prince Bladud of Bath, of whom as is well known, we have exactly opposite legends. On a former occasion I gave the imaginary cause of my leaving that famous Laurel Hill Institute of gentlemen cadets, in which I taught the young idea how to shoot; at present I propose to narrate the real cause of this separation. It is a melancholy affair, I assure you, from beginning to end ; and was all brought about by means of that truly insignificant and despicable animal which is known by the name of a mouse. My story shall be told in as few words as possible, let the final catastrophe serve as a warning to all ambitious school-teachers.

Well, gentlemen, you must know in the first place, that the situation of the Laurel Hill Institute is one of the most pleasant I ever saw in the whole course of my life. It is not like this Florida coast, low flat land, with nothing but palmettos, and yellow pitch pine on its surface; but stands, on the contrary, on the top of a hill, with a fresh green sward in front, while below the lawn is a lake on which the gentlemen cadets sometimes exercised themselves in sculling boats, rowing races, skipping flat stones over its surface, and other manly and warlike exercises. The head of the Laurel Hill Institute, the Reverend Dr. Skinner, was also a remarkable man in his way; learned in all the languages; a proficient in music, sculpture, painting, and the fine arts generally; orthodox in all matters of Church discipline and faith; and endowed beside with the very enviable faculty of blowing his own trumpet as loudly as any man in the State of which he is a resident. Talk of learning and ability—there never was such a family as the Skinners; speak of accomplishments and great natural gifts—the Skinners were absolutely without a parallel. And in order to give the place a greater reputation, it was noised about, that every thing around the Laurel Hill Institute was copied exactly after West Point. The cadets wore the same grey uniform in the one locality as the other; they all recited in a similar way, and were classified accordingly; the only difference between the two localities was this, that whereas in West Point, a certain number of bad marks is sure to expel a member; at the Laurel Hill Institute, on the other hand, justice was tempered with mercy, and a young man was permitted to undo his deficits by performing any useful piece of work that might be needed around the establishment. Sometimes the cadets at Laurel Hill were permitted to weed the garden; sometimes they were sent out to the Lake to catch fish for breakfast; at other times, it is said, they were allowed to peel the potatoes for dinner, just by way of variety; and if, in any of these cases, their efforts proved satisfactory, a certain number of bad marks were taken off their account, and then the happy recipient of this favor was allowed to go on as before. This much is offered by way of explanation.

Now it so happened that at the particular epoch of which I treat, a large colony of mice had invaded the premises occupied by Dr. Skinner; and had committed sad havoc among such eatables and drinkables as were to be found scattered here and there in it. Bread, flour, cheese and butter were all attacked; nay, even the old shoe strings that Dr. Skinner conscientiously gathered up, were assailed one night in a manner, as daring as it was perfidious. This outrage finally moved the anger of the chief personage in the establishment. "Betsy Jane," said he, one morning, to his wife, as they lay stretched on their marital couch, "I have an idea running through my head."

"What is that, Gideon?" said Mrs. Skinner, who had just awoke from her slumbers.

"It is this, my dear heart," said the Doctor, "these mice are beginning to be very troublesome; they have actually attacked the blue pill, which I now and then use, by way of medicine. If this thing goes on, they will drive us out of both house and home. I am resolved to wage war against them in every form I possibly can, and this very morning I intend to set the boys to catch mice, so as to rid ourselves of these troublesome invaders."

"Very well, my dear, do as you see fit," was the response.

"I'll exterminate them, even if it costs me an

empire," said the Doctor. So the very next morning the battalion was formed in line, thirty-five men in all ; and the Doctor then and there made proclamation that any boy who caught and killed a mouse, and would exhibit it, in due form to the principal in his study, he, the said boy would have five bad conduct marks taken off his list, and would, in addition, receive a day's leave of absence, before the end of the term."

"Well, how did the plan succeed ? " asked several of the auditors, who were evidently much interested in the recital which the bard thus presented.

"How did it succeed !" ejaculated Hogan, "why admirably in every respect. The thing simply worked like a charm. The Colonels, the Lieutenant Colonels, the Majors, the Captains and Lieutenants belonging to the Laurel Hill battalion of Cadets attacked the mice, in due order, and captured them by the dozen. Never was there such slaughter of rodents, from the days of the Pied Piper of Hamlin till the present. Meanwhile, the head of the Institute sat in his study, counted the spoils as they were brought in, and took off the black marks accordingly. Judging from the printed reports which were furnished them, there never was a better behaved set of young men than flourished under the care of Dr. Skinner. But in the long run, a disastrous result followed. The supply of mice at the Laurel Hill Institute became exhausted."

"Well, how did that affect the school ?" enquired Private Petersen.

"Affect the school!" was the answer, "it affected it badly in every way. The boys now knew there was no other method of effacing bad marks, except by going out once more into the garden to pull weeds, and that let me assure you, in the cold month of November, is anything but pleasant. The disappearance of the mice, sir, was simply disastrous.

"Well, what did they do?" asked Petersen, who still seemed somewhat interested, just then, in Hogan's narrative.

"What did they do!" was the rejoinder. "They could not have done anything at all, if it had not been for me. On the spur of the moment I made a suggestion."

"A suggestion—what was it, pray?"

"One, I think, that evinced both ingenuity and common sense. I simply said that since mice were beginning to get scarce, it were better not to attempt any very extensive captures. Let one animal be caught, taken in, and shown to the doctor, brought back and handed to the next student, and so on in succession, till the wants of the whole institute were served."

"How did that plan succeed?" was the next inquiry.

"Admirably, admirably," was the answer, "everything that I saw fit to hint, seemed to succeed. There sat Doctor Skinner, representative of the oldest, and noblest, and most aristocratic family in New Jersey, with his antiquated grey shawl around him, busily engaged in looking over a list of charges against each boy, and now and then effacing a demerit. The Doctor was satisfied, the boys were satisfied, I was satisfied, every one around the establishment was satisfied, till in the long run the principal person in the school, to use a slang phrase, literally began to 'smell a mice.'"

"Well, what was the result?"

"The result might easily be foreseen," was the rejoinder. "The Doctor stationed himself behind a door, in the way a New Jerseyman alone could do, watched one boy handing the animal to another, and was thus the discoverer of my ingeniously contrived plot."

"That was too bad," said Petersen.

"Bad! I rather imagine it was," responded the bard. "It put an end to one of the most capitally devised plans that I ever had the honor of inventing. The doctor, in particular, seemed very indignant, and told his wife that the double dealing and waywardness of young men of the present generation was simply beyond his comprehension, and this mouse affair, in particular, had a very bad look about it. Next morning he assembled all the boys in his study and gave them a long lecture on the numerous enormities of which they had been guilty. He told them that any body of young men, who would behave in such a disingenuous manner towards their teacher, as they evidently had done, could never expect to succeed in this world, and as to the world to come, their case was simply desperate. He then ordered the students to still continue their exertions against the mouse as a truly mischievous and destructive animal. "But boys," said he, by way of conclusion, "in case any more mice are caught, I shall insist on having the prize brought into my study. I shall place him lengthwise on a chopping block, and there and then, as a safeguard against double dealing, I shall instantly order his tail to be cut off !"

This cutting off the tail of a mouse, for the sake of good order and discipline, was rather too much for me. I was completely disgusted, in fact, with this sample of New Jersey ingenuity. So the very next morning I bundled up my effects, sought my beans in another quarter of the world, came into Newark and enlisted.

IV.

BUT notwithstanding the story-telling capacity evinced in this and in other similar narratives, the life in Florida began, in the long run, to pall. As to the natural curiosities of the State, the subject had long ago been exhausted; rattlesnakes had been killed, alligators had been caught with hook and line, and as to nests of scorpions, they had been exterminated again and again, till the thing had lost all novelty; nay further, even these wonderful epiphytes, which grow on the trees along the water-courses, and of whose beauty and variety your genuine Floridian is resolved eternally to boast—even these were dismissed as things of very little account. "Better twenty years of Europe than a cycle of Cathay" became eventually the prevailing sentiment. As to the progress of the " war," its history might be given in the words of the old song:

> For thirteen long months did I serve in the Everglade,
>   Neck deep in debt, and full waist-deep in mud;
> O'er dirty lagoon, and through streams I could never wade,
>   Battling it bravely but spilling no blood.

As the summer wore on, the heat at Fort Myers

became at times oppressive, and a good many of the
men began to suffer from the complaints incident to
such a climate; indeed, Averall himself was a martyr,
for a while, in this respect; and only escaped the
boneyard by the aid of liberal doses of quinine and
sulphuric acid, assisted by what must candidly be
set down as a good natural constitution. The experience already obtained of the interior of Florida,
back of Fort Myers, was not a pleasant one; and in
addition it was recollected that during the previous
war very grave blunders had been committed by the
officers sent in charge of troops, and the question
now presented itself, were these errors likely to be
repeated, in case it became necessary to drive the
Indians to extremities? Some of the soldiers had
heard the narrative of Private Ransom Clarke, who
went out as a member of the command under Major
Dade, in December, 1835, and who fortunately
escaped the massacre which took place on the route
between Tampa Bay and Fort King, on the 28th of
that month. Of the 117 men in that expedition,
three only escaped the general slaughter; and the
inquiry now was made, would officers be so ignorant
as to march men in solid column, through the
woods, without either scouts or skirmish line before
them. It was hoped not, and yet what guarantee
could be obtained against errors of a similar nature?
So all that was left to the Twenty-sixth Artillery was
to remain at their posts, like good soldiers; to do as
they were ordered on all occasions; and to preserve
even amidst the mosquitoes and rattlesnakes of
Florida, a cheerful, contented, and willing spirit.

As the event however turned out, the fortitude of

the Regiment was not put to a very severe test; for
the authorities in Washington, warned probably by
the expense and waste of life that were incurred
during the previous war, made up their minds not to
drive the Indians to hostilities. General Twiggs
again came to Fort Myers, another deputation was
sent into the woods, and again Master Bowlegs, and
some of his braves, entered into a fresh " talk " with
the pale-faces. This time it was proposed that any
of the Indians who would emigrate west, should receive a tract of land for their use, a year's provisions,
four blankets, a pint of beads, and a rifle; but any of
them who remained in Florida and ventured north
of a line drawn from Fort Myers to Lake Okee-chobee, would be hung. Mr. Bowlegs received the latter
part of the proposition in sullen silence, and then
said that Florida belonged to him and there he proposed to remain. Some of his people, however,
chose to look at the matter in a different light, and
finally about one-half of the Seminoles agreed to
accept the terms offered by the United States, and
emigrate west of the Mississippi. Mr. Bowlegs then
made his acknowledgments, and said he had no desire
to go to war, that bad men in Florida, for their own
purposes, had represented him as an enemy to the
Great Father, but such was not the case, that the
Seminoles had already suffered enough in encounter
with the United States, that all he desired was to be
left alone in the possession of his own dear swamps
and Everglades, and provided he were allowed to
hunt deer, and kill bear in that romantic locality, he
would ever remain as good and as quiet an Indian
as could be found between the rising and setting sun.

On these terms then a bargain was struck; Mr. Bow-legs returned to the country south of the Caloosa-hatchie, the Indians who had consented to emigrate came to Fort Myers, and in due time were dispatched to New Orleans by the Fashion, while to crown all, in about a month from this period, some troops who had been serving at Fort Pickens in the western part of the State, were sent to Fort Myers, in order to exchange stations with the garrison at that place. This change of posts, it may be observed, seemed almost a matter of necessity, for fully one-third of the garrison on the Caloosahatchie, at the time the transfer was made, were prostrated by a sort of in-termittent fever, which seemed to bid defiance to all the drugs and physic that could be employed against it. Even Spruce and Taper, gallant soldiers though they were, both vowed they had enough of the south-ern extremity of Florida.

A vast amount of sentiment has been expended on the Indians of America; and in particular their fighting qualities have been highly extolled, but if we examine carefully into the case, we will find that this particular characteristic has been much exag-gerated, and that in real willingness to face danger the Indian is, after all, decidedly inferior to the white. The savage is the creature of wiles, of pre-tences, of stratagems; give him the advantage of number and position, station him in a hammock or swamp, till his enemy is completely in his grasp, and he will soon exterminate him. But he is not the per-son to defy a whole host, by any means; or even to expose himself to marked danger, from a mere sense of duty, in the way that the professional soldier habitually does. Still as compared with other savages, the American Indian has, in many respects, the advantage. "Attentive observers," says Doctor Prichard, "have been struck with manifestations of greater energy and martial vigor, of more intense and deeper feeling, of a more reflective mind, of greater fortitude and more consistent perseverance in enterprises than is found among the volatile and almost animalized savages who are still to be found in some quarters of the old continent." All of this, of course, is in the Indian's favor; but when we attribute to the Seminole and Pawnee the elevated sentiments of the cultivated white man, in the way Mayne Reid or James Fenimore Cooper have done, the attempt at the very best is simply preposterous.

V.

THAT portion of the Twenty-sixth Artillery of which Guy Averall was a member, remained only a short time at Fort Pickens, when it was sent to Camp Twiggs in the State of Mississippi; and thence, after a stay of a few weeks, it was ordered to take post at New Orleans Barracks. At the latter place it remained about a month, when fresh directions came to pack up once more and proceed to its old rendezvous at Fort Columbus. During these changes of station, nothing of much moment occurred, as far as an immediate narrative is concerned, unless indeed we notice one or two trifling circumstances which certainly ought to have had some little influence in showing Guy Averall that there are rogues as well as honest men in the world, and that it will not answer to trust too much to specious pretensions. At

Fort Pickens was a Corporal, Alexander A. Brown by name, who gloried in the fact that he was an Englishman. The occupation of Corporal Brown was not a very elevated one, for by a strange violation of those orders which forbid the employment of an enlisted man in a menial capacity, he had been lately engaged as cook in the officers' mess. The Corporal, nevertheless, bore himself with great dignity, in spite of all that, and even ventured to boast, now and then, of that superlative honesty which is supposed to be the characteristic of every native of proud Albion. "Yes, sir, talk as you please, Hingland, sir, is the country where hall men are obliged to do right ; no chance of a man being a swindler there, with the Queen, lords and commons above him." And so impressed was Averall with this constant talk of the "Queen, lords and commons," that he fondly imagined the good Corporal to be one of the most honest personages in the world, spite of some warnings he had received to the contrary.

Now among the possessions of Averall, at this time, was a very pretty copy of Gray's poems, given to him by a relative, just before he set out on his adventures, and prized as a memento accordingly. Corporal Brown, on one occasion, when returning a visit from Guy, espied the volume as it lay in the bottom of Averall's locker, and immediately requested the loan of it. "I think a great deal of Gray as a poet," was his cunning remark, born in Lunnun on the twenty-sixth day of December, 1716, he died at Cambridge, of the gout, on the thirteenth day of July, 1771, aged fifty-five years. Gray wrote that beautiful poem they call the Helegy." Was it possible to resist an array of sentiment and statistics such as this? Guy could not, and when his friend asked permission to borrow the volume, Averall told the Corporal to take the book, retain it as long as he liked and afterwards return it at his convenience.

In about a fortnight afterwards, Averall heard that the non-commissioned officer was to be discharged, his term of service having now expired, so he thought it no harm to go over to the cook house and ask for the volume already borrowed. As soon as the word "Gray's poems" was mentioned, a blank expression passed over the features of the unfortunate Brown. "Oh, my friend, my friend, my very dear friend, I ham so sorry for you. I hintended to to return the poems before now, and should certainly have done so haccording to my intentions, but the book is stolen—the book is stolen—hand I now can find neither 'ed or tail of hit." Guy felt, at first, somewhat disconcerted at this untoward accident; he nevertheless told the Corporal not to pay any attention to the affair; that the money value of the article, after all, was not great, and since it was gone, there was now no use in uttering any further regrets on the subject.

Two days afterwards a discovery was made; for Averall, while passing the bunk occupied by a fellow-soldier, happened to spy the volume reported as lost, thrust between a pair of blankets. An explanation soon followed. "Where did you get that book, you rascal?" exclaimed the irate Guy, to the occupant of the place.

"Don't call me a rascal or I'll punch your eye out. I purchased that book this morning from Corporal Brown, for the sum of fifty cents."

" Purchased that book from Corporal Brown for the sum of fifty cents !" repeated the astonished Guy. " He told me the book was stolen from him a couple of days ago, and that he had been hunting high up and low down, for the missing volume, but could not find it."

" He did ! Why the sneaking, hungry, dog-robbing thief, he does not utter a word of truth in the matter. As to myself I did not care about purchasing the book at all, since it contains nothing but a lot of fool poetry; but the mean little hound came to me the second time, and said that in case I ever fell in love, the book would be a very nice present for a lady; so in order to get rid of the troublesome little insect, I gave him the money and let him go."

" Well, well," said Guy," this really astonishes me, I never will trust a human being, as long as I live. This man made the most specious pretences, and after all I find him to be the most despicable little rascal that ever I met. However, he has not got his discharge as yet, so I will go over to the officers' cook house and frighten him if I do nothing else."

Guy accordingly did go over to the officers' quarters, and found Corporal Brown there, who dared not deny a single word of the charge laid against him. At first Averall threatened to report the facts of the case to Brown's Captain; but finally, after thinking over the affair, he determined to let the matter go, rather than injure a man who was just on the point of leaving the service.

OLD FRIENDS.

I.

It was a bright and cheerful morning, in the early spring, when the Twenty-sixth Artillery, after an absence of some fifteen months, again reached their old quarters at Fort Columbus. As they approached Governor's Island, everything they saw seemed to remind them of their former residence at that place. The dear old barracks, in which they once were quartered, were still there; the familiar flag-staff, situated in one of the bastions of the fort; the row of poplar trees, near the water edge, where Guy Averall first met that Mentor, who had proved himself to be his best friend while serving in Florida; nay, further, the quiet, sleek-looking Quartermaster's horse, which was turned out to graze, near the foot of the glacis, all seemed to be unchanged since the Twenty-sixth Artillery had left the place. And let no one imagine that United States soldiers are destitute of love and affection as respects those localities in which they once more quartered. Indeed the contrary is well known to be the case, for in the absence of more specific ties they learn to cherish the memory of those particular localities in which any very considerable proportion of their life is spent. Every spot in such circumstances has its chain of associations; every nook and corner its little tale of adventure on romance; at one place the soldier, perchance, remembers he was entrapped, while passing a chain of sentinels, by a vigilant officer of the day; at another he actually succeeded in evading a wily Sergeant of the Guard, spite of the fact that the hour was long after tattoo, and that the adventurous runnagate had in his possession at the time, no less an article than a closely corked bottle of whiskey. But whatever sentimental notions the Twenty-sixth Artillery might have on this particular occasion were all quickly dispelled; for then and there, upon the wharf of Governor's Island, stood the gallant Brigadier herself, waiting anxiously to receive them. "Oh my dear good children, my dear good children, I am so very glad to see you," was her exclamation as the troops touched the shore, "why what a very delightful excursion you have had, during the past few months, in that very charming country, Florida. Why Sergeant Lawless, you are the very beau ideal of a noble-looking non-commissioned officer; and Averall, you are really, to my notion, the finest young soldier at present in the Army." And then, as the officers came up in succession, Mrs. Daisy threw her magnificent arms around each one in the most motherly way imaginable, and gave him a good sound buss, as expressive of the joy she felt at seeing her old Regiment once more in New York Harbor. This preliminary matter being settled, both officers and men were then informed that during the absence of the Regiment in Florida, she had met with an unusual piece of good luck, that Captain Daisy, "her own good Tom," the "best and dearest man that ever existed," had been promoted to a full Majority in the United States Army, and was now assigned to duty with the Twenty-sixth Artillery. "My dear Mr. Spruce," said the lady, after detailing this piece of good fortune, "I fully intend to celebrate the event, in a manner befitting the occasion. I propose that Tom shall apply for a six months' leave of absence, and as soon as he can obtain it, I intend we both shall set off, in order to visit some of the principal cities of Europe. A trip of this kind I'm sure would be delightful, and it is nothing more than the Major's due, considering his rank and length of service. This morning, by the way, I had quite a little excursion of my own. I was visiting that dear and delightful country, Switzerland; and in the course of an hour or two, I had already seen Lake Zug, and climbed on the top of Mount Righi, and sailed on the Lake of the Four Cantons; and after taking Unterseen and Interlaken in my way, I came down to Vevey and the Castle of Chillon, where I spent a short time, and I finally got into the vale of Chamouni, by way of the Tête Nôire, nor did I rest for a moment till I ascended the top of Mount Blanc, which we all know to be the very highest mountain in the whole of Europe. The trip was delightful I assure you."

"I dare say it was," rejoined the officer, "but did you not find it somewhat fatiguing, to travel so very far during one cold morning?"

"It was all done in the imagination—it was all done in the imagination and I was perfectly charmed with it. Tol-de-re-lol-lol, tol-de-re-lol-lol, oh the vale of Chamouni. Tol-de-re-lol-lol, tol-de-re-lol-lol, the vale, the vale of Chamouni." And in a thrice, the good Mrs. Daisy began rattling off a well-

known air from Linda di Chamouni in a way that
was perfectly astonishing.

In the course of a short time, the men had un-
loaded their effects from the transport ; and on their
way up to the barracks, it was noticed that Miss
Davis, the lady whom Averall had particularly
observed the night of the *Chapeau bras*, was on her
way in the direction of the wharf, accompanied by a
somewhat obstreperous specimen of humanity in the
person of young Hector Daisy. The boy was shouting in a way which was almost terrific ; his precept-
ress, however, endeavored to pacify him as well as
she possibly could, and then shook hands with such
of the officers as she knew, by way of welcome to
their old station. And the officers if the truth must
be told, were somewhat glad to see Miss Davis, for
in spite of the love and affection displayed by her
aunt in meeting them, they could not forget that the
younger lady was generally recognized as the more
evenly balanced personage in the domestic establishment of the good Major; although as far as questions
of taste and talent and *bon ton* were concerned, the
Brigadier of course, was acknowledged to be the
better authority. And Guy Averall, it must be confessed, shared in this feeling to some extent also ;
for as he looked for a moment at that pretty and
sensible face, he felt inclined to take a good deal on
trust in the case of its owner ; even admitting that
as far as fine manners were concerned, Mrs. Daisy
was decidedly the superior woman.

The first few days after the arrival of the troops,
they were occupied in putting their quarters in order;
this work completed, Guy applied for leave of absence

for twenty-four hours, and was fortunate enough to obtain this indulgence.   The time employed in this vacation passed away very pleasantly ; for after reaching New York, our young friend saw fit to cross the North River, and before very long, he gained the commercial capital of the Jerseys.   The farm occupied by Mr. Gore, his former employer, was soon reached, and there he met with a very hearty greeting.   " What kind of a place is the Army ? "   " Are soldiers severely punished in it ? " "Is there much chance of a person who enlists becoming a General ? "   Guy endeavored to answer these questions as well as he could, but was compelled to acknowledge that the chance of an enlisted man obtaining a commission in the Army, as things now stood, was very small indeed ; that not a single promotion of this kind has taken place for several years, and in short that some of the authorities seemed rather indisposed to advance enlisted men in this way.   This information, which was correct enough just then, served to create considerable surprise on the part of Mr. Gore, who added that if this were so, the American Army was not a fit place for any decent, respectable, well disposed young man. In response, nevertheless, Averall endeavored to explain, that in spite of untoward circumstances, many soldiers were both honest and honorable men.   But the farmer chose to exhibit his prejudice by saying if they were honest and honorable men, the service was no place for them.   To which remark Guy made answer that he was sorry to hear Mr. Gore express himself in this way, and thus the subject was dropped. Still Averall was doomed to disappointment in another direction. During his absence, he had occasionally imagined that perchance his former flame, Miss Jones, might remain true to him. But Jessie, that dear, sweet Jessie on whom Averall had once so fondly doated, had gone the way of all flesh—that is to say she had undertaken the responsibilities and care of wedded life. Some months previous to this time, she and her old admirer, John Harry Blasedell, had been married.

II.

On returning to Fort Columbus, after his visit to the Jerseys, Guy Averall began cogitating on the present aspect of his affairs. He still felt somewhat annoyed that his old flame had got married, but on reflecting on the subject for a moment, he had to acknowledge that in all probability the thing was for the best. "If I were to get mated," said he, "what would become of my wife? Descend to the grade of laundress in the Company? Well, that to Miss Jessie and also to me would certainly be a step in the wrong direction. So as to this thing of marrying or giving in marriage, while serving in the ranks, I suppose I will simply have to give it up. Still I have some of my old resources at hand; and books, we must admit, are never quarrelsome companions. By the way, would it not be well to take up some subject, as a study, instead of wasting my time in desultory efforts? There is Moldwell, for instance, a well informed and sensible man, perhaps I could get him to join me in some one line of investigation. And yet, *per contra*, does it follow that this pursuit of knowledge under difficulties, is worth one-half of the pains expended on it? Will it make me more contented with my lot; or better able to discharge such duties as I am required to perform in the Army? Might I not say with Milton:

> Alas! what boots it with incessant care,
> To tend the homely slighted shepherd's trade;
> And strictly meditate the thankless Muse?
> Were it not better done, as others use,
> To sport with Amaryllis in the shade,
> Or with the tangles of Neæra's hair?

And with this quotation, which Guy had picked up by accident in his miscellaneous reading, all effort at mental improvement for the present terminated. In truth, an event occurred, just then, which gave the thoughts of Averall an entirely new direction; for that very evening he was informed the gallant Major Daisy had selected the youth as his orderly.

Guy received the intelligence implied in this announcement in the way that a good soldier is bound to do. He accordingly spruced himself up, so as to look as neat and tidy as possible, and on reporting at the quarters of the commanding officer, he was received by the amiable Brigadier herself, in a manner which sufficiently expressed her usual goodness of heart. "Oh, Averall, I'm so glad to see you. How do you do? Just take a seat in the hallway, after you report to the Major, so as to be within call. Why, Averall, I understand you are very much interested in some of the young ladies in Rotten Row."

"I was not aware of the fact," responded Guy very meekly.

"Well I must have been misinformed," was the rejoinder, "but then, I have so little curiosity, that I seldom take the trouble of making any inquiry on these subjects. I really never concern myself in the affairs of a garrison."

In spite of the self denial implied in the foregoing remark, it was evident to Averall that Mrs. Daisy would gladly have prosecuted her inquiries on the present occasion. But at this juncture, unfortunately, the catechising was cut short, for the gallant Hector now made his appearance, howling as usual at the top of his voice.

"Mamma, mamma, mamma [howl] I can't stand this—I can't stand this—I can't stand this. Cousin Eleanor has taken away my cake. She says I can't have any sponge cake for breakfast, and that's a shame. I want my cake—I want my cake—I want my cake." And here the gallant Hector emitted a series of bawls which made the house resound from basement to garret.

"Why, Hector, Hector," said Mrs. Daisy in reply. "Sponge cake, you know, is not a proper article to eat so early in the morning. The night before last you ate a whole plateful of it, and the consequence was, you were very sick indeed, and had to take medicine, and that you know is not pleasant. You should strive to be a little man, and not think so much of eating. Before very long we intend to send you to West Point, to be educated for an officer, so mathematics is the thing you ought to be thinking of at present, not that vile sponge cake. Now go to cousin Eleanor, and commence saying your lessons. You will be a great, brave, noble, and gallant officer yet; one that will do excellent service for your country."

"Bah, bah, bah," was the rejoinder. "I don't care about mathematics, or I don't care about being an officer, or I don't care about West Point; all I want is cake, cake, cake, and you wont give me a bit of it from morning to night. Bah, bah, bah. You have just made up your mind to starve me."

And with these words the noble Hector started down the hallway, howling all the time, till finally Miss Davis took him in charge, and commenced her usual morning task; drumming a little music into Master Daisy's head, and teaching him the variations of the verbs *avoir* and *etre*.

III.

During his tour of duty at the quarters of the commanding officer, Guy Averall had frequent opportunities of observing, once more, those customs which obtain in polite society; and was moreover pleased to find that although somewhat eccentric in her ways, a sincere desire for mental improvement was very evident on the Brigadier's part. One day, for instance, it was noticed that Miss Eleanor and Mrs. Daisy were closeted together, with a big book before them; and that the latter lady seemed much interested in the science of astronomy.

"Now Eleanor," said Mrs. Daisy, "there is one question in which I am very much concerned. What does the word ecliptic mean?"

"Why aunt," said the other, by way of explanation, "the plane of the ecliptic is that plane in which the earth revolves in the course of a year."

"And the equator?"

"The plane of the equator is a plane passing through the centre of the earth, perpendicular to its axis."

"Then the ecliptic and the equator are not the same thing, are they?" asked Mrs. Daisy.

"By no means," was the response. And here Miss Davis, who seemed to have a very good knowledge of the subject, vouchsafed an explanation which seemed to set the matter in a very clear light. That explanation was not lost on the Brigadier, for the very next morning, when crossing over to the city, the lady broached the subject of astronomy to Messrs. Spruce and Taper, and astonished both the officers by a discussion on the nature of the ecliptic which would almost have done credit to the great Newton himself. In point of fact the information extracted from Miss Davis, was given word for word, with such addenda as her aunt saw fit to interpose. Could any one say, after this deny the fact that the Brigadier was destitute of scientific attainments?

Before very long indeed, Guy Averall had reason to suspect that a very considerable proportion of the knowledge possessed by Mrs. Daisy was supplied second hand the same way; for whenever the elder lady was at a loss for information on any subject, the intelligence of the younger one was pretty sure to be called into requisiton. "Eleanor," said Mrs. Daisy to her *vade mecum* one morning, within Averall's hearing, how do you pronounce h-u-i-l-e, the French word for oil?"

"Why aunt, that word is pronounced almost as if written *wheel*," was the reply.

"And olive oil is called—"

"Wheel-dole-leeve," said Miss Davis.

"Wheel-dole-leeve, wheel-dole-leeve," repeated Mrs. Daisy, as if to impress the pronounciation on her memory. That repetition was enough, for during the afternoon the orderly was sent over to the "sutler's secretary," who resided in Rotten Row, in order to make inquiry as to the present price of wheel-dole-leeve in that establishment. After obtaining the desired information, Averall came back to the Brigadier, repeated the current price, when the lady ordered Guy to procure a bottle. But such incidents as these, familiar though they be, should not be spoken of outside the pale of aristocratic society.

The only person who caused the good Mrs. Daisy any annoyance at this time was the irrepressible Blodgett. That person was an officer *sui generis*, a man who would uphold his rights on every possible occasion, and consequently, would not permit anybody in the land to dictate to him ; even supposing, by Jupiter, it was the great Brigadier herself. And truth to say, the Lieutenant was as good as his word, as our friend Guy happened to know. One morning Blodgett was in charge of the Company on drill, when Mrs. Daisy sent word over to him, with "her compliments," that she would like to have Averall at her quarters. This request or command, as the case might be, immediately excited the officer's sense of duty. "Go and tell Mrs. Daisy, with *my* compliments," was the rejoinder, "that Averall is turned over to me for the purpose of military instruction, and that I intend he shall remain here till the customary re-call is sounded." This response on the part of the Irrepressible, was the occasion of an indefinite amount of chagrin, as far as Mrs. Daisy was concerned. "I always suspected," said she, "that Lieutenant Blodgett was a low-born and impolite man ; and further than this, I now say that any one who calls habitually on the god Jupiter, in the way he does, is utterly destitute of the grace and dignity of a gentleman, and as such should be instantly discarded."

IV.

AFTER a short term of service Guy Averall became tolerably familiar with his sphere of duties at Headquarters; and found them on the whole to be not of a very exacting nature ; much lighter indeed than those that fell to his lot, when he carried logs or helped to load or unload the steamer Fashion in Florida. To run to the commissary on an errand; to ask the price of wheel-dole-leeve at the sutler's ; to procure Mrs. Daisy some erudite volume at the public library, or to ask that " dear man," the doctor, to pay the wife of the commandant a professional visit, such were some of Averall's tasks at this period of his career. As to pulling the gallant Brigadier in a boat round the Island, that for the present was fortunately discarded, as Mrs. Daisy now looked for amusement and exercise in a different way. The great trouble at this time was with Hector; and indeed the very day after the encounter with Blodgett, Guy Averall had quite a little adventure with that worthy. Miss Davis required the youngster, so as to set him to work in studying his lessons. But Hector was not to be found, and in spite of Miss Eleanor's assertion that she saw the boy go into the

17

garden, a short time previous, Guy was unable to discover him in that place. The orderly then shouted for Master Daisy by name; but no answer was made, and in the end every one became somewhat afraid that Hector was lost. A grand hunt was now the result; and although each person in the garrison was questioned concerning Hector, yet no one could give any information about the absentee. At this juncture the entire family began to be really very uneasy, but finally their anxiety was set at rest, for just after sundown Guy Averall went once more into the garden, and while there he noticed that an old vinegar barrel, stuck in one corner, which had been used of late as a resting place for Mrs. Daisy's hens, began to move. This of course excited Averall's attention, and on going up to it, the orderly was much surprised to find the gallant Hector crouched up in the straw, with a piece of plum-cake in one hand, and a book of fairy tales in the other, resting and reading as contentedly as possible. Guy naturally felt somewhat provoked at the conduct of the greedy little rascal; so he jerked him out of the barrel in an instant. " Did you not hear me calling you, sir," said Guy, after Hector was on his feet, "you have occasioned us all a nice amount of trouble. I want you to go into the house at once, and say your lessons to Miss Eleanor." But the gallant Trojan was in no humor to submit. " I don't care about my lesson, and I don't care about Miss Eleanor, as you call her," was his immediate reply, "and more than that, I'll complain to papa, about the way you have pulled and dragged me round, just for nothing. And I'll see if I can't get you put in the guard house too, you

Averall." It subsequently appeared that the noble
Hector had indeed entered a complaint against our
friend, and fully expected, no doubt, that Guy would
suffer condign punishment as a necessary consequence; but fortunately the commandant did not
pay any attention to the matter, and Averall continued to discharge his duties as heretofore. So much
for domestic affairs in the household of Major Daisy.

On one occasion, while serving as orderly at
Headquarters, Private Averall was the recipient of
some very well-intended advice on the part of Miss
Davis, the substance of which may as well be set
down in this place. To begin at the beginning, it is
perhaps necessary to state, that our friend having
expended his best efforts on the subject of ghosts
and disembodied spirits, without coming to any very
definite conclusion concerning them, began cogitating within himself if there was no other study to
which he might properly direct his attention. Filled
with these thoughts, he happened to saunter into the
hallway one day, and noticing a book lying on the
stairway, he took it up and began to read. The volume was in French, and proved to be a collection of
short stories, which the immortal Hector was supposed in the course of time to study. Guy glanced
at the first chapter which proved to be a translation
of Addison's paper, the " vision of Mirzah," and after
a little examination he found he could readily turn
tho narrative into English. At this instant Miss
Eleanor made her appearance, so Guy laid down the
book and stood at " attention," as was always his
custom, when any member of the family entered the
room where he was.

"Never mind, Averall, you need not trouble yourself about me. I'm only Miss Davis," was the observation which escaped in a half involuntary manner from the lady. But recollecting herself she instantly added, "I see you are examining one of Hector's books. Do you understand anything of French, Averall?"

"A little, very little, I should say, Miss," responded Guy.

"Where did you study the language?"

"What little I know was learned a very long time ago, long before I became a soldier."

"Where was that, Averall?"

"If the truth must be told on the subject, Miss, it was in the Kingdom of Ireland," said Guy.

"In Ireland indeed!" exclaimed the lady. "Well I should never connect the study of the French language with Ireland. But now that you are in America, why do you not keep up your knowledge of the tongue, by reading, occasionally, a French book?"

"For the most obvious reason in the world," was the rejoinder. "I'm nothing but a soldier, and in the Army I find that any one who deviates from the beaten track, which soldiers usually follow, is sure to meet with a good deal of contempt. I might tipple after pay-day, get into the guard house, spend my money, and even occasionally be the subject of a garrison court-martial, and no one would think the worse of me on that account; but if it were known that I was in the habit of poring over a French book, or hunting up words in a dictionary, why every one would set me down as an odd fish at the best; and that is a reputation which no enlisted soldier cares to sustain.'

"Yes, Averall, but on the other hand let me assure you," said Miss Davis, "that no sensible person will think the worse of you, even if you do not choose to follow the beaten track ; but will rather honor you for keeping away from it, when that track appears to be wrong."

"I know, I know," was the rejoinder, "but officers and their families, Miss Eleanor, can afford to be more independent than members of the rank and file. There are a number of good men in the company, it is true, who do not care to dissipate ; but there are others of a very different disposition, and it actually seems, at times, that no one can stand well in the estimation of these latter, unless he chooses to follow exactly in their steps. These are the persons I am obliged to contend with."

"Why Averall," was the rejoinder, "I see no necessity for contending with them, at all. Try and do what is right, and let your own character vindicate itself. For my part, Averall, I shall always consider you as a gentleman, as long as you behave well. And as to this matter of French, I certainly should not let the opinion of a few men prevent me from studying it, if I felt so inclined. Any books I have on the subject are at your service ; and if you have any grammatical difficulty, at any time, why I should always be glad to assist you, as far as it lies in my power."

"Thank you, Miss Eleanor," said Averall, who at that instant spoke from the bottom of his heart, for the truth of the matter was, the bearing of Miss Davis toward our friend was different from that which he had experienced from any other lady at Fort Columbus, as yet ; and this to Guy at the time, was a very great consideration. And then our adventurer could not help reflecting that if all the other ladies in the Army only acted and spoke in the way Miss Davis did, the service would be greatly improved, and every one around them would remain much better satisfied. "Yes," said he, but this was after a long pause, and only when he had secured possession of the hall-way to himself, " I am sorry that Mrs. Daisy, who pretends to be a gentlewoman, and who is always boasting of her fine acquaintances, both in New York and else-where, cannot treat me as though I were a civilized being, instead of spending her eternal soft soap over my countenance. I'm not a savage, I wasn't born in the wilds of Africa, even supposing my name is Pat. But here comes the gallant Hector with his books in his hand, prepared, I suppose, to fight for an hour or two over his lessons. The day before yesterday I heard him make an honest confession. as far as his geography was concerned, for he said that as to those two nations, Russia and Prussia, he never could distinguish the one from the other. But as to Turkey in Asia, he knew all about it, for that was the country where figs were produced ; and no one who had once eaten good, nice figs out of a round box, could possibly forget anything about them.

VII.

BUT let us abandon this theme and proceed to other subjects. As to the chief non-commissioned officer in Company " E," Twenty-sixth Artillery, he certainly deserved all the encomiums which his friends and admirers showered on his head. Sergeant

Lawless was, in fact, the beau ideal of all that is graceful in the ranks, and amply deserved the favor which many of the fair sex were disposed to bestow on him. Handsome, active, and well-proportioned, with sufficient self-appreciation to create the impression that he himself sufficiently understood the merits of his own case, he habitually sought the shades of Rotten Row, just as soon as evening parade was dismissed, and there continued till the first call for tattoo was beaten. He was a prime favorite among the young ladies of the garrison, that was evident; although they themselves, if questioned as to the reason of this preference, could hardly give a very satisfactory answer. Sergeant Lawless was not learned, he was not intelligent, he was not honest, and no person certainly thought him good, and yet every unmarried female in Rotten Row seemed to idolize him. Some may perchance ask the cause of this strange infatuation. As far as this inquiry is concerned, we must candidly admit we cannot tell, it is a mystery to us, all we can say by way of explanation is simply this, we have frequently heard of such things before, and only know that there are certain women, in all stations of life, who will fall head and ears in love with any man, let his general character be ever so worthless, provided he is in outward appearance, a handsome, dashing fellow, observes a tolerable regard for the proprieties of life, and, above all, enjoys the reputation of having some deviltry in him. This, after all, was the characteristic feature in the case of Sergeant Lawless, and to it his success as a gay cavalier, must in the main be attributed.

There was only one person in Rotten Row with whom Sergeant Lawless was not quite successful, and, as might naturally be expected, it was on this particular person that his heart was most set. Miss Kitty Traynor knew that she was good-looking, just in the same way as Sergeant Lawless was acquainted with his own graces; and what was still better, she loved a little flirtation too. She was careful not to give the non-commissioned officer any good ground of challenge, but kept playing him off and on, with all the arts of a coquette. Once, indeed, she told Sergeant Lawless that she had almost half made up her mind to become a soldier's wife; but the very next evening when the case was mentioned, the little minx chose to laugh in his face, said she had only spoken in fun, and as to this thing of turning washerwoman in the Army, just for the sake of a living, it had never entered her calculations. And then, on the following evening, she was careful to invite all the non-commissioned officers, she could find, to her uncle's house; and Sergeant Lawless, to his chagrin, discovered that he was not treated one whit better than anyone of the others.

This treatment on the part of Miss Kitty disconcerted the handsome Sergeant a good deal, he bit his lip, it is said, and looked anything but pleased, when the fact of this indifference was mentioned. But the Sergeant, during life, had been too much of a lovemaker to venture on any very active demonstration. Indeed, he very gallantly vouchsafed the opinion that in this matter of flirtation there was no royal road, that he or any other man on earth could follow; that women in this particular province were resolved to have their own way; and that in the peculiar circumstances in which he was placed, there was no resource left for him except to behave himself in an even, modest and good-tempered manner; and then accommodate himself according to future developments.

At length the good Mrs. Daisy, hearing of the facts of the case, resolved to take Kitty Traynor to task on account of her manner towards such a dashing non-commissioned officer as the Sergeant. " Why Kitty," said the Brigadier one day as she stopped the unoffending girl on the sidewalk, " I hear that ever so many of the Sergeants and Corporals of the garrison are so very attentive to you." The first impulse of poor Kitty was to resent this unwarrantable intrusion in the way it deserved; but on second thought she determined to answer Mrs. Daisy according to her folly, and with a quickness of manner, that did her infinite credit, she assumed at once a sufficiently innocent demeanor, and stood ready to respond to such questions as were propounded by her amiable protectress.

"Among other things, I hear that excellent man, Sergeant Lawless, is disposed to be very attentive at Rotten Row, is he not?"

"Perhaps he is," was the rejoinder, "but really, Mrs. Daisy, you don't expect I should know all about Rotten Row. Why, I am nothing but one person in that place, and have not the faculty of discovering what happens among my neighbors."

"I commend your prudence in that, my dear child," said Mrs. Daisy, who in her quality of protectress of the military establishment at Fort Columbus, thought it her duty to advise the commonality on all sorts of subjects.   I commend your prudence, indeed, for if there is anything I utterly despise, it is this inquisitive, meddling disposition.   I have always held the notion that in this busy world of ours, every one has enough to do to attend to his or her own proper vocation.   But is Sergeant Lawless so very attentive, after all ? "

"Indeed, I cannot answer for Sergeant Lawless," was the response, "I just know as much of him as of any other non-commissioned officer in the garrison."

"I saw Sergeant Lawless standing among several soldiers the other evening ; and I really thought him the most handsome man in the Fort.   So Sergeant Lawless is not the favored one then ?   How is it with the Steward, Petersen ?   He is very attentive also, I hear."

"I really dont know," said Kitty, giving a very significant shake of her head.

"Upon my word," said Mrs. Daisy, "I really think that Petersen is a very excellent man.   Some persons was saying, the other day, that he was studying medicine, so as to be in time, a doctor; and that I am sure, is a very commendable thing.   Then there is another very good man, Sergeant Ryan, what may I ask, do you think of him ?"

"I know nothing of Sergeant Ryan, any more than of any other soldier in the garrison," was the answer.

"Oh, I see how it is, Kitty," said Mrs. Daisy, "Sergeant Lawless, after all, is the favorite."

"Well, since you speak of Sergeant Lawless so highly," replied Kitty with a cunning little smile, "I certainly must acknowledge that I am inclined to take him on your recommendation. He is, as you say a remarkably fine-looking soldier, and may possibly make a very good husband. At any rate, I should never think of venturing on marriage, without taking you in as my counsellor, for do you know what, Mrs. Daisy, you have the reputation of knowing more about the affairs of the garrison than any other person in it."

The good Mrs. Daisy was a woman of vast and very accurate erudition, as is well-known, yet in certain directions, she was not so very high spirited, spite of all that. She thought that the words of Kitty sounded somewhat strangely, coming as they did from a "camp woman," and the concluding part of the girl's speech seemed to be intended as a quiet cut. Still Mrs. Daisy could not absolutely take offence at it; and as Kitty was a very proper subject for catechizing again, the Brigadier resolved to take the whole thing in good part.

"You are a very excellent girl, Kitty," said she with a most engaging smile, "and I have always taken the greatest possible interest in you, ever since I first saw you at this Fort. Of one thing, in addition, you may be certain, that whenever you do get married, I certainly shall dance at your wedding."

VIII.

It was not among the enlisted men alone, that the baby god, Cupid, played his cunning tricks at this time. Both of the subalterns of Guy's company felt the power of his dart. As soon as the Twenty-sixth Artillery had returned to their old quarters, Messrs.

Spruce and Taper immediately started to New York city, in order to pay their respects to those " fine girls " on whom their best affections were placed. Spruce, on this occasion, it is said, indited a set of verses, which subsequently found their way into print, and which eventually became quite popular among the gallant young officers of the time.

Lady, no cap is on my head,
  No visor on my brow,
I've lost my plume, and lost my heart,
  I'm not a soldier now !
My uniform I've taken off,
  My " cits " I've just put on.
And silk I've substiuted for
  The leather stock I've worn.
No more the sound of cannon grates
  Upon my ear, as when
It waked me up at break of day—.
  I was a soldier then.

As to Taper, he was every bit as devoted as Spruce, the difficulty in his case was to decide which one of the two "·fine girls " he had then on hand was the more eligible—the one who played the piano so delightfully, and affected to despise the Army ; or the one who did not play, and seemed to have a sentimental inclination for the stars and stripes. Both of them had " rocks," and that was the great recommendation in this particular case, so Taper, prudent little gentleman that he was, determined to keep both of the " fine girls " in leading strings.

I

He who wears the regimental suit,
Is oft as gay as a raw recruit,
  But what of that ?

The girls will follow when they hear the drum,
To view the tassel and the waving plume,
   Which decks his hat.

CHORUS.

Off, off, we go and say that we're on duty,
Smoke our cigars, or flirt with some new beauty,
Vive, vive l'amour ! cigars and cogniac !
Hurrah ! hurrah ! hurrah boys ! Vive le bivouac !

2

When we march into a country town,
Prudes may fly from us and dames may frown,
   But that's absurd !
When we march away, we leave behind,
Prudes and dames who've been vastly kind,
   Pray take my word.

CHORUS.

Off, off, we go, and say that we're on duty, &c.

Such was the song which Messrs. Spruce and Taper still chirruped at this time, with renewed vigor; as they wandered once more round the borders of Governor's Island, and occasionally pulled out the picture of this " fine girl " or that " fine girl " in order to show her visible form and likeness to one another.

And yet in spite of their self-appreciation, it must be acknowledged, that neither one of these gallants were insensible to modest worth; even when that undemonstrative quality was not connected with the possession of glittering pelf. One day, Guy Averall had the luck to be sent with a message from Major Daisy to the young officers, and on entering their quarters, both Messrs. Spruce and Taper were discovered in a state of dishabille, the first with cravat untied, being engaged in looking over a novel, written by that most famous of authors, Monsieur

Alexander Dumas, while the other, in slippers and dirty smoking-cap, was putting the finishing touches to the letter which he was in the act of penning to his lady love, at that instant. After selecting a sentence which seemed particularly fine, and reading it to his companion, Mr. Spruce assured Mr. Taper that no woman living could read such gushing expressions as the ones just enunciated, and at the same time remain insensible to the claims of the writer. This assurance seemed to gratify Taper immensely, but on a sudden the young man heaved a sigh, and then on the instant laid down his pen.

"Do you know what Spruce," said Taper speaking in a low tone, "when I was a Cadet, at West Point, I missed a glorious chance."

"How was that, my boy," asked Spruce as if somewhat interested.

"I'll tell you all about it," was the rejoinder. "It was the year before I graduated, when I accidentally became acquainted with a young lady from Rochester, in the State of New York. She was an angel I assure you if there ever was one on the face of this earth."

"I am sure she was," responded Spruce with a sympathetic air, "else you would not say so."

"I might have been a Count of Monte Cristo, or something of the sort, and achieved all manner of magnificent things, if I had married that girl at the first start. Her father, a wholesale druggist by profession was as rich as Croesus; and would have given her two hundred thousand dollars, if he would have given her a cent. The girl was desperately in love with me beside; in fact, she as much as offered herself to me, not less than half a dozen times."

"You were in bad luck on that occasion," said the other speaker. "Why did you not take the woman at her word?"

"Because I was a confounded fool, that is all, and it is now that I am sensible of my mistake. But that creature was an angel if there ever was one on earth. Her heart was as pure as crystal and——"

"Also as cold," interposed Spruce.

"No it wasn't, it wasn't cold, one bit," replied Taper, with much ardor. "I might have had that woman, as I said before, any day that I liked, but I was a fool, and hadn't sense to properly press my su't. Indeed, the only thing that my flame had against me was my unfortunate name; and even that would not have made any difference, had it not been for the sneers and banter of a certain little miscreant from Massachusetts, who ran away with my prize."

"Who was that?" asked Spruce, who was evidently interested in the recital thus offered by his friend.

"Why do you not know?" was the rejoinder. "It was that little whelp Twitchell, belonging to the Twenty-first, who was then acting as assistant Professor at the Academy. I'd pistol that fellow just as readily as I'd eat my breakfast, on account of the way he treated me. By some means or other he scraped acquaintance with my inamorata, and immediately began to twit her with my name, Theophilus Zanguebar Taper, till he laughed her out of what I almost considered an engagement, and then finally married her himself."

"That was unfortunate," said Spruce, "But wont the lady on Twenty-fifth Avenue, to whom you

are at present so much devoted, possibly object to
Zanguebar also ? My dear fellow, do you never think
of that ?

"Of course I do, of course I do, I think of it
every day," was the rejoinder. "But I'll never inform
any women on the face of the earth that Zanguebar
is part of my name, at least till I'm married. After
that event it wont make much difference."

"You are right, my boy, you are right," responded
Spruce, who now commenced twitching his moustache
with a pair of silver-handled tweezers. "But supposing Taper," said he at length, "that by some accident
your present undertaking should fail, what then ? "

"Why, try again my boy, try again, like a good
soldier, what else should I do." And here Mr.
Taper came to a pause and then added. "Perhaps
in a fit of desperation, I might be tempted to marry
a girl, poor but worthy, like Miss Eleanor then, who
as far as I know, would make a rough Artilleryman,
like me, a most excellent wife."

"Right Taper, right, I say, I admire your pluck,"
was the instant response. "Only I would recommend
you to expend your efforts in another quarter, for do
you know what, I've half an eye on Miss Eleanor
myself."

"Pshaw ! nonsense ! Now Spruce that is all
fudge," responded Taper. "How in the world can
a person have half an eye on one woman, and at the
same time be wholly devoted to another ? "

"I have always considered Miss Davis an excellent lady," said Spruce.

"So have I," responded Taper, "and possessed,
by the way, of a very thorough education beside."

" She understands the parley vous like a native, at least so I've been told," said the one.

" While her skill, in music, is beyond all question," replied the other.

" She manages the whole household as a kind of deputy general to her aunt," said the first speaker.

" And looks after that greedy young Hector, in addition," remarked the second.

" I wonder if she has any of the ready?" asked Spruce, who now gave his beautiful little moustache a contemplative twist.

" Oh hang the cent, hang the cent," was the answer, " and that is the vexatious part of the subject; for her father, as I understand the case, had saved a sufficient amount, out of his pay, to provide for his family ; but unfortunately before setting out to Mexico, he put all his money into the hand of one of those wretched sham bankers, who infest New York city. After a while the fellow failed and insisted on turning the funds that were delivered to him, as a trust, into an asset for the benefit of his creditors ; and Miss Eleanor, having no one to defend her rights was forced to give up all she had. The consequence then is, that the girl is now obliged to teach French for a living ; while the rascal who defrauded her is looked on as a paragon of excellence; has his fine house on Twenty-fifth Avenue, his liveried servants and all that sort of thing, and finally as the crowning act of a swell, his aristocratic "coat of arms." But who in the noble Twentysixth cares for this vulgar display on the part of a shabby pretender? Not you or I, my dear fellow, certainly not you or I."

18

"I'll tell you what, if I was'nt already half engaged," said Spruce, "I don't know that I could do any better than spend my evenings at Headquarters."

"The very remark I was going to make," responded Taper, as if moved on a sudden by a noble generosity.

"But we both cannot marry the same girl," said the one.

"No, not in this civilized country," rejoined the other.

"Let us then arrange the thing between us, so as to see who will go in and win," suggested Spruce.

"Arrange the thing! oh, Spruce, hang it, there would be no sentiment in that. If we don't succeed in New York, according to our expectations, let us both rather try for Miss Eleanor, so as to give the girl a fair chance."

"Right, my boy, right. The suggestion is in every way worthy of your own noble heart," responded Spruce. "And, in short, there is nothing left for us but to let events take their course, and feel assured, with Pope, that 'whatever is, is right.'"

"That's it, my boy—that's the very plan," rejoined Taper. "I'll follow the idea suggested just as you do."

And with this judicious remark, and the quotation from the Essay on Man, just noticed, this famous conversation between two of the younger officers of the Twenty-sixth Artillery, came to a conclusion.

IX.

IT was at this particular juncture that the irre-

pressible Blodgett, as a bold and ardent spirit, resolved to take the affairs of the garrison in charge
and conduct himself accordingly. " By Jupiter,"
said he to himself, one evening, just after he had
completed the plan of some wonderful machine or
other, which was destined to revolutionize the world.
" By Jupiter, I don't see why I should not have a
little pleasure, just as well as any one else; and if
Spruce and Taper enjoy the felicity of making love
to their girls, I cannot see why I myself should not
have the same satisfaction also."

So on the spur of the moment he buttoned up his
coat, and away he started to Headquarters. But
here his progress was barred by an untoward event
The good Mrs. Daisy still recollected that Blodgett,
when on drill, had denied her the services of Averall, and the insult still lingered in her memory.
So she quietly stole into the drawing room, during
the interval that Blodgett was in waiting, and
informed him, in the first place, that her niece was
not at home; and secondly, that any one who went
about in a careless, indifferent manner, calling on
the god Jupiter in the way Mr. Blodgett usually did,
gave proof sufficient by that single act, that his spirit
and disposition were anything but those of a gentleman, and till he had learned more agreeable manners
he had better not come into her presence.

" By Jupiter, ma'am, I will keep away then," responded the irresistible. And off he bolted in an
instânt.

A few days after the foregoing event, while Guy
Averall was going round the Island, in company with
the bard Hogan, the latter saw fit to introduce the

name of the Brigadier. "Do you know what," said he, "I have a very pretty story to tell in relation to our lady Glumdalclitch."

"What is it pray?" responded Averall, somewhat interested, for to him about this time, the leading traits and peculiarities of his lady patroness began to be pretty well known.

"The thing is characteristic," said the Bard, "but is told *sub rosa*, for I would not for my life, that a single word by way of disparagement, in regard to so excellent a woman as Mrs. Daisy should be repeated. You know she is very fond of us soldiers, she calls us her dear children, and never troubles us for anything, except just what she wants; still, at the same time, I don't know but I should like her much better if she were a little less profuse of her compliments, and exhibited some consideration for those immediately around her. She occasionally pretends, I believe, to be very charitable; but to my mind the way she prevaricates and fibs, whenever it suits her purpose, is perfectly shameful. You have heard of her hunting Blodgett away from her house; because, forsooth, he swears by the god Jupiter. Now that is all fudge—Mrs. Daisy does not care one whit about Jupiter, any more than anyone else, except just as the notion strikes her. The truth of the matter is, she is so much afraid of Miss Eleanor getting married, she will stoop to any kind of meanness to prevent it. Accordingly it so happened that when Blodgett made his call, Miss Davis was made to appear as if away from home, while the officer was sent about his business. The story was told last night on kitchen authority; and now the whole affair is spread among us Philistines."

"What an atrocious piece of imposition!" said Guy, who uttered the exclamation, be it observed, from the very bottom of his heart.

"The truth of the matter is," said Hogan, "that in the Army those terribly aristocratic personages play the very mischief with us, once they get into power, since there is absolutely no way of keeping them under control. Such persons as Mrs. Daisy could hardly exist in civil life. People before long would get tired of her, some would even express their opinion in a way that could not possibly be misunderstood. But with us the case is different, Everything in the service is regulated by authority; and if a woman, like the Brigadier, has an indolent, easily led husband, she can inflict a great many annoyances on every one in the place where she is quartered Like the trumpeter in Æsop, she may remain guiltless of war herself, but blowing the blasts which set other people fighting. Why I recollect one incident which happened at a post where I was serving, some years ago; and which, although perpetrated by a so-called lady, seemed such a piece of stupid barbarism, that even at this distance of time I occasionally recall it."

"What were the circumstances, pray?" asked Guy.

"The thing took place before the Mexican War. At the place mentioned the wife of the commandant bore a general resemblance to the Brigadier, was always boasting of her family connections, and other claims to consideration. One day she missed a silk dress, and immediately charged a colored servant with taking it. The negro denied the implication, when the mistress reiterated the charge, and then told the servant that if the dress were not produced immediately, the person who took it would be whipped."

'I don't care whether I am whipped or not,' was the reply, 'that will not make me produce the dress. I never took it and know nothing as to where it is.'

'You did, you huzzy,' was the response on the part of this Brigadier, 'and now I'll get you punished for your insolence, if it were for nothing else.'

'Very well, I can't help it,' was the reply on the part of the darkey. The mistress, however, carried out her threat, the servant was sent to the guard house, and there she received a most outrageous lashing, under the direction of the husband of the mistress, who was himself present on the occasion. Three or four days after, the dress, which was the occasion of all this clamor, was discovered in the bottom of an old trunk, where the wife of the commandant had carelessly thrown it. So much for plebeian aristocracy."

"Well," said Guy, "such things are atrocious, although as far as our Brigadier is concerned, boastful and imperious though she may seem, I hardly think she would be guilty of such conduct as that. But why are all our officers so infatuated about their New York acquaintances? Are all the excellencies of the earth concentrated in a little spot of Manhattan Island, three-quarters of a mile long and one-quarter broad? Our marriageable officials are young, handsome, agreeable, and have their salaries, at least, as a means of support. Mrs. Daisy cannot chase them all away, and as to Miss Eleanor, I'm sure she

would make any person in the Army a good wife; a
much better one, in all probability, than some of
those 'fine girls' on Twenty-fifth Avenue, to whom
both Spruce and Taper seem so very, very attentive.
On one occasion, indeed, I heard them both speak
very favorably of Miss Eleanor."

At this suggestion which was put forward in the
utmost good faith, the bard gave a shrill whistle, then
came to a halt, and afterwards commenced beating
his knees, in imitation of the gallop of a horse.

"Quadrupe-dante pa-trem soni-tu quatit-ungula-
campum. They are all in a trot, up Broadway, to
those blessed abodes, where nobody save saints and
angels are supposed to dwell. I dare say you have
heard of the famous doggerel, which was perpetrated
by the English footman."

> When the Duke of Leeds shall married be,
> To a fine young lady of high quality,
> How happy will that gentlewoman be,
> In his grace of Leeds good company.
>
> She shall have all that is fine and fair,
> And the best of silk and satin to wear,
> And ride in a coach to take the air,
> And have a house in Saint James' Square.

Now reverse the *she* for the *he*, and you have the
precise situation. In short, sir, I do not wish to be
severe on any one; and as to our officers, I do not
accuse them of any very flagrant crime. They do
not usually dissipate, they do not gamble, they are
reasonably attentive to their military duties, and if
the country were in danger, I'm sure they would all
do their duty towards it. But at the same time they
have the prevailing fault of the age, unmitigated

selfishness in money matters, and I am afraid in this universal hunt for wealth, Miss Davis, even in spite of her good qualities, will receive but scant justice from them. Fifty or a hundred years ago, according to current reports, young men had their failings, but they were somewhat different from those that now exist. They roystered, they got drunk, they fought duels, and made beasts of themselves generally, whenever they got the opportunity. At present we have changed all that. But the question still remains, is the change for the better?"

"I understand," responded Guy, "the general conclusion from what you say."

"Is what?" asked Hogan.

"It simply is this," replied Averall, "that Miss Davis, for want of a better offer, will turn round some bright morning, and marry that scatterbrain Blodgett."

ALL FOR LOVE.

I.

PREVIOUS to this time a somewhat untoward event took place. A man who had been confined, as a prisoner, at the guard house, met with his death in consequence of the harsh treatment he received at that place. The unfortunate fellow, whose name was Grady, had been on leave of absence for twenty-four hours; and at the expiration of his term, he came back from the city, pretty drunk. He was accordingly thrust into durance vile, and while there was undoubtedly very noisy. Taper, at that time was officer of the day; and finding that the man's bellowings could not be stopped, he ordered Ryan, who was then Sergeant of the Guard, to take him out of the prisoner's room and make a "spread eagle" of him. This operation, which was then quite prevalent, but has now fortunately been laid aside, consisted in taking the offender and pinioning him on the ground, so that he could not stir, his arms and feet being extended as far as possible for that purpose. Still the man continued his ravings; and among other things he charged the Sergeant of the Guard with that familiar crime of selling the provisions belonging to the men, and then sitting down, with certain other non-commissioned officers of his own stamp, and squandering the proceeds over cards. Whether the accusations were true or not, in this particular case, is not known; the charge, however, made the Sergeant furious, so without any more ado, he thrust a big stick into the prisoner's mouth, and secured it there as a gag.   Meanwhile the man was lying exposed to the rays of the sun, but before long, either the whiskey or the heat produced its natural effect, for he was senseless.   Seeing him in a state of coma, Guy Averall instantly ran for the doctor, who on his arrival ordered the prisoner to be untied. Such remedies as were available, were now employed to restore Grady to his senses, but unfortunately with little effect, for the man died in the course of a couple of hours.   A report of the case soon reached Headquarters, a paragraph or two on the subject appeared in the newspapers, a clamor was raised, and an investigation was ordered in Washington.   Before long down came old General Fuzzy, the same official who on a former occasion had reviewed the troops; intent no doubt on enquiring into all the circumstances of the case.   After the usual review and inspection, the men were dismissed, and then the Officer of the Day, and Sergeant of the Guard was summoned into the presence of the old chief.   What explanations were made in regard to the matter is not positively known; this much appears certain that the officer was not by any means allowed to go scot free ; the General, in fact, was reported as administering a pretty severe reprimand in the connection, and eventually an official order was published forbidding the use of the " spread eagle " in the future, and limiting punishments on prisoners, to those which may be regularly inflicted by sentence of an appropriate courtmartial.   As to Lieutenant Taper, he was only too glad to get rid of the affair on such easy terms; for since Grady had died he was somewhat apprehensive of being tried for manslaughter. But Ryan being of a different temperament took the thing very unconcernedly; in fact he swaggered about, day after day, just as if the loss of an odd soldier or two, through his brutality, were a thing of the most trifling consequence.

Meanwhile the good and amiable Mrs. Daisy resolved to mitigate this little unpleasantness in as effectual a manner as possible; and in pursuance of this design she finally determined to give another *chapeau bras.* Invitations were accordingly issued in the accustomed form, and the Hospital once more was put in order. The floor of the dancing hall was waxed, so that you could almost see your face in it, such bayonets as could be spared were arranged in the form of a heart on the ceiling, the name Daisy, in large Roman capitals, was painted directly over the spot where the hostess intended receiving her guests, while to crown all, Messrs. Spruce and Taper both went over to New York and ordered another suit of clothes, so as to appear properly in mufti. As to the Garde Imperiale, that of course could not be omitted, for Corporal Sullivan had already acquired ample credit in that role, and Hogan, Averall and Moldwell were all detailed in order to pay proper respect to her Imperial Highness on the occasion. When the guests began to arrive, it was noticed that a very large number of staff officers were present, for Mrs. Daisy seemed resolved to crush all adverse criticism in regard to the management of the post, as far as her gallant husband was concerned. She did not condescend to wheedle or deal in elaborate compliments, as other ladies would do in like circumstances, be it observed; her mind was altogether too lofty for any such pitiful attempts as these, her great strength lay in her capacity as a gusher, and as far as this quality was available, it was certainly exerted to the utmost on the occasion. "I understand Madam," said Captain Triangle of the Topographical Engineers, who probably understood what subject was most agreeable. "I understand, Madam, that it is your intention to go abroad during the ensuing summer." These words were spoken in the interval between two successive dances, and were intended as a very delicate compliment on the part of the speaker; for to go abroad, as the phrase is understood in New York, implies both wealth and leisure, the two greatest gifts that fortune can possibly bestow.

"I intend to visit Europe, most certainly," was the reply of Mrs. Daisy to the inquiry made on the part of Captain Triangle. "I intend of course to go abroad ; that is provided Major Daisy is willing to enter into those arrangements which I propose. And in case I do, I certainly intend taking Hector with me, so as to give him every possible advantage. Do you know that I really believe Hector to be one of the most extraordinary boys I ever met. His genius for foreign languages and mathematics is perfectly astonishing."

"Does Miss Davis intend to accompany you, may I ask?" said Triangle, who chose to exhibit some curiosity in regard to that somewhat obscure personage.

"Of course, of course, as my assistant," replied Mrs. Daisy. "We both intend to take care of Hector, and give him all the advantages that a tour on the continent of Europe can possibly confer."

"A very judicious resolve indeed," responded Triangle, "I'm sure the advantage will not be lost, on Hector. By the way, somebody or other mentioned to me that you intended to remain for several months in the city of Paris."

"Of course I do, of course I do," rejoined Mrs. Daisy, I should be a monster to neglect doing so. La belle Paree! La belle Paree, what would the world be without its belle Paree! We would be monsters, savages, Hottentots—whatever you like— anything, in fact, rather than civilized beings. Really and truly I think it is to France we are indebted for almost all that is elegant and great in this present age. Look at the progress of that country in the fine arts ; look at the majestic personage who at present rules that realm ; look at the painters, the poets, the sculptors, the dramatic writers, the musicians, and everything else, which we find in *la grande nation.* Really, Captain Triangle, you must forgive me, if I feel a little enthusiastic on this subject."

"I have no doubt that France, in Mrs. Daisy, will find an appreciative spectator of her greatness," said Triangle with a very polite bow. And with these important words this very elaborate conversation came to a termination.

The programme for the evening consisted of the usual mixture of round and square dances; and the supply of delicacies on the supper table was both varied and abundant; for Mrs. Daisy, to do her justice, had a certain animal love of good eating, and as long as every person around her did exactly as she wished, and gratified her whims in every possible respect, she was certainly the most liberal woman, as far as provender was concerned, that probably ever existed. During the festivities it was noticed that Miss Davis, by some strange mishap was absent; and the Brigadier on more than one occasion was obliged accordingly to explain. " The poor dear child, whom I love so very much, has one of those miserable headaches, to which she is constantly subject; and knowing the state in which she usually is, on those occasions, I could not help insisting on her returning home." Then turning to another officer whose well-cut chin, although half hidden by a moustache, served to denote the man of resolution, the amiable hostess continued :—

"Oh, Mr. Square, I am so very glad, indeed, to see you here—I hope you are enjoying yourself this evening. I should be very glad to welcome you back, at any time, to the Regiment; but then your position, as a member of General Scott's military family, is so very desirable, that I do not imagine you are particularly anxious to join us in either fort or field. By the way, what are all those stories which I have heard of you lately? I am told you are quite attentive to that very pretty little cousin of yours, who lives half way between Twenty-fifth Avenue and Gramercy Park—report indeed says it will be a match, as a matter of consequence. I should wish you all happiness, in the connection, I am sure ; and am certain you could not select a more accomplished lady for a wife."

"My cousin is indeed a woman of intelligence," was the reply, "but then you must not pay too much attention to what report says, for Madam Rumor, you must recollect, is a great gossip. To tell the truth, I have enjoyed my bachelor freedom so long, that I almost hesitate to give it up for any consideration. Am I not right in delaying somewhat in this matter?"

"Why no, I cannot see that there is any necessity for delay," was the answer. "Judging from my own experience, I should certainly give my opinion in a contrary direction. There is my own good Tom, the best and dearest man that ever existed, and I'm sure we have had a good deal of happiness together. He was the only person whose attention I ever encouraged, he married me after a courtship of a fortnight, and in spite of the shortness of an engagement, we certainly have had nothing but unalloyed pleasure ever since, in each other's society."

Here the officer was forced to smile on account of this very candid confession on the part of his hostess. As he turned away his head, Guy Averall caught a glimpse of his face, standing as the latter was in the hallway. On a sudden it occurred to him that he had seen that same personage before. Where could it have been? Somewhere, he felt certain, in New York. At length the truth flashed across his mind. It was the same individual who, long ago, had delivered him from the mock auction, in Broadway.

II.

By instituting proper inquiries during the next

few days, Guy Averall was enabled to ascertain a
few items in regard to the previous history of his
benefactor. Lieutenant Square, was a man whom
fortune had favored in many respects; and who, at
the same time, had not abused her gifts. His ancestors, the Squares of Madison Square, were of an
old Knickerbocker stock; and as such, had occupied
a somewhat prominent place in the history of his
native State, at a time when family influence, and
perhaps we may add, personal merit, passed for more
than they do now. As to himself, the Lieutenant
had received all the advantages that a liberal training could give. He had passed through the usual
fitting schools in a creditable way, and had already
graduated at one of our eastern colleges, when the
tender of an appointment to the military academy
was made, and this, after a little hesitation, he saw
proper to accept. His course at that institution was
such as to gain him the good will of both instructors
and cadets. Of studious habits, and attentive to his
duties, he, at the same time, avoided that offensive
smartness, which seems to take delight in "pinking"
a brother soldier; and as a natural consequence he
was regarded as a "fine fellow," who was justly entitled to all the favors that the institution heaped on
him. His friends visited him occasionally while at
West Point; and among others, that little cousin of
his, to whom report said he was now engaged, had
frequently met him there. After receiving his commission, he served for a couple of years with his
regiment, and at the termination of that time, he
was selected by General Scott, as a member of his
staff. Here, he had the honor of being entrusted

with several missions of a sufficiently delicate and important nature to testify the esteem in which the General himself held him. Such advantages as study and travel could confer, were not meanwhile neglected by Lieutenant Square; he had crossed the American Continent, on two successive occasions, for the purpose of examining its topographical features, and on his return from one of these, had made a very elaborate report on the subject to his military superiors. Nor had good luck neglected him in other regards—an uncle of his died about this time, who left him a very considerable sum of money, safely invested in a United States loan. And thus, on the whole, it may be said of him, as was formerly said of the Danish King, he had

> A combination and a form, indeed,
> Where every god did seem to set his seal
> To give the world, assurance of a man.

And is this account, laudatory although it may seem, an exaggerated, or an unnatural one? Do we not, every now and then, meet in the Army men who seem to unite in themselves all the good qualities attributed to this officer? Are such persons as Bayard and Sidney now extinct in the military profession? We hope not, even in this time serving, money making age of ours. For our part, we utterly despise that sneering, fault-finding disposition, which refuses to see anything good in those by whom we are surrounded. It is only the fiend Mephistopheles himself, and his followers, who habitually exhibit this unenviable trait.

As to the officer's *fiancee*, nothing was known at

19

the time by Guy Averall, beyond the fact that she was reported pretty; and like Square himself was believed to be wealthy; indeed the union of their respective fortunes was commented on, as a thing of mutual advantage.   Further than this neither Guy Averall, nor any of the enlisted men then serving at Fort Columbus knew anything of the lady; although it was a fair matter of inference, that a person like Lieutenant Square would never seek an alliance with any one whom he could not esteem and value as a friend.

III.

THE *chapeau bras* was now over, the inquiry as to the death of Private Grady was ended, the indignation of the Inspector General was satisfied; so Mrs. Daisy had an opportunity to expatiate once more on those amiable dignitaries in Europe, on whom her mind as an aristocratic member of society seem to constantly dwell; while Guy Averall once more took to his studies with renewed vigor.   He commenced mathematics, and having a natural aptitude in that direction, he soon made considerable progress in these studies; in a year indeed, he was able to go through the entire discussion of curves of the second degree, as deduced from the expression between two variables, a fact which indicated a very considerable amount of geometrical skill.   In French, the want of a teacher was somewhat severely felt; for although he read his Gil Blas and Charles the Twelfth in due order, his pronunciation of the language was really no pronunciation at all, while his knowledge of the niceties of the tongue was, like that of most foreigners who study it, never very accurate. We all remember the criticism of Macaulay, as applied to this subject, when speaking of Frederick the Great. Some encouragement Averall received, at this time, from looking over the grammar of William Cobbett, who gives a very interesting account of the way he studied French. Cobbett was like Averall, an enlisted soldier, but while serving in the ranks he indulged in none of the dissipation common in barrack life. Among other circumstances which the Englishman mentions, is an expedient, adopted while serving with his Regiment in Canada, in order to impress on his memory the various forms of irregular verbs. This was a piece of pasteboard containing a list of these words, written alphabetically, which was carried round by Cobbett in his pocket, and whenever a particular termination was forgotten, the card was always forthcoming to refresh his memory. And the industry and self restraint, implied in such a course as this, ultimately obtained its reward; for many years from that date, William Cobbett, once Sergeant Major of the 54th Foot, stood up as a candidate for the borough of Oldham, and for that borough was elected a member of the British Parliament.

But there were other students beside Guy Averall at the Fort, and while discharging his every day duties as Orderly at Headquarters, our friend had frequent opportunities of observing the wonderful genius of Hector, not only in regard to mathematics, but to such other subjects as he was taught. "We will have to send the child to West Point, on his return from Paris, he has such commanding talents, that it would be a pity to neglect him," was the con-

stant exclamation of Mrs. Daisy; and certes the
talents of Hector were of a most extraordinary description, as far as Guy was capable of judging. One
day the Brigadier went over to town, and Averall
was told to assist Miss Davis, in fixing a set of
window curtains in the parlor. Hardly had he began
the task, when Blodgett, who in spite of his declaration to keep away from Headquarters, apparently
took advantage of the absence of Brigadier to play
the dearly devoted to Miss Davis. In he came to
the parlor, sat down to the piano, and commenced
drumming away in a very brilliant style, his hair as
long and as fiery as usual, and his shirt, if the truth
must be told, very clean indeed for a person of his
habits. The piece chosen was one from a selection
of miscellaneous music, and as the irrepressible
stretched himself back on the music stool, he gave
Guy and Miss Davis his rendering of the following
song:

I

In days of ancient chivalry,
  A Knight of noble name,
Had lost his lordly lands and state,
  But not his well-earned fame.
" I care not for my vanished wealth,
  " My gold and silver flown,
"I still can wield my trusty sword,
  " And honor's still my own.
" I still can wield my trusty sword,
  " And honor's still my own."

2

His life blood ebbing fast away
  Upon the battle plain
That Knight still grasped his gallant sword,
  Though human help was vain.

" My soul to God, my heart to her
  " Who fills this bosom's throne,
" My life is for my country given,
  " But honor's still my own,
" My life is for my country given,
  " But honor's still my own."

"Well by Jupiter," said Blodgett, when he had finished the last line, " if they had only given me a fair chance, when I was a boy, in the way of a musical education, I would have been one of the greatest of opera singers, by this time, that was ever heard, either in this or any other country."

" Do you really think so," said Miss Davis as if somewhat amused at the officer's appreciation of himself.

"Certainly," said Blodgett again returning to the charge, " I have naturally one of the best tenor voices that ever was known. I can go over a good two octaves and a half—all the way from A flat to D sharp—just hear me." And in an instant the irrepressible Lieutenant was running over the notes, just as if he were at a New England Singing School.

"Why, Mr. Blodgett," said Miss Davis with a smile, as if determined to humor the foible of her visitor. "I really had no idea that you possessed such a magnificent organ. Why if you only had a proper training, you might go on the stage at any time, and acquire a reputation in opera."

"By Jupiter, so I might Miss Davis," said Blodgett, who accepted the compliment without a moment's hesitation. "And you, by the way, are not the first person who has told me the same thing. Why, I have a friend in New York, who assures me that Brignoli is no singer at all in comparison to me; and that if I had tried the part of Manrico, I could have beat him all hollow. Miss Davis, I have a proposition to make. I can get an arrangement of *ah che la morte* in the city; and let us both see what we can accomplish in that duet. I'll do my best I assure you."

"I have no doubt, Mr. Blodgett," said Miss Davis, "that a person of your musical skill, would be able to acquit himself in a piece, such as that, with great credit."

"By Jupiter, Miss Davis," responded Blodgett, who now threw back his head, and gave himself an appreciative shake. "By Jupiter, Miss Davis, it does me real good to hear a sensible woman, like you, talking in that way. Other ladies of my acquaintance might repeat my praises from morning to night, and from night to morning, and yet their words would be to me mere phrases, signifying nothing. Miss Davis, I do not know that I can express my feelings, on this occasion, in any more appropriate way, than by saying that I am willing to sing duets with you, not only when serving on Governor's Island, but also during life. Miss Davis, just think of these words for a moment. During life, Miss Davis, during life!"

"Oh dear me, Mr. Blodgett," said Miss Eleanor, who did not care apparently to take the words of the irrepressible Lieutenant in the way these were evidently intended. "I like a little music, now and then, and shall be always glad to have you to accompany me, when at your leisure. But singing duets through life, I'm afraid, would be a somewhat monotonous occupation. For my part, I should certainly desire a more varied existence than that."

"Then I am willing to make it as varied as you please, Miss Davis, provided you give me the chance, I'll dance, I'll sing, I'll ride with you. I'll do everything in the world to make you happy, if only—"

"Oh dear me, Mr. Blodgett," said Miss Eleanor, somewhat embarrassed. "I have always been sensible of your politeness as an officer at this post." And then as if to change the subject, the lady asked the irrepressible how he liked some music which had been given the week previous in New York?

"Very well, indeed," responded Blodgett, who was now all aglow on one subject, "I like the performance very much, the barcarolle, for instance, was very fine; although, as I've said before, I'd beat that ass of a Brignoli, in this matter of singing, completely. But that was not the matter, Miss Davis. we were discussing, just now, if you recollect. We were simply speaking of singing duets together. Miss Davis, you do not know how happy I should be, if only I were able to sing and talk, and play accompaniments, on the piano, with you, whenever I like."

"Let us change the subject to something more agreeable," said Miss Eleanor, who now began to perceive that Blodgett was in no humor to be put off. And at the same instant our friend Averall, who overheard all their conversation from his seat in the hallway, was angry enough with the pertinacious fellow, now arguing his cause, to take him bodily, and throw him out of the house. But the Lieutenant was in no humor to be put off.

"Oh! Miss Davis," exclaimed he in a way that

was almost irresistible, "why do you talk in that cruel, cruel manner! You do not know how long I have cherished you as the queen of my inmost thoughts! You do not know how long I have doated, have dreamed on you; how during the silent watches of the night I have dwelt on your image; how even in my midnight sleep I have—"

"Mr. Blodgett," said Miss Eleanor with some indignation, "have I ever done or said anything to encourage such a declaration as this?"

Such a question as the foregoing, put to any ordinary mortal, ought to have been sufficient; but Blodgett, as the reader is probably aware, was one of those consumate asses, spite of his vast scientific knowledge, who would not remain satisfied with a mere refusal, so he resolved to carry the fortress by a *coup de main*, and down he went accordingly on his knees. Miss Davis would willingly have told him that the subject he had insisted on was really a very painful one ; but Blodgett would not listen to any remonstrance on her part, so with hands clasped, and head thrown to one side, he began pouring out his phrases in the most extravagant way. But at this juncture the interview was cut short; for Averall, hearing the uproar in the parlor, determined at all risks to come to the assistance of his mistress, and therefore *sans ceremonie*, he strode into the room. As soon as Guy made his appearance, Blodgett jumped to his feet, and Miss Eleanor as if anxious to terminate the interview in this way, directed the orderly to put a few sticks of wood on the fire.

"You wont listen to me then," said Blodgett to Miss Eleanor, by way of a parting shot. But the latter simply looked at the officer, without saying a word, and the other understanding the silence of the lady as his *conge,* quietly left the room. At the same time Guy Averall was ready to give him his blessing.

"You greasy compound of dirt and braggadocio," said he to himself, "if you had a little cleanliness and modesty; just like any one else, you would pass muster well enough. However, as the case now apparently stands, I'm not much afraid for Miss Davis."

V.

IT was some little time after the disappearance of Blodgett, before Miss Davis could recover her usual self-possession ; the matter nevertheless was set at rest in a very commonplace way, by the appearance of young Hector, who now made his entrance into the room, and began shouting at the top of his voice, "Bah! bah! bah! bah! I want some cake, I want some cake. Bah! bah! bah! bah! wont you come away at once and get me some cake?"

"For heaven's sake, Hector," said Miss Davis, as if distressed beyond measure at the obstreperous noise, "go and get your book, and study your lessons, and dont think eternally of your stomach. Where is that little French grammar of yours? Go and learn your lessons in it, as soon as you can, and I will be ready to hear you in a few minutes."

"Yes, but who can study his French lessons, or anything else, without his cake. I cant, I tell you cousin Eleanor, I cant, so that is an end of the matter." In twenty minutes or therabouts, however, the gallant youth again made his appearance, with a dog-eared book in one hand, and a slate in the other. Miss Davis sat down on a lounge, and commenced teaching school.

"Come now, Hector, go on with your French, let me hear you read," was the first expression on the part of the promptress.

"I want some cake, I want some cake, I cant read French without my cake." And forthwith Hector opened his book.

"Juh ai un bon ——"

"Not jah ai, Hector—*j'ai* is the word, pronounced as one syllable."

"Very well, j'ai un bon pere, et un bonne mere."

"Not un bonne mere, Hector, une bonne mere—mere, you must recollect, is feminine."

"Very well, une bonne mere. Mon pere a vu la maison et le jardins."

"Not le jardins, Hector, jardins is plural—les jardins is the word."

"Very well, les gardins. J'ai une grammaire, une ardoise, et une crayon."

"That will do, now shut your book, and let me ask a few questions in grammar. How many numbers have we in French?"

"Two," said Hector quite boldly.

"Two, that is very well. Now what are their names?"

"Masculine and feminine," responded Hector with great alertness.

"Masculine and feminine numbers!" exclaimed Miss Eleanor, "why Hector, you surely know better than that."

"Well the books says so, that there are two numbers, masculine and feminine, and if the book is wrong I don't know what to say."

"Hector! Hector!" replied Miss Davis. "I almost despair of you. There are two numbers, singular and plural, now try and recollect that."

"Very well, two numbers, singular and plural, go on," said Hector, who evidently cared less for his lesson than for something to eat.

"How many genders have we in French?"

"Three, masculine, feminine, and neuter. That is all I can think of, though there may be more."

This was rather too much for Miss Eleanor. She had been using her utmost endeavors to drum a little French into a greedy, stupid, boy, for a period of six months, and behold the result! Finally she told him to take his slate, and set down a sum in addition, according to her dictation.

"Twenty-eight."

"Very well, twenty-eight," said Hector.

"Three hundred and twenty-four," said Miss Davis.

"Three hundred and twenty-four," repeated Hector, setting down the sum at the same time.

"Sixty-two," said the one.

"Sixty-two," repeated the other.

"Five hundred and ninety-eight," enunciated Miss Davis.

"Five hundred and ninety-eight," rejoined the other.

"Very well, now see how much the sum total is," said Miss Eleanor.

Hector rubbed and worked, and added for a while, and finally announced the result as sixty-seven

thousand one hundred and ninety-eight, as clearly
appears by the following count :

$$28$$
$$324$$
$$62$$
$$598$$
$$\overline{67198}$$

Sixty-seven thousand one hundred and ninety-
eight, sixty-seven thousand one hundred and ninety-
eight" exclaimed Miss Davis in absolute despair;
while Guy Averall, in spite of his best efforts to
appear unconcerned, was forced to laugh outright at
this elaborate specimen of stupidity. The Brigadier
for the last four or five months has been commending
Hector's powers of calculation, on every possible
occasion, and now behold the evidence of this important fact. For ourselves, as historians of this
simple but well authenticated narrative, we have
nothing more to say than to recommend Hector
Daisy's method of addition to all imaginative mothers,
in the Army, who contemplate sending their sons to
this or that scientific institution.

VI.

And yet Miss Davis had opportunities enough to
exercise her patience with other personages beside
Hector. During the week following the *chapeau bras*
a call as a matter of duty, was obligatory on those
who had participated in the festivities at Governor's
Island ; so Miss Eleanor had another opportunity of
seeing the guests who assembled on that eventful occasion. There was Captain Le Froy, of the Twenty-
sixth, an excellent soldier in every respect, who

strange to say, passed through the war of the Rebellion without attracting any marked attention, in spite of the fact, that he was almost constantly in the field. There was Colonel Guliston, per contra, of the Engineers. a big, broad, fat, red-faced old man ; of coarse, ungainly manners, who was always talking of the way that a certain Major Switzer of his corps, contrived to rob him of the reputation he had acquired at the seige of Vera Cruz, by toadying, in the most infamous manner, to the whims and caprices of a well-known General officer. There was Doctor Lambert, of the Medical Staff, a small, dark visaged wiry little fellow, who enjoyed the reputation of being a great manufacturer of puns—a man who would twist the most commonplace expression into any conceivable shape, in order to have an opportunity to give vent to some jingling resemblance of sounds, in words and ideas which have no possible resemblance to each other. There was Captain Backus, a rather undemonstrative individual, in ordinary matters, although considered learned in the law. Captain Backus was a firm supporter of a Judge Advocate's Department in the Army ; and certes he lived long enough to see it established too ; although considered rather too old, when this event took place, to receive any of the appointments which that branch of the Service then offered. There was Forkes, the Paymaster, a fat, happy-looking personage, who took the world easy. Major Forkes got his place on account of the way he had voted during an election for Senator in the legislature of Pennsylvania ; and held on to it ever since, in the way that a sensible, witty fellow might naturally be expected to do. There

was Colonel Cotters of the Subsistence Department;
a regularly trained soldier at West Point, whose strong
point, when discussing military matters was the vast
and illimitable distance that lay between an officer of
the Staff and an officer of the line, and how much
more polite, affable and intellectual the former class
of gentlemen were, than the latter.   There was
Square of the Twenty-sixth Artillery, with whose
merits the reader is already sufficiently acquainted.
There was Triangle of the Topographical Engineers,
who made himself somewhat obnoxious to the good
Mrs. Daisy, the night of the chapeau bras, by asking
for her niece, on that momentous occasion.   Now
regarding the characteristics of Captain Triangle, a
few words will suffice.   He was really, a good sub-
stantial, hard-working fellow, with a very tolerable
head and heart, a man in short, to whom a sedulous
matron might well entrust the keeping of a ward, be
the latter niece or daughter.   The habits of Triangle
were regular, he had saved a considerable portion of
his pay, his temperament was such that there was no
very great likelihood of his ever indulging in whimsical follies, and although he could hardly be called
brilliant, yet he certainly had sound sense sufficient
to acquit himself with decent credit, in any matter of
duty that was ever likely to come under his cognizance.   In short, Triangle had a great many points in
his favor; while the objections that could be urged
against him, as a marrying man, were not of very
great moment.   But this only caused Mrs. Daisy to
be more careful in the way she received him, and
after his name was announced, Miss Eleanor, as if
by accident, was directed to superintend some house-

hold work, which "that dear Irish servant girl,"
according to Mrs. Daisy, was then perpetrating in
the kitchen. So away went Miss Eleanor to her task,
and in the mean time the lady of the house did her
very best to entertain her visitor ; and after he was
gone she even saw fit to congratulate herself, that
she had contrived to circumvent both the officer and
her niece without exciting the suspicion of either
the one or the other. As to the officer, she certainly
did out-manœuvre him ; for Captain Triangle was
too honest and upright a man to believe that any
person, worthy the name of a woman, would throw
obstacles in the way of the settlement of a relative,
merely because the one had heretofore secured in the
person of the other a useful drudge around her
household. But Miss Eleanor understood her aunt
pretty thoroughly, and after she had discharged her
school-teaching and culinary duties that day, with
even more than her customary care, and had retired
in the evening to her own little room, the girl being
in a soliloquizing mood, saw proper to give scope to
her reflections in the following way,

"Well, well," said she, "it will not be the fault
of Mrs. Daisy, if anything happens to disturb the
serenity of this household, at least, as far as I am
personally concerned. I don't know but I should
feel complimented in having so much store set on
my services. I suppose, if I were careless or untidy
or ill-tempered, or were even blessed with a headache *all* the time, my aunt would be glad to get rid
of me. But because I have none of these things,
my connection with her is indissoluble. She need
not have been at the trouble, though, of sending me

down so abruptly to the kitchen, when Captain Triangle made his appearance, for I have heard so many
sneers and innuendos, of late, on this subject of
husband hunting, that I declare I would hardly move
two inches out of my way to catch the best man in
the universe. My aunt imagines, forsooth, I am
somewhat afraid of descending into the category of
old maids! She never committed a greater error in
her life. Old maids! Why should this thing of getting married, I ask, be made the be-all and end-all
of our feminine existence? For my part I could
never see that there was any reason or justice in the
sentiment. Some of the best women I have ever
known were old maids—women who have been an
honor to their sex, and whose shoe latchets, I feel I
am unworthy to loosen. In short, as far as being a
nun is concerned, I neither court the condition, nor
on the other hand do I fly away from it. One thing
is very certain, if it is the wish of heaven for me to
remain as I am, I shall never indulge in repining or
ill natured thoughts on that account. Let me rather
strive to grow.old well, and with good words and
charitable thoughts, endeavor to diffuse a spirit of
contentment and forbearance among those that sur-
round me. For the present, therefore, let a faithful
discharge of my every day duties be my first object,
and a firm trust in a protecting providence my chief
consolation, under any little annoyance to which I
may be subjected."

VII.

DURING the progress of the foregoing events, the
bard, Mr. Hogan, saw fit to entertain the enlisted

men of Company "E," of the Twenty-sixth Artillery, with a very pleasant little expedition on his part. At one end of Rotten Row, as already hinted, was a trader's establishment, kept by a man called Colegate, which place was famous for the exorbitant charges levied on the rank and file, belonging to the post. Every thing in it seemed to be sold at a rate fully one hundred per cent. over New York prices. Cheese, for instance, ten cents a pound in town, twenty with Colegate; butter fifteen cents in one place, thirty in the other; crackers five cents in New York, were charged at double that sum on the Island. In addition to all this, Mr. Colegate had the privilege of issuing credit tickets to the enlisted men for one-half of their pay, and afterwards collecting the amount charged from the paymaster, a system of undoubted benefit to himself, but at the same time of very questionable advantage to the soldier. Disputes frequently arose in the settlement of these accounts, and as the charges of Colegate were well known to be extortionate, it is easy to conceive that the sutler was anything rather than a prime favorite with one part of the military establishment at Fort Columbus. "If I could browbeat that old rascal out of a few dollars at pay day, I should consider it no sin, in any sense of the term," said a member of the Company on one occasion.

"That man has no feeling, in any one way," said another. "He charged me two dollars and a quarter for that bottle of cogniac," here the complainant held up a bottle, which at one time contained the liquor—"and I know if the same article were sold to an officer, the price would be only one-half."

20

"Let me look at that bottle," said Hogan with a smile. "It is empty I see—all gone. Allow me to say you have no feeling, yourself, to drink it up in that way, without dividing it properly with your comrades."

"I did divide it, though—I divided the brandy as far as it went; but, confound it, when every one in a squad room has a swig out of such a bottle as that, the thing will not last a great many minutes."

"I forgive you," responded Hogan. "I take back every word that I said, and in proof of my sincerity I promise to procure you a bottle of the same article, from Mr. Colegate, for the small sum of seventy-five cents, provided you will share the contents with the four persons who are in this room at present."

"I accept your proposal, the money will be forthcoming, in due time," was the reply.

"Hand me the empty bottle," said Hogan. The bottle was immediately produced.

"Where is the cork and the tinfoil that was over it?"

"Here they are, if you want them," was the rejoinder.

"Very well, that will do."

And immediately Mr. Hogan went over to the bucket that was standing in one corner of the squad room, took a quantity of water out of it, filled the empty bottle, put in a small portion of brown sugar, which he procured in the cook house, gave the mixture a shake, corked it securely, put on the tinfoil so as to make it look as if the bottle had never been opened, and then pronounced the contents to be brandy of first rate quality!

" Let me see if I cannot persuade friend Colegate as to the genuineness of the article," said the bard. And forthwith the so-called brandy was whisked under the skirt of his great coat, and the clerk sallied out in the direction of the trading establishment.

Before long Private Hogan was face to face with that august personage whom Mrs. Daisy had designated the " Sutler's Secretary. " After a few winks given in his own facetious style, the " Secretary" was induced to come into a little back room, that opened from the trading establishment, and there and then Private Hogan opened his case.

" I want you to sell me a bottle of your best cogniac," said the bard.

" Dare not do it—in fact there is no brandy in the place," was the reply.

" Oh nonsense, hold your tongue, I know a great deal better. There is Private So-and-So, who got a bottle from you this very morning, for two dollars and a quarter."

" Two dollars and a quarter, did you say—well perhaps he did. At any rate I must speak to Mr. Colegate himself, for he has forbidden me strictly to sell any liquor to enlisted men, unless with his permission."

" Well I will wait here till you see him on the subject. I am very dry, have been sitting up all night finishing a set of muster rolls, and would give almost any amount of money for a drop."

The secretary now disappeared, and in a few seconds returned with the intelligence that he had spoken to his chief, who had only one bottle of liquor left but for it he must ask the sum of three dollars and a half."

" Pretty big price," ejaculated Hogan ; still, as I have come after the beverage, a dollar here or there won't frighten me. Hand me the bottle."

The brandy was now presented to the bard, who on receiving it, thrust the bottle under the skirt of his coat and immediately walked off.

" Hold on, hold on," said the secretary, " you forgot to pay for that. Three dollars and a half, my dear sir, if you please."

" Don't you credit ? " asked Hogan with a look of infinite disgust.

" Credit—no—brandy is a contraband article, as you well know, in this place ; and it would never do to put such an item as that in an account rendered at a pay table."

" Well if you don't credit, I don't want the brandy," rejoined the bard. And in an instant the bottle or one very like it, was handed back to the sutler's deputy. The latter took the article in happy unconsciousness as to the real merits of his present possession, which was simply the water and the brown sugar already concocted by Hogan in the squad room, while that worthy personage marched back to the garrison with the genuine article under his coat tail, very much elated, no doubt, at the success of his scheme. He indignantly spurned the offer of the seventy-five cents, which was made him by his brother private, but spoke of pilfering a sutler, as if it was no great enormity, considering the charges which the latter constantly imposed on members of the rank and file.

We have it on record that before the bard Demodicus commenced his song, they gave him wine ;

and under the influence of such stimulant as he obtained that evening, Private Hogan recited a combination of Tom Moore and himself, which as an illustration of his peculiar genius may as well be inserted in this place.

1.

Lesbia hath a beaming eye,
   But no one knows for whom it beameth,
Right and left its arrows fly,
   But what they aim at no one dreameth.
Sweeter 'tis to gaze upon
   My Norah's lid that seldom rises,
Few her looks, but every one
   With unexpected light surprises.
Oh my Norah Creina dear !
   My gentle bashful Norah Creina !
Beauty lies in many eyes,
   But love in thine my Norah Creina !

2,

Lesbia's daughter I knew well,
   She was endowed with many graces,
And yet with spirit oft would tell
   How womankind should keep their places.
" Where is the use of slinging darts
   From eyes, since now they're ineffectual,
Here we can't pierce lover's hearts
   Unless we don—the intellectual."
Oh my Norah Creina dear !
   My gentle bashful Norah Creina !
You are fine, but more divine,
   I deem your daughter Norah Creina !

3.

Lesbia wore a robe of gold,
   But all so tight the nymph had laced it,
Not a charm of beauty's mould,
   Presumed to stay where nature placed it.

Oh my Norah's gown for me
   That floats as wild as mountain breezes,
Leaving every beauty free
   To sink or swell as heaven pleases !
Yes my Norah Creina dear !
   My simple graceful Norah Creina !
Nature's dress is loveliness,
   The dress you wear my Norah Creina !

4.

Lesbia's daughter had a dress
   But what it was I cannot state it,
Still I know her loveliness
   Was such that you could seldom mate it.
Still her elders air she blamed,
   As o'er the wash tub she kept rubbing,
When a nymph at nonsense aimed
   That nymph she thought deserved a drubbing.
Oh my Norah Creina dear !
   My gentle bashful Norah Creina !
For solid sense, without pretence,
   I laud your daughter, Norah Creina !

5.

Lesbia hath a wit refined,
   But when its points are glancing round us,
Who can tell if they're designed
   To dazzle merely, or to wound us,
Pillowed on my Norah's breast,
   In safer slumber love reposes,
Bed of peace, whose roughest part,
   Is but the crumpling of the roses.
Oh my Norah Creina dear !
   My mild, my artless Norah Creina !
Wit though bright, has not the light
   That warms your eyes my Norah Creina !

6.

Lesbia's daughter always said,
   That none but flirts in wit kept dealing.

Hands for honest work were made
   And hearts should not be got by stealing.
Still, if Lesbia were no prude
   Against her fame no word I'd utter,
Wit and love to some are food,
   While others ask plain bread and butter,
Oh my Nora Creina dear !
   My gentle, simple Norah Creina !
While I bless your loveliness,
   I'd wed your daughter Norah Creina !

But halt Mr. Hogan with thy nonsensical witticisms ! Dost thou not know that at this very date, a fitting model for that Lesbia whom thou endeavorest to turn into ridicule, assumes the most important step that it is possible for a woman to take. Yes, Miss Kitty Traynor, the belle of Rotten Row, the little flirt whom Mrs. Daisy endeavored to patronize, and who would not be patronized by her, the admired of many admirers, assumes the yoke of matrimony ! And the person to whom she is married is not the gay and festive Lawless, the dashing white Sergeantt who is acknowledged by every one to be the handsomest man on the Island. On the contrary, thal very plain, unpretending matter of fact and entirely unsophisticated member of Company " E," Corporal Jeremiah Sullivan is the fortunate individual !

PRACTICAL ETHICS.

I.

THE career of Mrs. Daisy on Governor's Island had hitherto been one of unalloyed pleasure, it now becomes our duty, as historian of this narrative, to record a melancholy event. Those bright anticipations of a visit to Europe, in which that lady had indulged for some time past, were doomed to a sudden collapse. In the first place it was ascertained that the War Department, at Washington, was somewhat unwilling to give leaves of absence to officers at that particular juncture. But even worse than this, was the fact that Major Daisy, after a critical examination of the situation of affairs, expressed an entire unwillingness to enter into that "financial arrangement," which his beloved wife had proposed with reference to the journey, involving as it did the pledge of his pay accounts for several months in advance, and also the disbursement of the small sum of money then in his possession, and which he had saved from his salary as an officer of the Army. In short, Major Daisy said that to Europe, under present circumstances, he would not go; and as the gallant Major was now and then sufficiently obstinate to adhere to his resolution, when once taken, his wife quickly saw that there was no likelihood of moving him. So all that was left to the Brigadier was to accept the situation with amiable resignation. "As to that dear foreign tour," said she, on one occasion, to a particular friend, "on which my heart was set, I am willing, perfectly willing to give it up, since my husband, the best and dearest man that ever existed, thinks it injudicious for us to undertake it, under present circumstances. Of course it would be charming to visit that beautiful city of Paris, which all Americans admire so much, but what is Paris to that love which a true and faithful wife owes to her husband! It is absolutely as nothing I assure you." And then, to show that she appreciated worth, and that devotion to duty was sure to be remembered, the good Mrs. Daisy was pleased to tell Guy Averall that since he had been such a faithful, diligent orderly, he could always get a pass to visit New York, whenever he liked; while Miss Davis was made happy by receiving a photograph of her aunt, in that pale pink dress, which she wore on the night of the *chapeau bras;* along with a copy of a volume which the elder lady had been examining of late, and which in her opinion contained a great deal of very useful and agreeable information, to wit, the justly celebrated and erudite Lemprìere Classical Dictionary.

One morning, shortly after this time, a boat was seen approaching the wharf at Governor's Island, and on its landing, no less a personage than Guy's old protector, Lieutenant Square, came on shore. The advent of the officer, at that very early hour, for it was not yet guardmount, occasioned considerable comment among the enlisted men, then stationed on the Island. "I wonder what is up, that Square is stirring so early? Perhaps General Scott has sent him over to make an inspection of the command, and report its general condition." These surmises, however, were set at rest toward evening; for it then became known that the Twenty-sixth Artillery had to pack up their effects and proceed at once to the South, their immediate destination being the post of Charleston. This change of quarters was occasioned, in a great measure, by the belligerent attitude which several of the states chose to assume, just then, on the question of slavery. Long before the great rebellion, as it is called, broke out, there were occasional indications of the tempest that was brewing; and at this particular time, the Legislature of South Carolina saw fit to adopt some highly censurable resolutions in regard to the fugitive slave law; declaring, among other things, that if their property in negroes was not amply protected; it was the duty and the privilege of that portion of the country to secede immediately from the Union. The admission of California, as a state, was also a bone of contention at this time; one party claiming the right that slavery should be recognized in its constitution; and another denying the privilege. The growing dissatisfaction which was thus manifested, received a fitting notice from the then President, Mr. Fillmore, in his annual message to Congress. "Cases have arisen," said he, "in which individuals have denied the binding authority of Acts of Congress, and even states have proposed to nullify said acts, upon the ground that the Constitution was the supreme law of the land, and that these acts of Congress were repugnant to the instrument; but nullification was now aimed, not so much against particular laws, as being inconsistent with the Constitution, as against the Constitution itself; and it is not to be disguised that a spirit exists, and has been actively at work, to rend asunder this Union, which is our cherished inheritance from our forefathers."

All this was uttered in the year 1851. It was ten years from that time ere these threatenings assumed a definite shape, and the first gun in the conflict was fired. Meanwhile, on receipt of orders to move, the usual scene of bustle and confusion was presented on Governor's Island. Furniture was sold, trunks were packed, and adieus were made, all of which being completed, the Twenty-sixth Artillery took their departure for the Sunny South, once more. As General Scott desired a special report on the condition of the country, he ordered his aide, Lieutenant Square, to accompany the command, so as to obtain the best possible information that could be furnished by an intelligent observer regarding the condition of the country in that particular State to which the troops were sent. For some time Lieutenant Square was regarded as on the staff of the General in Chief; but finally he was assigned to duty as Adjutant to that command which was under command of our old and venerated friend, Major Daisy.

II.

THE transport which conveyed the Twenty-sixth Artillery to Charleston was an exceedingly rickety one, the space between decks, allotted to the enlisted men, was both dirty and confined, and the conveniencies for cooking were anything but satisfactory. All, however, put up with the annoyances, incident to such a situation, in a truly admirable manner; and even the pretty Mrs. Sullivan, then a passenger, did not seem to complain any more than the others. As a means of amusement, the old custom of story-telling was observed on board in due form; and among others the Steward Peterson, on one occasion, saw fit to favor the Company, then assembled on the forecastle, with his narrative, which as well as can be recollected ran in the following style :

You must know, gentlemen, said he, that I have had my little adventures as well as others; on one occasion, indeed, my zeal for scientific knowledge got me into a rather serious difficulty. You have doubtless noticed a particular skull which I usually carry in that box. Now thereby hangs a tale, and for reasons which will presently appear, I can hardly pay a visit to Burlington, in the State of Vermont, at least for the present. Not but I like Burlington, which is in itself a very pleasant place, with a College set on its highest hill, and a broad expanse of lake at its foot, and majestic mountains around it on every side, while the inhabitants thereof are as pleasant a set of people as you will find anywhere in New England. And yet, as I remarked before, I can hardly hope to return to that place in the course of my natural life, for while there I was so unfortunate as to incur the ill will of a certain Frenchman, called Antoine, who has taken a high oath, before all the saints in Heaven, to embrace the very first opportunity that is offered, to arm himself with a loaded pistol and then and there to shoot me.

The reason of this state of affairs may be told in a few words. As already hinted, it was partly owing to the desire I had to secure this particular skull, and partly owing to that inherent propensity to blunder, which in spite of my best efforts to the contrary, occasionally breaks out as part of my nature.

It is something more than two years since I first made my entrance into Burlington, and then engaged as a journeyman printer in the office of the daily newspaper published in that place. As companion in my labors I had a little fellow from Connecticut, by the name of Caffee. Now Caffee, if you please, was a very lively little cricket in his way; and among his vagaries he was somewhat desirous of being a Doctor. So one evening he came to me with a proposition that we would both start to a graveyard, steal a body from its last resting place, and then make a fair divide of our plunder; that is to say, that he should take the trunk of the cadaver as his proper proportion, and I should have the head.

At first I felt horrified at the proposal. To steal a body out of the grave, after it had been confided to its last resting place by sorrowing friends, was to my mind an act that was simply sacrilegious. I presented my views on the subject to Caffee, with proper force, but it was all in vain—the man only laughed at my scruples.

" My dear fellow," said he, " what is this poor carcass, once life is gone ? Nothing, I assure you, but a heap of air and ashes. The only possible use of the human body, after life is extinct, is to forward the cause of science. Why the doctors, up at the Medical College, on the top of the hill, get their subjects from New York, at the rate of five dollars apiece ; and shall we, who are every whit as

desirous of knowledge as they, shall we, I say, be
debarred the same privilege? As to this reluctance
to avail ourselves of such means of information as
are within our grasp, it is nothing but mere senti-
mentalism. To my knowledge, a certain little carter
in Frenchtown has died within the past few days,
and is now buried near the church of St. Joseph, on
Geoch Street. Let us go up to the cemetery this
very night, and steal the body for dissection. In
case we are successful in exhuming the remains, I
will surrender to you the man's head, as a proper
reward for your trouble."

"Let me take an hour or two for reflection,"
said I. "The head, I'll acknowledge, is a temptation; but to steal a body out of the grave for its
sake, is an act of which I never have been guilty."

Without compromising myself any further, I now
went down to my boarding-house, and on making
inquiry there, I discovered that the Frenchman, then
defunct, whose name, by the way, was Cabana, was
a real curiosity when alive, in regard to his capacity
for eating. Eat did I say! He hardly seemed
capable of any thing else. Sitting on his little
vehicle, near the Market house, waiting for an occasional job, surrounded by a crowd of eager, gossiping
Canadians, he rarely allowed his jaws to rest for a
minute. That trait in the character of Cabana, determined my action. I resolved, on the instant, to
get possession of the head, if it were only to examine
his bump of alimentativeness. I accordingly com-
municated my design to my associate.

About two o'clock the next morning we set out
on our expedition, each one being equipped with a

shovel. It snowed quite heavily at the time, although it was only the beginning of November; but then in Burlington, it must be recollected, there are only six months of winter. The storm which was falling did not in the least interrupt our labors; we worked away like a couple of railway hands, exhumed the remains of poor Cabana, hoisted them over our shoulders, and in this style we proceeded to a little out-house, back of the Free Press office, and there deposited our treasure. No sooner was the corpse laid on the ground than Caffee, with a big carving knife, cut the head off the unfortunate man, and delivered it immediately to me. I put it in a carpet-bag, and carried it to my boarding-house. But what became of the trunk, which remained, I never could discover.

That portion, however, which was delivered to me was in itself a treasure; for if I ever had any doubt, as to the truth of phrenology before, that doubt was removed by an examination of this cranium. As soon as I had pickled it and got rid of the superfluous flesh, I instantly began to look out for that organ which Spurzheim and Gall have indicated as the proper concomitant of a generous appetite; and let me assure, in all honor, gentlemen, my search did not end in disappointment. Caution was full, philoprogenitiveness was large, inhabitiveness was moderate, adhesiveness was fully developed, but when you come to alimentativeness you had the bump in the shape of a mountain! And if any one should doubt the accuracy of what I say, I will produce that same individual skull, which I have ever since carried around with me, and then let him dispute, if he will, the virtues of cranological science.

But meanwhile, without being conscious of it, a difficulty arose. The dead Cabana had a brother called Antoine, who owned a lot of ground in the cemetery where the defunct carter had been deposited, and on going up to look at it one day, he accidently stumbled against something in the snow, which on examination, proved to be nothing either more or less than the head dress of his brother Lewis, that by some extraordinary mistake had been dropped by Caffee and me, when on our way homeward as resurrectionists. Soon the news spread far and wide over Burlington, that a certain vestment belonging to the defunct Frenchman had been discovered. Some said one thing, and some said another by way of explanation, and finally Antoine, a strictly religious man, thought it better to make the case known to his priest. He found the good curé walking backward and forward, in his hallway, reading his breviary, and taking off his hat in the most reverential manner possible, Antoine opened his case. The father heard him patiently, and after all was over, he quietly replied : " Soyez tranquille, soyez tranquille mon fils, votre frere est parmi les saints—he is in paradise, and that head dress was left as a token that all is well— restez content, restez content, la chose est un vrai miracle," And then he recited some instances of extraordinary signs which had happened in recent times, and which certainly went to show that the age of special manifestations was not yet past. As soon as I understood that the good father had pronounced the finding of the head cloth an indication of the will of heaven, I was delivered from a sore tribulation ; for I knew but too well that if my share in the matter were discovered, I certainly would be subjected to some serious consequences. So I again resumed my work in the printing office, and was only too glad to have escaped the danger with so little apparent difficulty.

But I had not as yet escaped, as I found to my cost. The pertinacious Antoine kept running backwards and forwards among the inhabitants of Frenchtown, exhibiting the head dress wherever he went, as proof positive that his brother was now in glory, and lauding the extraordinary gift which had been vouchsafed on the occasion. But eventually he encountered another Frenchman, called Chauvin, who having travelled a good deal of late, as a tin peddler in northern Vermont, had, as a consequence, lost something of his faith in extraordinary events. "Le diable! bétise!" exclaimed he "that article was never sent to you in that way. I'll tell you the miracle that has happened. Some person, not a loup garou either, has violated your brother's grave and has dropped that head dress when going away from it. Go, get a spade, and examine the grave at once, and I'll venture to say you'll discover nothing in the place but an empty coffin." As soon as I heard of that speech, I began to bundle up my effects, for I did not know what might be the next step in the adventure.

. Before night set in, down came Antoine, with a pistol in his hand, swearing like a trooper. He had been to the grave, had discovered that the body of his brother was gone, and what was still worse, he suspected that d——d phrenologist, as he called me, of making off with the plunder. I met the fellow in

21

the street and asked him why in the world he should leave the charge on me ? "

" You ! ventre bleu ! " was the response. " because you are always going round with your box of old skulls, exhibiting them as such strange objects, and offering to feel the head of any person you meet for the sum of twenty-five cents.   Who else but you could have robbed the grave, and if I were only sure of the thing "—here the rascal flourished a pistol in my face—" I'd blow out your confounded brains, before you are many minutes older."

I endeavored to pacify the mad Frenchman, as best I could, but he still kept twirling his pistol round and round, and on one occasion I really thought he was going to shoot me. On returning to my lodging that evening, I opened the case to Caffee, and told him candidly that he really had been the means of leading me into a very embarassing situation.

" I'll acknowledge it," said he, " there is however one consolation in the matter, we typo's are by nature a wandering race, and one town is about as much a home to us as another. As the thing now rests, I am fortunately not suspected, so in order to make the best amends possible, I will make a tender of my purse, so as to afford you a fitting equipment for your travels. Here it is, you will find twenty-five dollars in it—that sum, I am sure, will serve to keep you going till you get employment somewhere else. And in case you ever attempt to rob a grave again, let me give you a word of advice. In the first place, be careful about leaving any tracks in the snow ; and secondly don't be too anxious to establish your reputation as a scientific expert."

I took the purse from the fellow in the spirit in which it was offered, started from Burlington that very night, stopped in Troy, where I worked a few days, and at the end of a weeks time, I found myself in the city of Newark, and there I enlisted.

III.

THE indulgent reader who has followed us so patiently in the course of this narrative may possibly object that Guy Averall, who is dubbed a hero, does not exhibit any very adventurous spirit after all; and that he should initiate, as far as possible, the example set by his countryman, Con Cregan, even so far as to make love to Spanish beauties, go to Algiers and become a general, and finally sip tea in the Tuileries in company with the Princess of Verneuil. But Averall and Cregan it must be remembered are two very different personages; for while the one rushes into the most perilous undertakings, the other adheres conscientiously to the most common-place facts. Still Guy, we maintain, is a hero in spite of all that; his bravery being shown by the willingness with which he accepts the situation in which he is placed, and endeavors, so far as possible, to discharge his duties in a creditable way. He does not grumble unnecessarily, he does not tell long stories about that venerable aunt of his who might accomplish all sorts of things for him, his ragamuffin father is never mentioned, he knows he is a private soldier, in the American Army, nothing more, and as a private soldier he is determined to perform his duty. His spirit is further evinced by the care with which he chooses his associates. Whatever is good around

him he accepts, the muck-rake, on the other hand,
he carefully avoids, his companions are the very best
his company contains, and by conversing with them
occasionally his understanding is improved, his observations of right and wrong become more accurate, and he gradually becomes conscious of what
are his duties, his privileges, and his opportunities
as a man and a citizen.

During the voyage to Charleston, Guy Averall
held a conversation with his old friend Moldwell on
the subject of liberty, which conversation deserves a
short notice in this place, not only on account of its
connection with subsequent events, but also because
of the sentiments therein contained. At several
times, during his period of service, our friend had
heard that divinity lauded in the most exalted terms,
by certain members of his barrack room acquaintance;
he hardly knew, however, what value was to be
attached to these encomiums; for in the first place,
he was occasionally inclined to distrust the judgment of those who were loudest in liberty's praise;
and again, he now and then had occasion to notice,
that persons who are strong supporters of freedom
as a sentimental illusion, are often the very ones to
show themselves to be the most arbitrary and tyran-
nical, once they are invested with supreme power.
There were Ryan and Lawless, for instance, who
could hardly be considered patterns of correctness;
and whose faults in certain directions, we have rather
hinted at, than attempted, with anything approaching accuracy, to sketch. And yet these men were
always talking about "freedom and independence,"
just as if these were the most exalted of virtues.

The question which now presented itself was simply this, could men, like Lawless and Ryan, be intrusted with supreme power in any condition of life, regard being paid to the welfare of those by whom they are surrounded?

"My dear sir," said Moldwell in reply to the inquiries of Guy, "the subject you have broached is one that admits of a very lengthened discussion, Liberty may be a good, or it may be a very bad thing, just as it is entrusted to those who are capable of using it, or are not so qualified. As to personal liberty, there are certain obligations due to the state which protects us; and after these are discharged, enlightened opinion would say that every person has a right to act as he pleases, provided that in so doing, he inflicts no harm on any other member of the community. As soon, however, as he does this, his liberty must be restrained. We cannot allow thieves and murderers to go at large; we are obliged to confine and even to punish them, as a protection to the rest of our associates. The first restriction then on personal liberty is this, that injurious acts cannot be permitted, and that those who commit them, do so at their peril."

"What is your notion of political liberty, may I ask?" said Guy.

"Political liberty is a good thing, in itself, when admissable," responded Moldwell, "although at the same time, it is somewhat difficult to define its exact limit. It is not of necessity the first thing that a state need attain, indeed in some countries, such as Hindoostan, its existence is clearly impossible, while in other places, such as the United States, we have political liberty in an almost unlimited degree. But of one thing we may be certain, these institutions, on which political liberty depends, and without which its existence is but temporary, are in themselves things of slow growth, and cannot be created in a day. It is in this sense that Burke's observation holds good, that constitutions grow and are not made. Our own Constitution was not formed in the year 1787, but had been growing for centuries. Its foundation was laid in those laws which were brought from the mother country, in the right of trial by jury, in the equality of all classes before the law, and in unwillingness to submit to taxation without representation. The American Constitution, in short, is but the embodiment of principles that have existed from time immemorial among English speaking people. So it is with the British Constitution, which is not a written article at all, but a collection of usages that have been in process of formation, from the time that the first parliament was summoned in the thirteenth century. On the other hand we sometimes express surprise at the want of order in the so-called South American Republic. The true explanation of this condition of things is the simple fact that the Spaniards never allowed free institutions in their colonies ; and as yet such countries as Mexico and Ecuador have been unable to create them."

"What do you think of the progress of liberty in France," said Guy. "They had a Republic there a few years ago, and now, it appears, they have an Empire."

"No country," was the reply, "could furnish a

more appropriate illustration of the principles just laid down. 'Tis true, the general tendency of the present age is towards freedom; and yet, at the same time, it must be remembered that in France, free institutions, as we understand them, have had only as yet a limited existence. As a natural consequence they cannot be established at once in full, by the mere fiat of a new government, even should that government be a Republic. The well known writer, De Tocqueville, has taken the trouble to explain that France has always been a centralized government, and has so continued under successive changes. He shows that under the ancient regime, for instance, a road could not be constructed, a bridge built, or a clerk appointed in a petty office without sanction from the central authority in Paris, and the result has been that Paris has continued to rule the nation ever since. The same remark applies to other countries on the continent of Europe. Constitutions and liberal forms of government were established in several of them in the year 1848, but we all know how many of these so called republics now exist. One thing we should never forget, that truth and honor and respect for the rights of others, are essential requisites in those who would derive any benefit from the operations of independence. To be free men must be moral. In short I would say that the steps from servitude to absolute equality with a governing class, is a sheer impossibility, and those who look for the sudden regeneration of States, by a mere change in the form of government, are doomed eventually to be most bitterly disappointed.

IV.

THAT portion of the Twenty-sixth Artillery, of which Guy Averall was a member, remained but a short time in Charleston, for almost immediately after its arrival, Companies "E" and "I" of the Regiment were ordered to take post at a place know as Camp Scott, some forty or fifty miles northeast of Charleston, near the mouth of the Santee River. Some four or five years previous, when a somewhat similar trouble was brewing, the place had been selected as a station for United States troops; and on the arrival of the Twenty-sixth Artillery, at their new halting place, it was discovered that the so called "camp," consisted of a series of low, one-story houses, facing the river, and a town of some five or six hundred inhabitants back of it. The country in the neighborhood, like that found everywhere along the Southern coast of the United States, was extremely sandy; with the eternal pitch pine as the principal feature in the landscape. Guy Averall and his comrades soon put their quarters in proper order, and after the lapse of a week or thereabouts, the good and amiable Mrs. Daisy was gratified by receiving the customary calls from the three or four heads of families who constituted the " real *elite*" of the place. · Of course, Mrs. Daisy was delighted to see them ; and after the usual preliminaries, in the way of conversation, were disposed of, the gallant Brigadier gave vent to those feelings which were ever uppermost in her mind. " Had it not been for circumstances, untoward in themselves, but over which she had no control, she intended residing

abroad that very summer ; her husband, one of the
best and dearest men in existence; was to accompany her, and in addition, an officer of the Regiment, Lieutenant Square, and his excellent wife,
were to be of the party." And then in a half casual,
half braggadocio way it was mentioned that the said
Square "was one of the most worthy and accomplished subalterns in the service, while the lady he
was on the point of marrying was a woman with
every charm that could possibly be named, and as
good and beautiful, as she was polite and fasci-
nating." Of course, the three or four persons who
constituted the true and leading aristocracy of
Jonesville, were fully impressed with the importance
of everything that Mrs. Daisy said, and wondered
how a lady of such parts and prospects as she evidently was, should at the same time be so extremely
gracious and condescending.

Meanwhile it must be noted that Miss Davis had
to attend, as usual, to most of the drudgery around
the house. She saw that the packing boxes belonging to her uncle's equipment were opened, the carpets put down, and the few pictures belonging to
the household were properly hung, and when young
Hector made himself sick, by eating too much cake,
she had all the watching and waiting to do, which
that amiable youngster required. She would have
attended to all these tasks nevertheless in a cheerful
spirit, if her aunt had only been willing to render
her common justice; but in spite of her gifts and
fine phrases, Mrs. Daisy, as has already been hinted,
was not a particularly kind woman, and as a necessary consequence Miss Eleanor had often to suffer.

Guy Averall was already pretty well acquainted with the whims of the Brigadier, and was prepared to believe almost anything in regard to her ; but one day, about this time, a little incident occured within the sphere of our hero's own observation, and which from the spirit of wilful misrepresentation which it exhibited, almost caused that young Artilleryman to hate Mrs. Daisy. During the forenoon, Miss Eleanor had been busy arranging the furniture in the drawing room, and having completed her task, she for a moment stepped out on the piazza in front of the quarters. Now on the piazza there happened to be lying a piece of rope, which had been used in bundling some of the household effects. "Averall," said Miss Eleanor, in her quality of manager of the establishment, "I wish you to put that rope in the store house, and here is a book that you may have, which will probably interest you." Guy opened the volume, as soon as his task was completed, and discovered it to be a copy of Sir Walter Scott's novel of Rob Roy, a work which has afforded pleasure to many persons both young and old.

"I think I shall read this book with a great deal of interest," said Guy, "I always have admired these old Scotch stories, there is so much romance and adventure about them."

"And I admire them too," responded Miss Davis, "and like Sir Walter especially—his sentiment is always the correct one on the subject of which he writes, and that to me is one of his strongest recommendations."

Guy assented, of course, to this observation, and at the same time could not help reflecting once more, how much better the Brigadier would appear, if she could only learn to talk in the sensible way adopted by Miss Eleanor, instead of bragging eternally about her Twenty-fifth Avenue, and other great relations. But just at this instant, Mr. Spruce was observed coming up the sidewalk. "Miss Davis," said he, "we are getting up a little party to visit the old wreck at Porter's Point—several of the young ladies in town are going—wont you do us the honor to accompany us?" Without thinking much on the matter, Miss Davis asked when the party intended to start, and then gave her consent to become a member. But hardly had the officer taken his departure when Mrs. Daisy saw fit to institute a series of inquiries as to the object of his visit, and when informed of the true state of the case, and that Blodgett and Taper would possibly both be members, that excellent lady proceeded to administer a most unmerciful lecture, telling Miss Eleanor, among other things, how that poor child Hector must be neglected every time her "assistant" took it into her head to thrust herself before gentlemen! Miss Eleanor endeavored to reply as well as she could, but the other lady would do nothing but sermonize on the "proprieties of life," just as if Miss Davis had been guilty of some terrible enormity in accepting the invitation. And when Miss Davis after listening to this long harangue went once more into her own room, and began thinking of all she had done for her aunt, how she furnished her with the French, and botany and astronomy and everything else, that was necessary to spread before company; how she watched over Mrs. Daisy's household, just as if it

were her own; and, in addition, took care of that
greedy young boy night and day; how she had done
everything for her aunt that it was possible for one
woman to do for another; and then to be abused and
misunderstood as she had been during that afternoon, it really seemed more than she could bear.
And yet before long her own good sense came to the
rescue. "Yes," said she, " my aunt can censure and
misrepresent as she likes, but my own heart tells me
I have endeavored to do what is right. And as long
as I think so, it would ill become me to indulge in
pitiful complaints. No one, not even uncle, shall
ever know but I am treated both kindly and justly
under this roof. And in spite of all that the so called
wise may say to the contrary, I fully believe in a good
Providence, who will reward me sooner or later,
according to my deserts."

V.

FROM these little incidents in the domestic affairs
of Mrs. Daisy to the career of Private Petersen, is
both an easy and natural transition; suffice it to say
in the connection that at this period the easy going,
good natured steward drove quite a flourishing trade
by examining the crania of such residents of Jonesville, as chose to present themselves for an inspection. Seated on a chair, in the dispensary, some
long, lank native of the place might be seen, while
over him stood the "Doctor," as he was sometimes
called, who with his fingers in his skull, in the position of a barber, was delivering a panegyric in something approaching the following style:

"Head well formed, sir, size twenty-two inches,

temperment somewhat bilious. In your case we have amativeness fully developed. You are fond of domestic life, would make a good husband, are naturally inclined to be affectionate to a wife; and if now a single man you certainly should marry."

"Is that so?" would be the probable question at this juncture.

"By all means—I should certainly advise you to marry. The next organ we have is philo-progenitiveness, or the love of offspring. In this case, also, the bump is quite full. You are naturally fond of the young, and have much sympathy with infantile weakness. As the head of a family, you would be an admirable man, since we find in your case all the organs necessary to constitute a good husband and father."

"How would I do as an astronomer?" would probably be the next inquiry.

"Astronomer! let me see. You have individuality, form, size, number, order and comparison all large. Why, sir, let me tell you, you would make an excellent astronomer; all that would be necessary is a little practice in the science, and a supply of the proper instruments." And on receiving this assurance, the latent star-gazer would pay his fee of twenty-five cents very readily, and only hoped that the time was not far distant when he would develop into an Airy or Herschel. It was evident that Petersen, spite of his simplicity, had read the story of Gil Blas and the Bishop of Oveida.

Whatever were the faults and failings of these "crackers" in the piney districts of the South, and they have been charged with poverty, shiftlessness,

ignorance, and fifty other things beside, they certainly were by nature anything but aggressive; and
it was only by the continual urging and suggestions
of the rascally politicians on the subject of slavery,
that the poor whites in the South were forced into
the position of hostility to the United States government, which they eventually assumed. Indeed, the
Twenty-sixth Artillery had not been quartered at
Camp Scott more than a fortnight, when evidence
was afforded of the dangerous character of these
political demagogues, whose leading principle of
action seems to be to intensify whatever discontent
may happen to be current at the moment, for the
sake of advancing their own interests. Right or
wrong it makes no difference; all is grist that can be
ground in their mill; the great end of the orthodox
"statesman" is to make himself "popular," and
provided this can be accomplished the ultimate consequences of his harangue, are to him a subject of
very little consideration. On the present occasion,
the Circuit Court happened to be in session; and the
country people for miles around flocked into Jonesville. That evening a political meeting was held in
the public square, and some furious resolutions were
passed, denouncing several of the Northern states in
regard to alleged violations of the fugitive slave law.
A light-haired, curly-headed little upstart, originally
from Pennsylvania, was on the platform; and in his
own glib way, was urging his "fellow citizens of
Jonesville," to resent the affront put on them, by
every means in their power; and if necessary to pass
an ordinance of secession, declaring their state free
and independent, and the federal compact broken !

This harangue had proceeded some length, when suddenly a voice was heard in the crowd.

"It will be a grave mistake if that ordinance of secession be passed," said the unknown stranger.

"Why so, may I ask ?" rejoined the orator.

"It will be the death blow of that very institution you seek to preserve," was the reply.

"It will be the beginning of a new and glorious era for the South," remarked the Orator.

"We will see," said the interlocutor from beneath.

"We will see also," said the speaker from above.

And thus the controversy ended. Who the person was that uttered this protest against the Orator, no one could tell; nor did any one in the crowd suspect that it was spoken by an officer belonging to the garrison, who certainly was neither Mr. Spruce nor Taper, nor yet the gallant Major Daisy.

VI.

IT now becomes our duty, as historian of this record, to relate an event of a sufficiently calamitous nature, an event well remembered by all officers and men who served in the Twenty-sixth Artillery at this time; and which may serve to illustrate the diabolical passions by which persons who pretend to be human are occasionally influenced. For some time back it had become evident that bad blood existed between two of the non-commissioned officers of Company "E"; for Sergeant Lawless, on the one hand, and Corporal Sullivan on the other, were constantly complaining and wrangling with each other. First one would run with a certain statement to Major Daisy, and then the other, so that it was impossible to decide between the rival contestants. The origin of the quarrel was involved in obscurity, although this much appeared evident, that at one time Lawless did all in his power to belittle Sullivan, both before his commanding officer and also in the eyes of the men of the Company. It had already been hinted that the education of Sullivan was somewhat limited; so Lawless took advantage of this circumstance, and on every possible occasion, ordered the Corporal on some duty where this defect would appear in as glaring a manner as possible. And then, if any error was committed, the unfortunate Sullivan was pretty certain to hear of it. One trick, much practiced by Lawless at this time, was to send Sullivan to draw rations; and on his return to cross-question him as to how many pounds of pork or rice he got at the commissary, and when the other could not give him the correct answer, to make some sneering rejoinder regarding the qualification of such a person for the grade of Corporal. At length it seemed as though Sullivan had determined not to be put down in that way; for he went into Jonesville, purchased a few books, and then, under the guidance of his wife, he proceeded to study the principles of numerical calculation. As soon as Lawless noticed this, he immediately changed his tactics in regard to the Corporal; for now instead of finding fault with him, on account of his want of knowledge, he chose to make fun of Sullivan for his studious habits. "There is Corporal Sullivan, if you please; studies reading, writing and the rule of three; is resolved to be a professor in a college, or something of the sort one of these days, I suppose." Sullivan stood this banter without saying a word, he knew very well that Lawless had the advantage in regard to rank, and that it would not serve any good purpose to crack jokes with him. He therefore paid no attention to these witticisms on the part of his superior, but simply did his duty as he was bid, and on one or two occasions, when he thought he was somewhat imposed on, he lodged a complaint with the commandant, who in spite of his habitual indolence, really endeavored to render him some justice. At length an unexpected advantage was thrown in Sullivan's way. One night it so happened that he was acting as Sergeant of the guard; when Lawless, having sold a half barrel of pork, belonging to the Company, sat down with a few friends, so as to enjoy a sociable game of cards. They gambled away till tattoo; when having answered their names, they again returned to the room, and putting up a blanket in the window, so as to conceal the light, they all sat down in order to continue their operations. Sometime during the night, Lieutenant Square, who was acting as officer of the day, visited the guard, and then and there called Sullivan aside. "Corporal," said he, "I think there is a candle burning in the quarters of Company "E." It is your duty as noncommissioned officer, in charge of the guard, to see that it is extinguished. I wish you to go over at once, order the light out, and then report to me." According to directions Sullivan started to the quarters, and there, around a blanket, spread on the floor, he discovered both Lawless and Ryan, with three or four other gentlemen of like

22

stamp, all engaged in the innocent amusement of "poker."

And here it is necessary that an explanation should be made. Lawless was undoubtedly a very unprincipled man, and anything rather than a fit person for the position he held in a Company, yet in spite of these drawbacks, he had some qualities which made him a favorite with a certain proportion of the men under him. Every scoundrel, unless he is an arrant coward, is sure to have his followers, who look up to him, applaud his bad deeds, and are ready to follow him, as far as their capacity will permit The present case was no exception to the rule, as to the reason of the preference extended towards the non-commissioned officer, it is not difficult to explain its origin. In the first place, Lawless was not very exacting in the way of duty; in the second place, he was liberal with every thing that he had, no matter whether he stole it or not; in the third place, he was a great "patriot," and that, we are sure, is the sum of all excellencies. With these recommendations in his favor, the man could not go amiss, for there were certainly a half dozen persons in the Company, more or less, who thought Lawless the *ne plus ultra* of all that was excellent, and who were ready to follow him, through thick and thin, on every possible occasion. In point of fact, it so happened that these worthies had established a code of honor of their own, in the Company; it was not considered wrong for Lawless to cheat, to bully, or to squander the earnings of others; but to utter a single word in disparagement of him, or to peach on him to the authorities, was regarded as simply infamous. When Sullivan, therefore, put his head into the room where Lawless was seated, the simple injunction was given: "Tell the officer of the day that everything is quiet, and that you did not see anyone here." And strange as it may seem, the first Sergeant of Company " E " of the Twenty-sixth Artillery, really expected that this command should be obeyed to the letter.

Sullivan, however, was in no mood to do as directed. He had already suffered enough from his superior to prevent him seeking to palliate his faults; and beside this, he considered it his duty, at all events, to tell the truth when questioned on a subject, such as the present. On reporting to Lieutenant Square, he informed him of what he had seen. As a consequence charges were preferred against Lawless and his friends, the following day; but owing to the listlessness or indifference of Major Daisy, these charges were never prosecuted, and the offenders in the affair were finally allowed to go scot free, with a mere reprimand.

A few evenings after this encounter, a group of soldiers were sitting in front of their quarters at Camp Scott. Some were smoking their pipes; some were speculating on their future plans, once their enlistment had expired; and others, again, were engaged in the customary occupation of story telling. Among these latter was Corporal Sullivan, who having just fought his way through some profound calculation in mathematics, thought it only proper and right to amuse those present with that old recital about Hudden and Dudden and Donald O'Leary; which, we need hardly say, was given with much gusto. Just

as the non-commissioned officer had concluded his
tale, some one from behind him, slung a brickbat
with murderous intent ; for the missile, after touching the cap of the Corporal, struck the ground a few
yards behind him, and hopped into the middle of the
parade, In an instant Sullivan turned round, and
noticing a group of soldiers, standing at some distance behind him, he immediately spoke up.

"Well," said he," I did not know that I had
given any occasion for this, but whoever has slung
that brickbat at me had better step up to the front,
and perhaps he will find before long, that I am not
afraid to settle with the gentleman."

And with these words the Corporal left his seat,
and proceeded a few paces in the direction of the
suspected aggressors. But just at that instant the
tattoo sounded, and all the members of Company
"E," the Corporal himself included, fell into the
ranks, and answered their names in the customary
manner. And after the ranks were broken, Guy
Averall, and most of the other soldiers proceeded
quietly to their beds.

VII.

NEXT morning it was reported everywhere
throughout the garrison that Corporal Sullivan had
deserted, and as a necessary consequence, the good
Mrs. Daisy saw fit to exhibit a very high state of
indignation. "Can it be possible," said she, "that
the dear child who has just wedded his wife, should
without provocation leave her in this undutiful manner ? I pity Katy Traynor, I really pity her from
the bottom of my heart, but then the poor girl was

determined to have her way, and now, as a consequence, she must suffer. Had she married some
intelligent, well-conducted soldier, according to my
advice, he would have protected and shielded her as
long as she lived, instead of deserting her as that
child Sullivan had done. For my part, I only wish
I were rid of the Army in general, and of Camp
Scott in particular, for ever since we came here I
have been subjected to all sorts of annoyances. First
it is one thing, and then it is another, so really, I
think, the sooner Tom and I make preparations for
leaving the Army, so much the better. But then the
misfortune is, that neither my husband or I have
means sufficient to enable us to do so, and therefore
we must stick to the service as best we can." And
with this most lame and impotent conclusion the
speech of the good Mrs. Daisy terminated.

Meanwhile the first Sergeant of the Company
went round, collected the equipments of the absent
non-commissioned officer, and turned them into the
store room, as the property of a deserter. When
asked if he could offer any explanation why Sullivan
had left his command so abruptly, Sergeant Lawless
shook his head, and said he did not know; but Ryan,
who seemed to take some interest in the case, saw
proper to observe that in his opinion the cause was
simply—jealousy—that Sullivan had taken offence at
some little attention shown his wife by the first Sergeant, and remembering that the latter, at one time,
had been a suitor for the hand of Miss Kitty Traynor, he chose to terminate the matter somewhat
abruptly by taking "French leave." But all the men
of the Company thought the story, thus told, to be

a very improbable one, for Sullivan, as far as was known, had never any occasion to quarrel with his wife, who was simply as faithful and devoted a creature, as any woman could possibly be, and seemed fully resolved ever since her marriage to belie those stories, in regard to her being nothing but a mere flirt, which at one time had been circulated against her.

At a late hour in the day, as Guy Averall, Hogan and a number of other men, were standing in their quarters, it was noticed that Ryan, on a sudden, entered the room and went directly to his knapsack. From it he took out some article of clothing, a shirt apparently, held it up for a second or two, asked the question "will not some one give me six cents for this." And before any answer could be returned, he threw the article into the fire. He immediately afterwards left the room, but hardly had he gone when Hogan gave a start.

"Did you see that fellow burn that shirt?" was his remark.

"I did," was the answer from several.

"And I noticed blood on it," said Guy.

"Well, depend on it," was the rejoinder, "there is more in that simple act than appears upon the surface. That fellow would never destroy his clothing unless there were some cause for it. I'll venture my life that this story of Sullivan's desertion is all fudge. The man has been foully dealt with, and the principal object with these two rascals, who are now non-commissioned officers, is to gain time so that this affair may blow over. Do you recollect that brick-bat which was fired at the Corporal last night? It certainly was done with some evil intent. I'll go this very instant to Major Daisy and give him my impression of the entire transaction."

This resolution on the part of Hogan was instantly approved by every one in the room ; so in a second the clerk put on his jacket, and after buttoning it up, away he started to the quarters of the commanding officer. After ringing at the hall door, in the usual manner, a servant directed him to remain, and before many seconds in came Major Daisy, with a slipper on one foot, and a shoe down in the heel on the other, rubbing his nose as was usually his habit.

"Well Hogan what do you want ? " was the fatherly inquiry on the part of the old veteran. The bard related his story in as few words as possible, and dwelt particularly on the fact that Ryan had destroyed an article of clothing, without apparent cause, that morning, and that blood had been observed on it.

" Vell, what if he did destroy his clothing ? " was the reply. " Any good soldier may destroy his clothing if he pleases. That's nothing pad. Ryan was always a goot man, when he worked with me, and that is the reason I made him Gorporal. Pad soldiers get trunk and goot soldiers do not. Ryan never got trunk and so he is a good soldier. However if you choose you can zee Lieutenant Spruce on the subject. I am not well to-day, and at any rate he is in command of the Company."

And with this recommendation ringing in his ear, away went Hogan to see that officer.

On reaching the quarters of Lieutenant Spruce,

the clerk again opened his case but without much success. Of course Lieutenant Spruce would not habor a suspicion against such a gentlemanly person as Ryan appeared to be. "Sergeant Lawless has been here already this morning," was the rejoinder, " and has reported the facts in the case. If I under- stand the matter rightly Corporal Sullivan had a quarrel with his wife, a few days ago, and had already made preparations for leaving the Company. However, I'll attend to the thing." And really and truly Lieutenant Spruce did attend to the matter in an admirable way ; for having just received a letter from that "fine girl " of his, on whom his heart was set, he turned the whole investigation over to his friend Taper, sat down to read his billet doux, and thus for the present the entire thing was neglected.

Disappointed in his endeavors, Hogan now thought of returning to his quarters, when fortu- nutely he met the Adjutant, Lieutenant Square, on the sidewalk. Again the old story was rehearsed, that Sullivan's absence had something mysterious in it, that instead of quarreling with his wife, as Law- less alledged, it was well known that both had lived very happily together, that a brickbat had been flung at Sullivan, the previous evening, as if for the pur- pose of provoking a quarrel, that Ryan's demeanor on the whole, was suspicious ; and his general character among the men was not good.

"Very well," said the other, " I'll speak to the commanding officer on the subject. I shall probably obtain authority to get a squad of men, and with them I intend to examine the neighborhood and see if any traces of Sullivan are visible."

While Hogan was employed in this way, Guy Averall was not permitted to remain in quiet, for some person, probably a confederate, chose to go to Sergeant Ryan and inform him that the bard had already paid a visit to the quarters of the commanding officer, and that Averall, in addition, had urged his comrade to do so. The occasion being one of importance, it was deemed advisable, on the part of Ryan, to try what a little bluster would do, and Guy was accordingly selected as a proper subject of attack.

"Well, parlez vous," said the Sergeant as he swaggered into the quarters. "How do you feel this morning?" The non-commissioned officer could sneer at Averall's attempts to study French, if he could do nothing else.

"I am quite well," said Guy, at least as well as could be expected under existing circumstances."

"Well, as could be expected under existing circumstances," said Ryan, repeating Averall's words. "Parlez vous, I understand you have been quite busy this morning."

"In what way?" asked Averall.

"In rubbing your musket, in whitening your belts, and in other affairs beside."

"Well," said Guy, "I'm sure it is the duty of a soldier to keep his gun and equipments cleaned, and as to the other affairs of which you speak, I really do not know exactly what you mean."

"What story was that you told to Hogan, before he started to the quarters of Major Daisy?"

"I told him," said Guy, "that the shirt which you offered for six cents in this room, and afterwards burned, had blood on it, and I now repeat the same story."

"Blood on it!" again repeated Ryan, "how do you know that there was blood on it?"

"Because I saw it with my own two eyes," said Guy.

"Might not your eyes deceive you?" asked Ryan.

"Not in such a case as that," was the answer.

"What business have you with me or my shirt! Cannot you mind your own business! Is not that enough for you!"

"Sergeant Ryan," answered Averall, "I did not thrust my head into a corner to spy into your effects. You took that shirt of yours, and burned it in the presence of several men in the squad room. I was a witness of the fact, and have an undoubted right to mention the circumstance to any one that I choose, and also to draw my own inference from the same."

"What is your inference?" asked Ryan.

"That I am not bound to tell," was the answer on the part of Averall," for it might possibly happen that my inference is wrong, and then I would be doing an act of injustice both to you and also to myself."

"You are a great raisoner, parlez vous," said the non-commissioned officer, "but do you know what, I think a good slap in the face, at this instant, would suit you as well as anything else." And at this juncture Ryan assumed an attitude, as if he intended to inflict bodily chastisement on Guy Averall.

The latter, however, understood the situation of affairs too well to be bullied. It was not an object with Ryan, at present, to provoke a quarrel with Averall, since such a course would be simply adding fire to the flames already in existence. His purpose was merely to frighten Guy with silence in regard to the burning of the clothing that morning ; and provided this end were accomplished, it was not his intention to strike a single blow. But the sympathies of Averall were already enlisted on the side of right and justice ; and as to Ryan, he was determined not to give him any advantage.

"Sergeant," said he, "there is no use in talking any further on this matter. A member of the Company is now absent, and some of us are determined to find out where he has gone, your bluster therefore, is of no avail, especially as I have now been long enough in the service to understand the difference between an official and a purely personal matter. As to the first, you are a Sergeant in this Company, and as such I will obey you. But when you attempt to provoke a quarrel, in the way you now do, I will give you to understand you are no better than any other man. Of course you are stronger and bigger than I, and in an affair of fisticuffs would doubtless have the advantage. But I, on the other hand, do not choose to submit to such an appeal as that. If · you strike me you do it at your peril. There is my musket and bayonet now standing in the gun rack. At present they are injuring no one. But if I am hit the case will be very different. I will then use them on you, just as I would on the meanest private in the Company."

As soon as Ryan felt satisfied that Averall could neither be frightened or cajoled, he instantly changed his demeanor. A smile spread over his brutal countenance, for he now wished to ingratiate himself as far as possible. It was better that Averall, under present circumstances should remain at least passive, than that he should become an avowed enemy. The sneering allusion to Guy's studies was accordingly dropped, and in its place was substituted a reference to the supposed locality of his birth.

"You are a brave fellow after all," was the exclamation of the non-commissioned officer, "well done for the Enniskillener, well done for the Enniskillener!"

<h2 style="text-align:center">VIII.</h2>

As far as the plan proposed by Lieutenant Square was concerned, the good Major Daisy at first seemed disposed to throw obstacles in the way, "I should like to obtain a detail, Major, to go into the woods," said the Adjutant while addressing his superior. "It has been reported to me that an attempt was made last night to pick a quarrel with Corporal Sullivan, now absent, and although nothing definite in regard to the matter is known, I should like to ascertain if any traces of him can be discovered in the neighborhood.

"I have already heard of this case of Corporal Sullivan, and have turned over the affair to his Company commander. Lieutenant Spruce has the matter in charge."

"But Lieutenant Spruce, as I understand the case, does not chose to exert himself in it. He has turned the whole thing over to Lieutenant Taper."

"Very well, I have done with it. I have done with it. I have given the necessary orders, and the responsibility no longer rests on me."

"Major Daisy, permit me to say," was the answer,

"that as long as a transaction of this kind remains in doubt, you cannot get rid of the responsibility. I have already been balked in an official matter, at this post ; but am determined not to be turned aside in this. As the case stands, a member of the command has disappeared in a way that no one can sufficiently explain. Now, allow me to say, that an affair of this kind is of too much importance to be hushed up. You may refuse me a detail of men if you choose, but be assured of this, if the circumstances are brought to the notice of the proper authorities, and I am asked for any opinion in respect to it, that opinion will be given without regard to the rank or position of any one in this command. Now you can act as you choose in the matter."

These words, which were uttered in a pretty determined tone, soon brought the gallant Major to terms. "Well, well, I will give you the detail—I will give you the detail. Mrs. Daisy will have to let her work go. Averall, go and tell the acting Sergeant Major to send a party of eight men to report to the Adjutant."

In less than an hour from that time the squad just mentioned was called out, and leaving Camp Scott, they took the road which led to Hammerton Court House. After proceeding for some distance a couple of negroes were met, and to these Lieutenant Square proposed a few questions, as to whether any soldier had been seen going that way? According to the answer then given by the "darkies," they had not noticed any enlisted man leaving camp. The next person addressed was the toll keeper of the bridge over the Santee River; but he, in like manner, was

certain no soldier had passed in that direction. The
conclusion then was, even in spite of the smiles and
assertions of Lawless, that if Sullivan had really deserted, he certainly had not taken the road to the
upper country. On the way back the party went
into some of the houses occupied by the "crackers,"
the name applied to the poor whites in the South.
These edifices were constructed of round, unhewn
logs, and covered with clapboards; the chinks between the logs that formed the walls, being large
enough for a dog to jump through, and a doorway,
that in one case, was covered with a dirty old quilt,
in default of the proper appendage. Spite of all
that is said of social progress in the new world, the
whole appearance of the buildings did not indicate
a very exalted civilization. On making inquiry of
the inmates, the same answer was always returned—
they had not seen any soldier going that way, nor
did they believe any had left for the other side of
the river. At length one of the residents suggested
that perhaps the missing man might have sought the
road to Hammerton, by a certain cross-cut which led
towards a little stream that empties into the Santee,
and which is known by the name of John's creek.
In this direction the squad accordingly went, and
soon met a couple of whites, who seemed to be out
on a hunting expedition, for they both carried rifles
on their shoulders. To them, in like manner, the
usual question was put, but neither of them seemed
to know anything of a deserter. And then one of
the men spoke up. "If it is a dead soldier you are
looking for, I reckon I know whar you'll find one,
for I saw a man in uniform, all haggled and cut,

lying in a heap of brush, near the creek this very morning." The nonchalant manner in which these words were uttered, seemed to indicate that a dead man or two was a thing of very little consequence in that part of South Carolina; on being requested, however, to do so, the stranger accompanied the party in the direction of Camp Scott. In doing so, it was noticed he kept pretty close to the creek, and when within a quarter of a mile or thereabouts of the barracks, he went into the brush, which lined the edge of the stream. There, sorrowful to relate, the dead body of poor Sullivan was discovered, cut and mangled in the most frightful manner. On his face were several gashes, his breast was stabbed in four or five places, some of his fingers were almost severed from his hand, while his legs and arms all presented evidence of the violence he had suffered. At this instant a feeling of horror was visible in the face of every one present, but after it had subsided to some extent, the body was brought back, placed in the Hospital, and after a little investigation, all the circumstances connected with the case were developed. From the testimony of several of the men it appeared, that after tattoo, on the previous evening, Sullivan saw fit to accuse Ryan of throwing the brickbat at him, a fact which the other did not choose to deny, and after a short parley, it was determined that they should both go into the woods, and ascertain which of the two were the better man. It was also shown that Lawless consented to act as umpire between the contestants ; and further, that a couple of knives were purchased at the sutler's establishment belonging to the place, these being the weapons with

which the fight was conducted. What took place
after this it was impossible to tell, as Ryan and Lawless when separately questioned, told different stor'es
from each other, and there was no reason to believe
that either of them was strictly true. This much,
however, was evident, that while Sullivan was cut and
mangled in a manner that was fearful, neither one of
the other members of the party received any injury, a
state of things which justified the suspicion that Lawless and Ryan, after exciting the anger of the Corporal,
by an unprovoked attack, got him into the woods,
and when within their power, they fell on him and
butchered him. Both of these worthies, as was well
known, had some cause for disliking Sullivan ; and
now, as a consequence, the poor fellow has met his
untimely fate. On the whole, the officer in command of the garrison, had no other alternative but to
place Lawless and Ryan in close confinement ; and
after an inquest was held on Sullivan's body, to turn
them over, for further prosecution, to the civil authority.

On examining the knapsacks of the prisoners after
their arrest, a number of interesting relics were discovered, which served to show that both of the non-
commissioned officers were men of a sufficiently
lively nature; for in that belonging to Lawless were
found a number of ladies' favors of various kinds,
kid gloves, billets doux and so forth; some of
which, by the way, had about them a certain strange
look of suspicion. Mixed with these gifts, per contra,
was a very well considered plan for the invasion of
Ireland, duly elaborated, in which it was stated that
a column of well-armed men, proceeding from the

Cove of Cork might advance north, and then be joined by another column coming from the west, that these united bodies might then proceed in the direction of the Capital, and when within a short distance of the hill of Tara might there defeat the English and then proclaim liberty to the Hibernian people. The other knapsack, which was the property of Ryan, was still more curious, for in it was found a humorous description of the celebrated Puck, of national fame, whose business it was to demolish Patrician landlords, from behind a hedge, at the rate of five pound sterling a head, provided he got in addition a sufficient supply of aqua vitæ to sustain his faltering courage to the trigger stretch. And then followed a number of signs, passwords, and grips, evidently belonging to a Molly Maguire, or other secret society. " Are you straight ?" " I am." "How straight ?" "As straight as a rush." " For what do you fight?" "For liberty." "Gracious heaven !" exclaimed Hogan, after he had examined this somewhat strange catechism, "liberty forsooth! Are we to hear of nothing but liberty ! Or rather, what has liberty in common with such lively gentlemen as these." The existence of this paper served to explain a curious paradox which had appeared for some time back, to wit, that every now and then a murderous attack was made on some member of the Company, in the dark, usually with a sling shot or some such instrument, and that the perpetrators of these deeds could never be discovered. Was it possible, that these non-commissioned officers, whom the good Mrs. Daisy seemed to estimate so highly, were after all nothing but a couple of vile Thugs; and

23

that a whole Company had to submit to the whims
and caprices of such a pair of rascals?

But the most pitiful sight of all was presented
after the remains of the unfortunate Corporal was
laid in the Hospital.   His wife appeared, threw herself on the corpse, and in phrases which it would be
impossible to translate, lamented the fate of her
husband.   "I know," said she, "how this has all
happened.   I always told him to beware of Lawless,
but the poor fellow had a spirit that could not brook
an insult; and so he died the victim of his crafty,
treacherous enemy." And then referring to her efforts
as a school teacher she would say, "up in his own
room is the copy book, on which he wrote his last
line, and the slate on which he did his last sum, for
after he was made Corporal he always wished to be a
scholar, and I was willing to assist him, as far as I
possibly could; but now he is gone—he is gone—
and I never henceforth will whisper a word in his
ear, or see, even for a moment the light of his eyes."

And then, when she began thinking on her hard
fate, it almost seemed as if the heart of the unfortunate woman would break.   She cried, and cried, till
she could hardly contain herself.   But where is the
use in repining—in all these matters there is but one
course.   The body of Corporal Sullivan was consigned to the dust from whence it was taken, and
after a little delay, his wife bid adieu to the scene of
these disasters.   A subscription was opened to re-
lieve her immediate necessities, to which both officers
and men freely contributed, and with the sum, raised
in this way, she obtained the means of defraying her
expenses to the north.

SUBSEQUENT PROCEEDINGS.

I.

THE events already narrated, disastrous though they were, had one good effect ; they delivered the well-disposed men of Company " E ". from an odious tyranny to which, for a long time, they had been subjected. The disgrace of Lawless and Ryan destroyed the power of a dangerous clique, and substituted a better class of men in power. No longer were there any offensive demands for the money of this or that person, under color of a loan, said loan to be afterwards repaid or not, just as the borrower might choose ; and if forsooth the money were demanded back again at pay day, the applicant was instantly set down as a mean spirited, penurious, low fellow ; insensible alike to the claims of generosity, and the code of honor of a soldier. A visit to Camp Scott was made about this time by old General Fuzzy ; and it was arranged, among other things, that the command of Company " E," should be entrusted to Lieutenant Square, Major Daisy being meanwhile left in charge of the garrison. As to Taper, he was detailed on duty as instructor in the science of ethics at the Military Academy, and the gay and handsome Spruce was made Adjutant. The affairs of the Twenty-sixth Artillery were now regulated on military principles. By a singular piece of good fortune, the Scotchman, Moldwell, was selected

as first Sergeant; and under his guardianship the
smallest private in the Company was treated as if he
had the same natural right as the biggest, instead of
being subjected to the whims and caprices of the
latter. As to Hogan, he was too irregular and careless in his habits to be entrusted with a military
command, but having pledged his honor, as a gentleman, not to get drunk more than three or four
times in the course of a year, he finally was assigned
to the charge of the commissary. Here the bard had
ample opportunities to exhibit his knowledge of the
value of beans, as part of the soldiers' fare; and ere
long the command was convinced that the various
proportions of that vegetable, along with the other
constituents of the soldiers' ration in America, pork,
beef, flour, rice, coffee, sugar, vinegar, candles, soap
and salt, were all as familiar to Private Hogan, as
were certain knotty points in scholastic divinity; or
the sayings, translations and imitations of his whimsical countryman, Father Prout. In short, in his
management of the Company, Lieutenant Square
seemed to act on the principle that all the virtues of
the organization do not rest exclusively with those
who happen to be possessed of vigorous arms and
muscles; that some remnants of common understanding and honesty are to be found even among individuals of less exalted mould; and that by making
a proper use of the sense of right and wrong, which
undoubtedly exists in all communities, it is possible to govern a number of soldiers very well,
without having constant recourse to such little whims
as "bucking and gagging," "tying up by the thumbs,"
manufacturing "spread eagles," and other little

eccentricities with which the United States private was unhappily but too familiar at this period.

As to the good and amiable Mrs. Daisy, her mind was greatly exercised at this time. In the first place, her spirit, as she herself said, had received a severe shock on account of the fall of those "dear children" Sergeants Lawless and Ryan; and in addition to all this, Mr. Blodgett, the irrepressible, still seemed to be a source of trouble. But the greatest annoyance of all was in reference to that dear Vale of Chamouni, on which her heart was still set, for her own darling Tom, as yet, seemed somewhat indifferent to the charms of that place, and having made up his mind not to forestall his pay, he felt disposed apparently to disparage that far-famed locality, whenever the subject was mentioned. "What fools our beople bake of themselves," he would sometimes say, "when they begin talking about these foreign blaces. Bale of Chamouni! My wife, Mrs. Daisy, is a perfect bonobaniac on the subject; and after all what is it! A kind of gully, I suppose, between a couple of mountains, with a road running through it, from end to end, and a few taverns stuck here and there, just by way of variety. Why I could find you plenty of bales, such as this, within fifty miles of New York, if Mrs. Daisy would only be satisfied with them."

"Oh Tom! oh Tom!" would be the rejoinder "you have not a particle of poetry or romance in your composition." And with this sage remark on the part of his spouse, the discussion usually terminated.

At length it seemed as though that kind Providence which watches over the destinies of nations, and has ever an eye on the deserving, looked down in pity on the good Mrs. Daisy, and actually relieved her from two of her principal difficulties. In the first place, it may be remarked that Blodgett, taking example apparently from Lieutenant Square, began to be somewhat attentive to a cousin of his at this time, a fact which did not remain long undiscovered, so Mrs. Daisy immediately came to the conclusion that all sources of anxiety on account of that scatterbrain subaltern were now removed; and that her ward, Miss Davis, was not destined to fall into his clutches. In the second place, it deserves to be recorded, that just about this time, an uncle of the Brigadier happened to die in New York; and on examining his will it was discovered that a legacy of a few thousand dollars had actually been left to his niece. It was with feelings of mingled joy and sorrow that the lady received the news. "The poor dear man!" said she by way of exclamation, "it pains my heart so much to think that he is gone. I always loved him very dearly, and had long looked on him as a second father to me, and so indeed he was, since my own dear pa took his departure to a better world than this. But now his struggles and anxieties are all over, he is laid at rest, and I shall never enjoy the felicity of seeing his dear face again. But Tom, Tom," continued Mrs. Daisy still sticking to her text. "I have one question to ask. As soon as I obtain the money, cannot we get that six months leave of absence, that we have been speaking of, for so long a time, and enjoy ourselves, by taking our little ramble as we originally intended in far off countries."

"Ramble as we originally intended in far off

countries! Ramble as we originally intended in far off countries!" exclaimed Major Daisy in despair, "I see we will have no peace or quietness till we find ourselves in motion. Yes, yes, Sophia, you can have your own way in this, as you already have had it in a good many other things. There is only one request I have to present. Don't mention Europe to me till we are ready to start; for I already have heard enough on that subject to last me my lifetime."

"Then I shall see the dear vale of Chamouni," said Mrs. Daisy, "with my own two eyes, and we shall both visit the Lake of Geneva, and the castle of Chillon, with Clarens, Vevey, Lausanne, and all the other localities.. Tol-de-re-lol-lol! Tol-de-re-lol-lol! Oh the vale of Chamouni. Tol-de-re-lol-lol! Tol-de-re-lol-lol! Oh the vale, the vale of Chamouni."

"Major Daisy I have only one word to say in the connection, I consider myself one of the most fortunate women in the world, and you as simply the best and dearest man that ever existed."

II.

BUT it must not be supposed that the good Mrs. Daisy depended altogether on those exotic pleasures as a means of enjoyment; on the contrary her mind was too well disciplined to rest entirely on foreign attractions, such as far off places afford, and hence it happened that as long as she remained in her own country, she resolved to participate in its society and customary gratifications. And in proof of this we would mention, that after remaining in Camp Scott for about three months, the troops were

ordered to one of the Forts in Charleston Harbor.
The third or fourth day after their arrival it was
reported that a boating party, having returned at a
somewhat late hour in the night, Lieutenant Square,
instead of going to his quarters, as he ought, was
actually seen with Mrs. Daisy on one arm, and Miss
Eleanor on the other, taking a moonlight stroll round
the brick covered ramparts of Fort Moultrie. Now
no one pays any regard to a midnight stroll in America, during the lovely month of August, when the
voice of the mocking bird is heard in the grove, and
the buzz of the mosquito is heard in the ear, and
the thermometer is standing at ninety; and yet this
particular excursion was regarded with a good deal
of suspicion. Why could not Mrs. Daisy, if sentiment-
ally inclined, go and plump at once into her downy
bed, and allow Miss Eleanor, who was a marriageable
woman, to have this little stroll · with Lieutenant
Square in quietude ? But no, such a thing as this
would be highly improper, so the Brigadier, who by
the way did not object to a little soft nonsense herself, would not subject the niece to this vile offence
of lovemaking.

"By all that is handsome," said a big recruit,
when the circumstance was mentioned, "I should
consider it the greatest joke in the world, if the
Lifftenant should steal a march on old Jazabel, and
marry Miss Eleanor, in spite of her teeth. It is the
greatest pity in the world he is not a free man, for
if Square and Miss Davis, by some accident, should
become husband and wife, I'm blessed but every
soldier in the company would dance a hornpipe on
the occasion. It is easy to see who is the real lady,

after all, in that house, even in spite of the Brigadier's mighty pretensions. I guess, if Miss Davis
left, the Brigadier would have to look after young
Hector himself, and teach him French too ; and as
to his face, it might remain dirty or not, just as
chance should direct, for by the powers above, the
mother is too lazy to trouble herself with such trifles
as that, in the way of household discipline. She is
always talking of Kings and aristocracy."

"Of course she does," was the reply from some
one else, " and well entitled is she to the privilege.
Do we not know, as she has often told us, that she
was brought up in the lap of luxury, all her life, and
how can a person who has enjoyed such privileges
as these, venture to attend to a few every-day cares ?
Didn't I hear her tell a rousing whopper, the other
evening, in addition to a few of the same sort, which
I have already set down in my catalogue."

"What was that ?" was the rejoinder.

"I will tell you, just as the lady herself rehearsed
the narration, for I heard her going over the whole
thing, from beginning to end. According to her
account, the present A. T. Stewart, of New York, is entitled to the family of the Brigadier for all his greatness. The 'child' was originally nothing but a boy,
very poor and very ignorant, who landed at New
York in a pair of corduroys, and afterwards went
about the street selling newspapers. The father of
Mrs. Daisy, seeing the urchin, called him in; gave
him his supper and sent him to school; and from
such humble beginnings as these, arose all of A. T.
Stewart's subsequent greatness. He never forgets
his old benefactor, be it told ; for any time that Mrs.

Daisy goes into Stewart's warehouse, the head book-keeper is sent immediately to wait on her. She can order as many goods as she likes, they are instantly sent down to her house, and she can pay for them or not, just as it suits her convenience."

"It is a wonder," said the other, "that a person like Mrs. Daisy is not ashamed to tell such fables."

"Fables!" was the rejoinder, "these are not fables at all—the woman has been telling these stories so very, very often, that she really now believes in the truth of them. Still after all, I will give Mrs. Daisy credit for one thing. She every now and then will release a soldier from the guard house, provided she requires some work from him. Perhaps after all, she will grow lenient towards one of her best friends, I mean towards Miss Davis herself."

"Oh, indeed she wont," was the reply. "The place of Miss Eleanor is fixed. Mrs. Daisy considers her niece as her own particular perquisite; and to allow the latter to leave her house, is a thing that a woman like the Brigadier will never consent to. She requires the service of Miss Davis now, particularly, in view of that foreign gallop on which she seems so much bent. Beside all this, I have my private reasons for supposing that Miss Eleanor has pretty thoroughly abandoned this notion of matrimony."

III.

It was subsquent to the foregoing events that the principal personage in Fort Moultrie was obliged to stand up and explain. The immediate occasion of this adventure was the inimitable Hector. One day his mother hearing that the Secretary of War was inclined to be propitious, resolved to take time by the forelock, and accordingly wrote that, when the proper time came, she was very desirous that her son should receive an appointment as a cadet. The Secretary, supposing that the request was an urgent one, posted off immediately to the President, and laid the claims of Major Daisy before him. That dignitary was disposed to be complaisant, and as a consequence, down came a letter from the War Department, saying that the President, in consideration of the services of Major Daisy, had been pleased to act favorably on the application for his son to a place at West Point; that all which was now necessary was to send the age of the boy, and the State in which he was born, in order to have his name properly entered as a candidate for examination. The brave and gallant Brigadier was now forced to apologize. Her son had not as yet attained the proper age, so that the boon she asked was a prospective, rather than an immediate favor. "If, however." said she, "a vacancy shouid be open, say five or six years from now, I shall be most proud to accept the favor, for I certainly consider the Army the noblest profession in the country.

As to those officers of the Twenty-Sixth Artillery whose names have already appeared in this history, their love affairs, let us assure the reader, now proceeded in as prosperous a way as could be expected. First, as regards the irrepressible, he actually did write a couple of letters to his cousin; but just at that juncture he happened to get hold of a book which caused considerable talk at that time, the "Vestiges of Creation," and noticing that an English

physicist, Andrew Crosse by name, while experiment-
ing with a solution of silicate of potash, and an ordinary galvanic battery, was surprised to see " as if
gradually growing from specks, between the poles of
the battery," certain animals of the genus *acarus !*
Now this notion of producing animals by means of
electricity, was too captivating in itself to escape the
attention of Blodgett ; for the irrepressible was one
of those half crazy individuals, who are always on the
lookout for anything that can militate against the accuracy of the first three chapters of Genesis ; and
provided they see something new in that direction,
they consider themselves to be immortal discoverers.
He accordingly dispatched an order to New York
for a galvanic apparatus, and as soon as it came to
hand, he commenced dabbling with his chemicals.
But somehow or other, the insects would not come ;
and although silicate of potash, cyanide of potassium,
bromide of silver, and carbonate of soda were all used
in succession, yet that did not mend the matter, for
the experiment was a failure.   So Blodgett had no
resource but to lay the blame on the means within
his reach.   " By Jupiter, Square," said he one day,
" I can make as big bugs, and as fine bugs, as any
person in the whole universe—all I want is the proper
kind of instrument."

" You can do anything, Blodgett, that mortal man
ever accomplished, except one," said Square.

" Except one," repeated Blodgett.   " What is
that one, may I ask ?"

" Persuade a woman, who is unwilling to do so,
to marry you," was the answer."

The irrepressible made no reply to this observa-

tion, but at the same time he colored as if his face
was a carrot. Was it possible that Square, even in
the midst of his nonchalant existence, had suspected
Blodgett of a more than ordinar good will towards
Miss Eleanor; and took this method of curbing the
somewhat ino dinat self-conceit of his brother officer? Or was the expression which had just escaped,
a mere hap-hazard phrase, which beyond its general
application signified nothing? For our part we must
confess that ha ing studied this problem for a very
considerable space of time, we are obliged to let the
whole matter rest, with the customary Spanish inquiry, *quien sabe?*

As to our old friends, Messrs. Spruce and Taper,
we have only this much to say that during their term
of duty, in the South, they were both as merry as
crickets. They carolled that song about "cigars"
and "cognac," just as usual; and after Taper was
transferred to West Point, he went a step further and
proposed, first, to that "lovely girl" on Twenty-fifth
Avenue, and some other street; and afterwards to
the other "lovely girl" who lived a square further
up town, but the answer, unfortunately, was alike in
both cases—kind papa thought Mr. Taper a very excellent young man, and in other circumstances would
be disposed to give him every possible consideration;
but then the profession which Taper followed presented an insuperable objection, and neither personage would consent that a member of his family should
adopt such a wandering, half-gypsy calling as that to
which the suitor was bound. So the officer was
obliged to take his hat in hand and make his departure. With Spruce, on the contrary, the result was

totally different. The father of that gentleman ; a cross, vinegar-faced old fellow, who lived in the neighborhood of Madison Square, had the reputation of being tolerably rich, owing to a fortunate speculation in Western lands. It was currently supposed that the officer, at some time or other, would be the inheritor of a considerable proportion of this wealth; a fact which was duly taken into account when that gallant young Subaltern presented his claim. The venerable papa, in this case, did not like the army any more than other persons did, but gold is omnipotent everywhere ; and the fact that Spruce had his great expectations before him outweighed all minor considerations. After the customary doubts and hesitations were removed, the reluctant head of the family assented. In a couple of months from that time, the marriage was celebrated with proper solemnity ; and the happy couple both started on their wedding tour. What presents they received and what places they visited, it becomes us not to say ; but after the lapse of a month or six weeks, the final result followed, for the gallant Lieutenant brought his wife to Fort Moultrie. After a due exchange of calls, examination of wedding gifts, etc., " bride is a lovely creature, you know," the lady herself came up as a proper subject for examination, and on a close and searching inspection, it was officially declared that Mrs. Spruce was a lady of many excellent qualities, a woman who was calculated in every way to make her husband happy ; and do honor besides to the Army, in every respect. All the ladies at Fort Moultrie were loud in their praise of Mrs. Spruce, but Mrs. Daisy was loudest of all ; indeed as far as that point was concerned, the way the Brigadier took Mrs. Spruce under her charge was one of the most touching sights that could well be conceived. " I'll be a dear, good mother to you, my child. I'll be a dear, good mother to you, as long as you remain in the service," was the affectionate exclamation of Mrs. Daisy after making her first call, " an innocent creature, such as you, wants some one to look after her interest. I'll never forget you as long as you live—your husband is a gallant officer and gentleman, who fully deserves any attention I may bestow on his wife."

" Thank you, Mrs. Daisy," said Spruce, with a bow.

" No thanks at all—no thanks at all—it is merely my duty as wife of the commanding officer of this garrison. Now, Mr. Square, when are we going to have the pleasure of bestowing the same attention on you ?"

" As far as that point is concerned, I really cannot say," was the reply.

" Bring the dear child here as soon as possible—bring the dear child here as soon as possible, don't make any delay, and I'll do all in my power to make it agreeable for her. I was brought up in absolute elegance; as I've often said, I was never controlled in any way when young, but I did not mind the change into the Army one bit. I willingly surrendered every thing I had in the world for the sake of my own good Tom, and now there is nothing that gives me so much pleasure as seeing his friends and my friends all together. Once Mrs. Square joins us in the Army, we will soon clear out the Hospital in the usual way, and then we all can dance the *chapeau bras.*

V.

As to Guy Averall, he had nothing whatever to do with love at this time; the truth of the matter being that the pay which he then drew as a private soldier, seven dollars a month, would hardly allow him to indulge in that somewhat expensive luxury. He still kept up his studies as usual; and after getting through his Charles the Twelfth and Gil Blas, he made a further advance in the usual French course, by translating Corinne, Louis Quatorze and two or three of the plays of Moliere. He now felt himself fully prepared to dip into those beautifu', though somewhat eccentric works, which constitute the great bulk of modern Gallic literature—George Sand and Paul de Kock, Monsieur Balzac, and the Author of the Mysteries of Paris. But luckily for Guy, he was saved from this degradation, for about this time he succeeded in making the acquaintance of Shakspeare. But here, perchance, some persons may ask, how does it happen that Averall, who seems to have a tolerable appreciation of mathematical science, and is even able to understand a political discussion, should yet remain ignorant of the greatest of English poets? But Guy, it must be recollected, was born in a curious part of the world, the north of Ireland; a region that for narrow puritanical prejudices is exceeded by none; and where these prejudices exercise a tyranny that in other places would be simply unendurable. In his youth the boy had access to books, it is true, and was occasionally allowed to rejuvenate himself by an inspection of such entertaining volumes as "Blair on the Grave" or "Harvey's Meditations Among the Tombs," but to think of glancing at the productions of an irreligious play actor, like Shakspeare, the thing was impossible! And the fact was, that while there was a tolerable collection of volumes of a miscellaneous character in his aunt's house, which he could read as he chose, yet Shakspeare, at that time, was to him a sealed book, so that till he was stationed at Fort Moultrie, he never read a single play of the greatest of dramatists. But this restraint, after all, was anything rather than an injury; for do we not become insensible of the force and beauty of the best passages of English poetry, by a mechanical repetition of them, at a time when our inexperience of life renders us incapable of appreciating their excellence? Almost any boy of fourteen years of age, for instance, has gone over the passage "To be or not to be," till it has lost half its meaning, and has become little more than a mere conglomeration of words. The same remark applies to other quotations beside the one mentioned; some of which, spite of their merits, are even parodied and ridiculed in every possible way. At any rate, when Guy Averall began reading the bard of Avon it was with the freshness of a new occupation, and certes the enjoyment and instruction which he received at that time, was a subject on which he long after loved to dilate. It was pure pleasure—pleasure of the loftiest kind—pleasure derived from sympathy and contact with beings higher than we meet on earth, but who had this much of humanity about them that they have loved and suffered, just as we have, and as a conse-

24

quence they present a reflex image of those feelings
which every one among us may claim as his own;
but as his own, intensified and beautified by the art
of the poet.

The first play that Averall read was King Lear,
a tragedy which, as an expression of sublime sorrow
has not, we believe, its equal in the world. Then
followed Macbeth, and Othello and lastly, Hamlet,
Prince of Denmark, works that were absolutely new
revelations of power to Guy, and full of the most
glorious imagery. Even in their minute aspects,
what evidence do we find of that divine ideality,
which all true poets possess in a greater or less
degree, but which none have exhibited with greater
opulence than Shakespeare. Here, for instance, is
sentence after sentence, which on account of its
appositeness and suggestiveness, has been quoted
again and again, but of whose origin Guy Averall
knows nothing till he discovers it in Hamlet or Macbeth. How universal Shakespeare seems, living in an
age when polemical and political controversy was
rife, he is neither Romanist nor Puritan, a friend of
the people or an admirer of kings; but nature's
great poet, who feels himself at liberty to illustrate
his sentiments by allusions drawn from the most
opposite sources. What exquisite pictures of external nature do we find here and there scattered
through his plays, of which the lines in which Horatio
informs Marcellus that daylight is approaching, are an
instance. In sketching a person what masterly power
is exhibited ; the disposition of Cordelia, for instance,
is revealed by the very first sentence which she
utters. This power of indicating a scene or a char-

acter by a few words, is the very highest excellence in poetic art, and is constantly exhibited by our great dramatist. But it is useless to attempt to enumerate other examples of the very highest qualities.

Guy Averall was not a critic at this period, and understood little or nothing about those varieties of time, place and action on which French writers lay so much stress ; he was conscious, nevertheless, even when first examining Shakespeare, that in his principal plays there is at least a unity of sentiment, from beginning to end, and to the illustration of this, all the incidents of the piece are subordinate. This characteristic has been duly noticed by the German critics and also by Coleridge. In Romeo and Juliet, for instance, we have youthful love and its unfortunate requital ; in Macbeth guilty ambition and its downfall ; in Lear the ingratitude of an old man's offspring is exemplified. Instead of there being a want of symmetry in Shakespeare, as many of the French writers seem to suppose, there is the most carefully developed plot, while his neglect of the so-called classic rules, gives his plays a freedom, variety and vigor to which those who write after the French model, can make no possible pretension.

It was the habit of Guy's aunt, as a strict Puritan, to disparage those works of imagination of which Shakespeare's plays are an example; calling them nothing, in short, but mere " bundles of lies " ; it is a noteworthy fact nevertheless, that some of these falsehoods, as she still chooses to designate them, possess a durability to which works of mere information can lay no possible claim. Nor is this fact difficult to explain. A play, a poem, or a novel is a work of art, and as such may approach perfection in its kind ; and hence become a source of permanent pleasure ever afterwards. But in mere science, the case is different. Books of that sort can be constantly improved. Knowledge is not only progressive, but it is yearly put into a more and more convenient shape; and hence it happens that the works of the early discoverers are first read, and after a time absolutely neglected. There probably was never a greater mathematical genius than Sir Isaac Newton, yet who is there that studies the Principia now? Absolutely no one, in its entirety unless perchance it is some historian of the progress of physical science, who examines the book from motives of curiosity. The fact is, the knowledge contained in that production has been put into more convenient shape by subsequent writers. But with Othello and Macbeth the case is different. These appeal to the feelings of the heart, which are permanent in - all ages and countries ; and as a consequence are sure to be always read and appreciated.

VI.

DROPPING Guy Averall and his Shakespeare for the present, and proceeding with our direct narrative we would say, that during the epoch under consideration, were still continued the most extensive preparations, by the good Mrs. Daisy, in view of that foreign excursion, on which her mind was now wholly bent, while Miss Davis, in her inferior and dependent character as an " assistant," was obliged to render her aunt all the service she could afford in the connection. Sometimes the former lady would spread out the map of Europe, and debate, within herself, which was the best possible route of travel to take. At one time, for instance, she would imagine herself going down the Rhine, examining those old castles and towns of which so many romantic stories are told ; anon she was stopping at Interlaken or Berne, or sailing at will on the Lake of Geneva. But it was not in these ideal rambles alone that her mind was exercised at this period ; for Mrs. Daisy was by nature too well informed and acute a woman to remain ignorant of the fact that in order to derive proper advantages from travel, much preparatory study is needed; and the history, language and literature of the country one proposes to visit, should all be subjected to a preliminary inspection. And the truth of the matter was, that the Brigadier, ill-trained and badly constituted personage though she might be, had yet a wonderful knack of gathering random misinformation on all sorts of subjects ; so that painting, sculpture, astronomy, the use of the globes, and a hundred other things beside, had all to pay tribute to her commanding intellect. In no one direction, as may readily be surmised, was her knowledge either correct or well digested ; she was erratic and wilful, but not a stupid woman by any means. Indeed the readiness with which she acquired a smattering of knowledge on this and that topic, was in itself somewhat remarkable. By glancing over a book, here and there, she was generally able, in a couple of hours, to obtain a tolerably accurate notion of its contents; and that was all that was required, for the time being, to gratify her curiosity. As to serious study, it was a thing of which she never had been guilty in the course of her life; everything was done by fits and starts, and once her curiosity on one topic was exhausted, another was taken up, to be pursued and dropped in the same desultory manner.

At the present period, Mrs. Daisy appeared to take a profound interest in the fine arts ; and whenever she happened to be in the dark, on any particular subject, her usual source of information, Miss Eleanor, was always on hand, and was sure to be called in to supply the desired information, if possible.

But it was, after all, when talking of those dear princes and princesses on whom the heart of Mrs. Daisy was so constantly set, that the superiority of this excellent woman became clearly manifested, and in his passages backward and forward between Fort Moultrie and Charleston City, Guy Averall had frequent opportunities of hearing how intimate Mrs. Daisy was with the Queen of Great Britain and Ireland, among other notables ; and also what a supreme interest she took in the affairs of her family. " There was that poor dear angel Victoria, whom I love so very much; and her good husband Prince Albert whom I esteem so very highly; and their children the Princess Royal, born on such a day in the year one thousand eight hundred and forty; and the Prince of Wales born on such a day in the year eighteen hundred and forty-one; and the lovely Alice, born on such a day in the year eighteen hundred and forty-three." And so Mrs. Daisy would go on, giving day and date for the birth of the queen's somewhat numerous family, till the whole list was exhausted.

After such a painstaking effort as this, it will readily be granted that if any one were entitled to rub noses with majestic royalty while paying a visit to foreign lands, the Brigadier was certainly that fortunate individual. But why Mrs. Daisy, as a stern republican, should ascribe such superlative honor to crowned heads, was to Guy Averall, at least, a mystery.

On some occasions it seemed as though Lieutenant Square took note of this little foible on the part of Mrs. Daisy; and endeavored to curb it as far as possible, while avoiding at the same time, anything that might seem absolutely offensive. One day, for instance, it was remarked that the Brigadier, who seemed to have been refreshing her mind on the topography of the west end of London, chose to ventilate her ideas on the subject.

" Oh Mr. Square," said she, " I have the greatest possible desire to ask you a few questions in regard to England. I believe Pall Mall is the great centre of the clubs in London, is it not?"

" Yes, ma'am," replied Square, "there are quite a number of them there. They frown like so many fortresses on you, in that part of the metropolis."

"And near the extremity of the street stands Marlborough House, where it is expected that the Prince of Wales will in time reside; and at some distance farther off is Saint James' Palace, where the good queen usually holds her drawing rooms and levees."

" I believe you are correct," said Square.

" I suppose the palace of St. James is a **very** beautiful structure," said Mrs. Daisy.

" It did not appear to me to be so," responded

the officer. "My recollection of it is, a somewhat clumsy-looking, brick building; in front of which I once saw the usual guard mounting, at about 11 o'clock, in the forenoon of a hot summer day. Still the place, in itself, is certainly anything but romantic."

"The dear brick palace, before which they mount guard at 11 o'clock, how much pleasure it would afford me to see it! And what a delightful thing a levee or a drawing-room must be!"

"It doubtless must, to those who are interested in such matters," said Square, "for my part, however, I was never much inclined that way. Indeed, I am such a believer in the natural equality of mankind, that if the fact of a presentation at court would subject me to the charge of toadyism to those who possibly think themselves better than me; why I, for one, would be the very last person to lay myself open to a charge of that sort. Like Lord Thurlow, I would say it is necessary for the peers to seek me, rather than I the peerage. I consider the upper classes of England, nevertheless, a very useful body of men, even in spite of all that."

"I am glad to hear you talk in that way," said Mrs. Daisy, "for do you know what, I am frequently annoyed and disgusted, when noticing the manner in which our penny politicians are in the habit of constantly disparaging every one who is not as commonplace and vulgar as themselves. I was brought up with certain prejudices, in favor of rank, as I am free to confess. My ancestors, long before the time of the Revolution, were among the best known and most aristocratic people in the city of New York; indeed, during the time that the Army under Sir

Henry Clinton occupied that place, its officers were always solicitous to be received at my great-grand-father's house, who usually entertained them in a truly magnificent way."

"Ah," said Square with a sympathetic sigh, "I understand now the true state of the case. Your great-grandfather was one of those unfortunate Tories I presume."

"No, I do not wish to be understood as quite conveying *that* notion," was the reply, "for as far as the Tories are concerned, I utterly despise them. But something, as you probably are aware, is due to those venerable old associations on which we fondly doat ; and such was the position of my great-grand-father, under the colonial regime, that he could not refuse certain civilities to the representatives of British rule ; although at bottom, I believe, a more sincere or true-hearted patriot than he, probably never existed."

Here the conversation ended, and the officer kept wondering at the warped ideas of Mrs. Daisy on almost every subject she mentioned. "What a woman this is," said he to himself, "and to how many false criticisms such a person as she is, must subject the better disposed and more sensible ladies of the Army. Yes, yes, take him all in all, man is an exceedingly peverse animal. The good and the bad are both equally open to the gaze of the world; but individuals and communities are almost sure to be judged by their defects, rather than by the pos-session of the opposite qualities. A stranger who should hear the Brigadier talk, would form a very queer opinion of the Twenty-sixth Artillery; yet

surely the great majority of the ladies of the Army
are women of genuine merit, and not fools and
pretenders like Mrs. Daisy.

VII.

WITHOUT being very much disconcerted, however, by the oddities of the Brigadier, Lieutenant
Square continued to visit Head Quarters now and
then as if for the purpose of whiling away his time,
and making himself as agreeable as possible to its
various inmates. Sometimes he and Mrs. Daisy
occupied themselves in playing a game of chess;
sometimes Miss Eleanor gave those present a little
music on the piano, anon the old Major would recite
some of those time-honored legends about the conduct of the Indians, during the first Florida war,
as for instance, how Mr. Bowlegs, on one occasion,
professed a great desire of peace, and even persuaded General Harney, then stationed on the Caloosahatchie, to send away the boats belonging to his
command, so as to receive some of the Seminoles on
the opposite side of the river ; and while the camp
was thus depleted of men, the crafty old savage, who
had collected all his braves for the purpose, made an
attack on the place, and commenced slaughtering
the soldiers within his reach, so that Harney only
escaped by taking to the swamps, clothed as he was
in a pair of old drawers and a night shirt. At which
rather ridiculous denouement the Major, although
relating the story for the fifteenth time, would
laugh most heartily. And to tell the truth, Lieutenant Squire was sometimes obliged to laugh quite
heartily too, not on account of there having been

anything said that was so very remarkable, but solely on account of the persistency with which the same identical story was repeated.

A well timed compliment paid now and then to Mrs. Daisy, served to put that lady in excessively good humor, and as a consequence of his politeness, Lieutenant Square had permission to take Miss Eleanor out, whenever he liked, and to chat and ramble with her, not only around the brick covered ramparts of the Fort ; but also in every other place in the vicinity. What words passed between the officer and Miss Davis, on these occasions, we have not the means of telling, but one fact was clearly apparent—they both seemed to enjoy these rambles, and laughed and chatted together, as if in default of more serious occupation. The only possible excep-tion that can be taken to all this was the somewhat unseemly levity on the part of a man like Square ; who, as every one in the Fort well knew, was now bound to propriety by ties of a more than ordinary nature. But here are some extracts from a diary which Miss Eleanor kept at this time ; extracts which may possibly indicate the cause of Lieutenant Square's course ; and show also how far he allowed his natural *bonhomie* to carry him beyond those boundaries which prudence seemed to prescribe for a person in his circumstances.

November 21st. A wet, unpleasant morning. The rain kept descending from the sky in a con-tinual pour, a big puddle of water is formed in front of our quarters, while the half dozen chickens which constitute the poultry family, in Major Daisy's estab-lishment, are huddled together, in forlorn looking attitude, under the wood shed. Attended as usual to my customary task—drumming a little French into the head of my worthy cousin. I really now have achieved a success, for after an effort of a couple of years, I have succeeded in getting him through the forms of the two principal auxiliary verbs, without his committing any very extravagant blunder. In the evening, Mr. Square came round and made a call. Brought a copy of Hazlett's Essays with him, and showed us also a few pencil sketches he had made the day previous. During his visit Mrs. Daisy took occasion to ask what the name of that heathen god, who descended from the celestial abodes in the shape of a golden shower, when Square told her it was Jupiter and gave the story embraced in the legend. I wonder if the officer is supplied with a duplicate of that wonderful present which aunt once made me—I refer, of course, to Lemprière's Classical Dictionary. Still, I admire the thirst for information possessed by my aunt; and only regret that ladies generally do not improve their time in the way she does.

22. Had a stroll with Mr. Square along the beach which extends north and south from the Fort, and which is used as a promenade by most of the people who live on the Island. Rather enjoyed the walk, for the officer rehearsed, in a somewhat amusing manner, a number of his West Point experiences; and in particular how his instructor in Cavalry Tactics, a certain formidable personage, Major Billings by name, made him "cut heads" in the riding hall. It seems that the cadets at the Academy are not, at heart, one whit more respectful to their superiors,

than are some of the soldiers in garrison; but the
rigid discipline enforced in both places served to
keep all within the bounds of decorum. Some of
the ballads and songs which I have seen, and which
are said to emanate from the young men at that institution, are very amusing in their way; and if collected together in a permanent form would make a
very interesting compendium. On returning from
our rambles the officer was pleased to pay Mrs. Daisy
a compliment which the latter evidently took in good
part. Finding her out in the garden, with a pair of
scissors in her hand, clipping some of the dead
leaves off her flowers, Mr. Square remarked that
whenever he saw Mrs. Daisy occupied in that way,
he always thought of the burden of a popular song,
which was neither more nor less than " love among
the roses." Aunt immediately laughed at this sally,
and afterwards told me that, in her opinion, Mr.
Square was one of the most polite gentlemen she ever
had met in the whole course of her existence.

25th. While rambling out with my escort this
afternoon, the subject of novel reading was introduced, and incidentally it was noticed that most
words depended on one theme, the passion of love,
to give them interest. To which observation I happened to reply, that if love were altogether omitted
in a novel, most readers would undoubtedly consider
it a very tame production. To this the officer made
answer, that talk as we would, love in itself was certainly not a silly theme; its universality indeed
proved quite the contrary. What he objected to in
most novels was this, that they gave false views of
life, and as a consequence they sometimes made

young people discontented with their present condition. I suppose what was then said is true, although
even if I read an occasional novel, I hope I am not
discontented with mine. Some fictions, in my
opinion, teach a very noble purpose—who is there,
for instance, that does not admire the conduct of
Jeanie Deans, who cannot be tempted to tell an un-
truth, even for the sake of saving the life of her
sister. I think there is something truly splendid in
this heroism, exhibited as it is by a person in humble
life.

30th. Have made an important discovery. For
some reason or other aunt is very much afraid of
Captain Triangle of the Topographical Engineers,
who has lately been ordered from New York city to
this place. This evening she introduced his name,
and said she "loved him very much," but at the
same time regretted that the "family connection" of
Captain Triangle should be so very indifferent. But
Lieutenant Square, who was present, chose to take
up the cudgels for his friend, and said he never
understood that the family connections of Triangle
were indifferent; and even supposing such to be the
case, he hoped we were sufficiently independent in
the Army to value a man for his own sake, rather
than for the sake of his relatives. My aunt seeing
the tone which the officer chose to adopt, appeared to
agree with him perfectly. I wonder, though, what can
be the objection of Mrs. Daisy to the antecedents of
the person whose name she had mentioned! Can it
be possible that Triangle has neglected to pay the
wife of the commandant at Fort Moultrie the proper
modicum of compliments? Or on the other hand is

she apprehensive that the topographical official should prove somewhat too attentive to this poor and unfortunate me?

Dec. 3. This being a rather unpleasant day, and having nothing in particular to do, I sat down and glanced over Madam de Stael's work on Germany. Without professing to be able to give an opinion of the book, as a work of information, I can admire, nevertheless, the genuine love of freedom evinced therein, and can readily conceive how the writer should be hated very cordially by such a despotic tyrant as Napoleon. It is often said by those who sneer at the better half of creation, that woman cannot generalize; but does not the existence of such a book, as the one I have been reading prove quite the contrary? And yet, after all, such a woman as Madam de Stael is almost sure to be anything rather than a favorite with persons of her own sex. She was undoubtedly looked on, during her day, as a noisy demonstrative talker; and as such was condemned by what was then known as "society." Woman, as a general thing, admire gracefulness, delicacy and a regard for the proprieties of life; and always account it much safer in their sisters to remain becoming, and even commonplace, rather than attempt or say anything which has the appearance of being unconventional.

4th. To-day I heard of a very contemptible act on the part of that elegant little gentleman, Lieutenant Taper, an officer who notwithstanding his dandified ways, I never saw much cause to admire. In spite of his constant bragging about his fine connections, his origin is really very unpretending, although that circumstance is certainly nothing to be ashamed of, but rather the contrary, and is anything but a reason why he should turn his back on his best friend. Such, however, is reported to be the case, for some time ago, when stationed at West Point, a plain, although a very decent-looking woman, called there, and asked for Lieutenant Taper, and when some person enquired who the visitor was, the contemptible little fellow chose to say, " a woman he once boarded with!" Boarded with! I imagine he did, for the visitor was neither more nor less than his own mother! If Mr. Taper only knew how much he has lessened himself, by this affair, in the estimation of his best friends, he certainly would never have committed this *faux pas.* But *noblesse oblige,* I am afraid, in many cases, is a very poor rule of conduct.

6th. Felt somewhat dispirited to-day, for Hector, somehow or other seemed determined to give me a good deal of trouble. Some time ago, I congratulated myself in having him thoroughly grounded in the forms of *avoir* and *etre,* but to-day he returned to one of his old errors, and would insist that *j'avais eu* signified "I had been." My cousin has curious humors, take him all in all. The other afternoon while I was absent in the city, he amused himself by taking the lock of my trunk to pieces, and scattering the works here and there over the house, so that I had to employ a soldier to put them together once more. Still I must exercise my patience with the boy as well as I can, although at times this is somewhat difficult. Yesterday he informed me that when he grew up he intended to turn pirate—that a pirate had nothing to do but to go aboard a vessel, and sail on the seas, and capture ships, with rich ladies on them, who would fall in love with him immediately, and this to Hector is the acme of felicity.

7th. To-day while walking out with Mr. Square, he made a somewhat strange announcement. He said Mrs. Daisy was constantly questioning him about his cousin in New York, and asking when he intended bringing her down to Fort Moultrie ; but in spite of aunt's belief to the contrary, he did not know if he should bring his cousin to Fort Moultrie at all. And then, after a pause, he added that if he could find some one whom he liked, and who would not feel dissatisfied with the haphazard existence one leads in the Army, he would set up his household gods without delay. I could not take the thing to myself ; and consequently felt somewhat at a loss in regard to a reply ; for the observation, which seemed to have a purpose in it, came to me very unexpectedly. I only know this much, that during the remaining half hour of our ramble we spoke to each other with less freedom than before; and as to any attempt at pleasantry, the thing had vanished. As to Lieutenant Square, he undoubtedly has my good will and respect ; for every one acknowledges that a more high-minded and honorable man does not exist in the service. But it would ill become me as a woman, and I trust as a friend, to do or say anything under present circumstances, which would influence his course of action in any way.

VIII.

FOR some time after the events recorded in the the foregoing chapter, the life of the various residents
25

at Fort Moultrie glided along without any very great
change. But at length a circumstance took place
which seemed to modify the bearing of Lieutenant
Square and Miss Davis toward each other. This
was the removal of the famous Triangle from Charleston Harbor; an event which relieved Mrs. Daisy
of a portion, at least, of her fears. Triangle was
gone, therefore there was no danger of Mrs. Daisy
being deprived of the services of her "assistant," at
least for the present. So the preparation for the
great European jaunt proceeded as heretofore, and
Mrs. Daisy even talked of taking a few lessons from
a dancing-master, who gave instructions in the Polo-
naise, as a needful requisite for a person whose
great aim, at present, was to cut a proper figure
among the crowned heads and other dignitaries of
the old continent. But at this instant, a strange
suspicion entered the mind of the gallant Brigadier.
What if Lieutenant Square had some sinister design
in showing so much attention as of late was manifested to Miss Eleanor? Was it proper that an
officer who was just on the point of getting married,
should carry on this unseemly flirtation with any one
but his *fiancée!* Or again, might not Lieutenant
Square also be in want of an "assistant" to his
future wife ; and knowing Miss Davis to be a useful
personage, might he not have a place for her in this
capacity? Yes, yes, that was the clue ; Spruce was
to be married before long, and Miss Davis was to be
a governess in his family. On reflecting on this
subject, Mrs. Daisy became convinced that both
Square and Miss Eleanor deserved to be watched.
And sure enough, before long the good and amiable

feminine who presided over the affairs of the garrison at Fort Moultrie, saw enough to confirm her worst suspicions. Lieutenant Square and Miss Davis were approaching the Major's quarters that very afternoon; the one looked very grave, and the other was evidently urging some matter on the attention of his associate for the time being. This circumstance was enough to determine Mrs. Daisy. So that very same evening the astonished officer was hurried out of Head Quarters, on some flimsy pretext or other, in the same way that Blodgett had formerly been discarded, while Miss Davis, for the future, was forbidden to take any more strolls in the vicinity of the Fort, and in short, was relegated, once more, to her ordinary duties with the noble Hector, as the proper subject of her keeping.

A few days after this event, spite of Mrs. Daisy's restriction, the Lieutenant and Miss Davis again met, when the former took occasion to denounce the Brigadier in the most unmeasured terms. "With all due respect to your aunt," was his exclamation, "I think her treatment both of you and also of myself, is simply outrageous. That woman is nothing more than a coarse overbearing tyrant, and if I were situated the same way Miss Davis now is, I would not submit to her imposition, no not for a single hour." But Miss Eleanor with that feminine regard for the proprieties of life which seemed inherent in her as a woman, simply shook her head as if she had no other alternative than to submit to her aunt's dictation, and then quietly walked home again.

This conduct, on the part of Miss Davis, served to arouse the indignation of the bard Hogan ; who of course, heard the whole story, on kitchen authority, almost as soon as it happened, and who could not understand those delicate scruples which prevented Miss Eleanor from acceeding to the Lieutenant's proposition, no matter what the nature of this proposition might be. "With all her piano playing accomplishments and pretty looks," said the bard, "I humbly give it as my opinion that the girl has no common sense, else she would accede at once to Squares' proposal, for the latter is too honorable a man, as every enlisted soldier well knows, to offer anything to Miss Eleanor that the latter could not with safety accept. And yet, forsooth, on account of some whimsical notion of her own, the lady chooses to disregard the offer of a man, who wishes to be her husband. She will never meet with a better protector than Square, no not if she should search the universe."

"Yes," said his companion, who for the nonce happened to be old Moldwell, "but perhaps Miss Davis does not like to give people occasion to talk—women, you know, are somewhat sensitive in that way."

"Talk be hanged," was the rejoinder, "why need Miss Eleanor care particularly about what people may say. All she need care about is to get out of old Jezebel's clutches as soon as possible; and provided this is attained, why Mrs. Grundy may talk as much as she pleases."

"Yes," said Moldwell, "but are there not such things as objections on another score. Supposing that the proposition of Lieutenant Square were a runaway match, or something else that Madam Grundy might not approve, would it be consistent with a proper sense of dignity for Miss Eleanor to accept it ?"

"Dignity be hanged," said the bard, "who in the world should care about dignity when dealing with such a selfish old blood-sucker as the aunt is. No sir, I'll tell you what the final issue of this whole affair will be. The occasion will pass; Lieutenant Square, who is now indignant with the vice-commandant, will suffer his resentment to cool; Miss Eleanor will still adhere to her prim, prudish ways; the officer, no matter how intent on matrimony, just now, will get tired of delay; some new whim will take his fancy ; and then as a final result, Miss Eleanor will be obliged to submit once more to her unthankful task-mistress, who will lord it over her supremely from morning to night, and from night to morning, just as long as she lives. Yes sir, that will be the whole end of the business—the whole end of the business."

IX.

FROM the dire catastrophe which Hogan predicted, Miss Eleanor was nevertheless saved by a fortunate event. Some resolute Jenkins or other who was prowling around the city of Charleston for news, accidentally got hold of the fact that Square was reported as about to be married, so availing himself of the circumstance he wrote a very elaborate account of the bridegroom and bride, sent the letter to the leading journal of fashion, the New York *Herald*, where it was duly printed, and in time was read by every officer and enlisted man at the Fort. The article served to throw the old Brigadier completely off her guard, for it distinctly stated that the future Mrs. Square was not only quite wealthy but was also one of the most practical women in the city of New York, and as to this thing of having an "assistant" in the management of her domestic affairs, she utterly spurned the idea. This statement on the part of the correspondent served to satisfy Mrs. Daisy, she saw in an instant that there was not the slightest danger of losing Miss Eleanor through the agency of Square, so she resolved accordingly to dismiss any unjust suspicions that she heretofore had entertained against that officer, and hold out the olive branch the very first time she met him. It was not long before the occasion was presented, for that very afternoon she came across Square, who was strolling out by himself in the vicinity of the Fort. "My dear good gentleman," was the exclamation of Mrs. Daisy, almost before the officer had time to return her bow of recognition. "I am so very glad indeed to meet you. But why do you look so disconsolate? In love, that is very evident! And how is it that you do not come over and see us now and then at Headquarters? Why both I and the Major will be delighted to see you; and Eleanor, the dear child, who always seems so willing to oblige, will give you a little music whenever you like." And thus, in spite of his protestations, the Lieutenant was installed in favor with Mrs. Daisy once more; and on visiting his old post he had the satisfaction of answering, at large, such questions as the amiable Brigadier propounded, and hearing, in addition, that famous story about Mr. Bowlegs and General Harney, just as if nothing had happened.

One day, about three or four weeks after the pre-

ceeding events, a party consisting of the officers and
ladies belonging to the Fort, were proceeding as
usual in an open boat, between the garrison and
Charleston ; when Mrs. Daisy who had already exhausted the city of London, in her numerous discussions, next resolved to invade the city of Paris.

"What a superb place, the chateau of the Tuileries must be !" exclaimed the lady, as if for the purpose of eliciting some remark, from some one of the
officers then in the boat.

"Yes, certainly," replied Square who happened
to be present. "Some of the architects, at least,
who have been employed on that edifice, have enjoyed considerable reputation. It is a very different
building from Saint James' I assure you."

"And on one side of the Tuileries," continued
the Brigadier, "runs that famous Rue de Rivoli, of
which we have all heard so much."

"As usual, Madam, you are perfectly correct,"
responded Square.

"The dear Rue de Rivoli !" exclaimed Mrs.
Daisy. "How I should like to to wander along its
arcades, and view the tasteful treasures that are exhibited in its magasins and boutiques."

"That surely would be delightful," said the
officer.

"Then west of the chateau, as I understand it,
is situated the garden of the Tuileries ; and beyond
it we have the Place de la Concorde ; and after the
latter comes the Champs Elysees, the usual place of
promenade for the Parisians."

"Your notion of the situation of those localities
is perfectly accurate," rejoined Square.

"The dear Champs Elysees!" exclaimed the lady. "What a romance there is in its winding paths! I already imagine myself mingling among the crowd, who frequent its sequestered shades."

"Yes, Madam; or perchance you might hear *Partant pour la Syrie*, in a cafe chantant, although that is not 'aristocratic'; or listen to the music at the Concert Musard, which is as fashionable a place as possibly can be desired."

"The dear Concert Musard! I hope the time may arrive when I can harken to the ravishing strains which float on its air—that is to say under the favor of the War Department, and my own good Tom."

"I hope so, too, Mrs. Daisy," said the officer. "Nothing like trusting in Providence. Whenever the War Department and Major Daisy prove propitious, I hope those of us who visit Paris may have an agreeable time."

"I anticipate as much," rejoined the Brigadier. "I have always been predisposed toward Frenchmen, and if I were in the chief city of that country, I should certainly feel assured of much pleasure, if I only had such an excellent guide and instructor as you."

"Oh Mrs. Daisy!" exclaimed Square. "You are pleased to compliment me. I am somewhat afraid I hardly deserve so much."

"On the contrary, I cannot imagine anything more delightful than to examine Paris under your auspices," responded the Brigadier. "You have not made your application for a leave yet, I suppose, but I'm sure if you put the thing in proper form, the

War Department will be perfectly willing to grant
you that indulgence, at the same time Major Daisy
is allowed his."

"And perhaps on the other hand the War Department might deny the favor," responded Square.

"Oh, no, that is impossible," exclaimed Mrs.
Daisy. "Such a highly deserving officer as you,
must certainly secure such a trifling favor without a
moments delay. But *apropos*, I have one observation
to make in regard to France. I think the Emperor
Napoleon a very great man. He seems so successful in everything he has undertaken, ever since he
ascended the French throne."

"In a certain way he undoubtedly has succeeded,"
responded Square. "Under his rule France has
remained quiet, and that is saying a great deal ; and
in addition he has shown himself to be a person of
capacity, as far as the development of the resources
of the Empire are concerned, and that is still another
point in his favor."

"I am glad to hear you speak in that way,"
replied Mrs. Daisy, "for do you know what, I have
frequently been annoyed and grieved to notice how
some persons attempt to belittle and disparage that
dear good *Louis trois* whenever they speak of him.
To me that sort of thing seems pitiful indeed."

"Yes," responded the other, "but, Mrs. Daisy, let
me ask one question. Has not the French Emperor,
by his conduct, laid himself liable to these disparaging remarks? When he was elected President, he
had a grand opportunity of showing himself a friend
of that constitutional freedom which the best minds
of the age recognize as the natural development of

this century. But instead of doing so, instead of showing himself to be a Washington or Henry the Fourth, Louis Napoleon, like a true Bonaparte availed himself of the position he held, to gratify his own selfish ends. The circumstances connected with his famous *coup d' etat* are odious and in fact infamous, and it will be very difficult to convince thinking people, either in Europe or America, that the French Emperor is a far seeing, much less an honest man."

"I'm sure I know nothing of the matter of which you speak," said Mrs. Daisy, with a distressed look, "I'm sure I know nothing about it at all; in fact I was never able to look at political economy or that sort of matter, in anything approaching a metaphysical way. Indeed I have nothing but my own heart and affections to guide me, when I think of so exalted a personage as the occupant of a throne. We all know, however, that the French people have never been able to govern themselves, and as a natural consequence have always been obliged to submit to some self-imposed master. That single fact seems to me to be an all-sufficient reason why the Emperor should be supported in his place. In addition to all this, I have, as I remarked before, a very deep affection for that dear child, the Empress, whom I love very much, and I'm sure as a mother myself, I may be allowed to say that I hope the young Louis Napoleon, now eighteen months old, may eventually inherit all the power and prerogatives of his sire."

"Why aunt," exclaimed Miss Davis, who could not help depreciating the insane admiration which her relative exhibited for persons with hereditary titles, "how can you speak in that ridiculous way, why one would almost imagine you were not an American at all."

Now Mrs. Daisy was a truly elegant and aristocratic woman ; a little loud, perhaps, in her manners and way of thinking, but such presumptuous insolence as was indicated by this speech of Miss Davis, was simply more than she could endure. She accordingly resolved to give the latter a good setting down, and as a necessary preliminary to this business, the gallant Brigadier drew herself up to a commanding height.

"Miss Davis," said she, "you entirely forget yourself, I was speaking to Mr. Square, not to you, when you saw fit to interrupt me. Any remark you made, under the circumstances was uncalled for, and entirely out of place, and I have only to beg, that in the future you will confine yourself to such matters as are within the proper sphere of your duty."

"I shall endeavor to do so," said Miss Davis, who at the same time bit her lip, lest some unguarded expression should escape her. "I'll strive and observe a discreet silence as long as I possibly can."

*   *   *   *   *

Miss Davis had heretofore been snubbed pretty frequently ; but her aunt unfortunately attempted that manœuvre a little too often that day ; for before very long a very important event transpired in the quarters occupied by the commandant. That evening his amiable spouse was there, arrayed in most resplendent style, while on one side of her stood Hector, the invincible, who wore on this occasion, a truly commanding look. After a while Mr. Square was announced, and Mrs. Daisy, who had been reading both history and biography that afternoon, chose to dilate on the character of Oliver Cromwell as a very extraordinary man ; but heaped the most unmeasured abuse, per contra, on that guilty wretch, Voltaire, in consequence of his attacks on such religion as prevailed in France during his time. At this point in the conversation, Lieutenant Square, who still seemed to fill the role of instructor, saw fit to draw a distinction.

"The character of Voltaire," said he, "has been the subject of frequent debate ; he was doubtless a man of some virtues and of many faults ; and as far as these latter are concerned, I certainly do not care to extenuate them. As to his books, one of them is justly considered a scandal to French literature, while in questions connected with religion he was the very genius of irreverence, and hence the hostility with which his memory has been followed. But on the other hand Voltaire's manliness, love of justice, and hatred of oppression must never be forgotten in the general estimate ; indeed his conduct in such cases as that of the persecuted Protestant, Jean Calas, shows that his notions of right and justice were immensly in advance of some of the ecclesiastical authorities in his country during the age in which he lived."

Mrs. Daisy received this statement with perfect astonishment; for she never supposed that a word should be spoken by a Christian gentleman, in favor of such a despicable fellow as Voltaire. But at this instant, Miss Davis, who had previously been absent, entered the room, when immediately she was attacked by Hector. "I want some cake—I want some cake. I'll go and rub out my exercise, so that you can't read it, if I don't get some cake." Miss Davis without minding the clamor raised by the prospective candidate for West Point, went over to the piano, opened her music book, and commenced playing one of her usual pieces, with the evident intention of •driving away her little annoyance. But the aunt, somehow or other, did not care to condone this apparent neglect of Hector, for hardly had her niece touched the keys, when the Brigadier went over to the instrument, and attempted to shut it down with the customary formula.

" Don't play that cherished thing; don't play that cherished thing, ' Home, Sweet Home,' Eleanor dear. 'You wound my most tender sensibilities whenever you force me to hear it. Mr. Square, you can hardly understand the associations connected with an early hearth from which I have long, long been separated." But hardly had the Brigadier commenced her oration about her wounded heart, than Square, to whom the words were addressed, jumped from his chair, and going over to the seat which was occupied by Miss Eleanor he quietly said :

"I can stand this nonsense no longer. Miss Davis, I have had the desire for some time past, to take a moonlight stroll with you. Can I avail myself of that privilege now ?"

The denouement was now a surprise to every one present, not excepting the gallant Brigadier herself. Miss Davis glanced at the officer for a moment, as if there had been some previous understanding with him, and then to the astonishment of those looking on, she accepted Mr. Square's invitation, and the two left the room.

But when she returned and it was formally announced that the two were now engaged to be married, was there not a pretty fracas! In the first place Mrs. Daisy seemed greatly shocked at what she designated this sudden resolution; and then she enquired if the officer had not compromised his own cousin in a very unseemly way? To this the answer was given that Square had not compromised his cousin at all; that nothing but mere civilities, such as are common between relatives, had passed between himself and Miss Madison; that he had once stated to Mrs. Daisy she must not trust Madam Rumor in these matters; and, in short, that a previous engagement having existed between himself, and any person living in New York, was all assumption on Mrs. Daisy's part.

"And so the gentleman has availed himself of my misinformation, in order to worm himself into this family and deprive me of the legitimate prop on which I depend during my declining years!"

"I do not know that I have been guilty of any social or moral impropriety," said Square, "in paying my addresses to Miss Davis in the way I have done."

"And must I wander alone and unattended through that beautiful Paree, with no one but the child Hector by my side?"

"Why you'll have bee Sophia," said Major Daisy, who now deemed it proper and right to speak up. "I'll act as your escort through Paree, as you call it. As long as you have bee, you need not care for any one else." And here the Major indulged in a sly little laugh, and then added, "But couldn't you see all along, for the last three or four months at the least, that the fellow was after Eleanor ?"

"I could see nothing of the kind, Major Daisy," was the appropriate reply, "the man has completely deceived me, and having said this much, I wish you to remain perfectly quiet, till I have finally disposed of this case. In the first place I wish to inform myself, before going any further, respecting this double dealing and want of candor on the part of Mr. Square."

"But aunt," replied Miss Eleanor, "Mr. Square says he forewarned you, long ago, when we were stationed on Governor's Island, not to place too much reliance on current rumors; and even intimated that he and his cousin might not be engaged after all."

"If that be the case," said the Brigadier," the man has wilfully deceived me, and I have only a few words more to say, and these words are expressive of my opinion of Mr. Square. That subaltern is a clown, an ape, a monster, an intruder into an innocent household, a person in whom no confidence should be placed, a boastful hypocrite, an officer unworthy of the position he holds, an arrogant pretender, a man that has not a drop of aristocratic blood in his veins, a low born pest, a peeping scoundrel—yes and worse than all that, since he has chosen on one or two occasions, while in my presence, to make light of those feelings of reverence and devotion which we all possess ; and has even gone so far as to laud an unhallowed infidel like Voltaire ; I hereby pronounce Mr. Square to be a person of an unbelieving and sceptical turn of mind, one that has not a particle of true religion in his heart, and is utterly destitute of the grace and charity of a Christian ! I pity you, Eleanor Davis, I pity you from the very bottom of my heart, there is nothing in this world but misery in store for you."

A CHANGE OF QUARTERS.

I.

AFTER a while orders came for the Twenty-sixth Artillery to pack up their effects, and proceed to one of the stations on the Northern Lakes, which was then known by the name of Fort Pleasanton. This shifting of quarters was attended with one or two changes. In the first place the gallant Brigadier, having been made the actual recipient of that legacy to which she was entitled, on the settlement of her uncle's estate, was now enabled to indulge in her peregrinating proclivities ; and accordingly Major Daisy, Mrs Daisy, and the young Hector Daisy, all set out on their travels. What places they visited and what fine acquaintances they made, while abroad, becomes us not to say ; meanwhile Captain Square, now promoted to this rank, and Miss Davis had been married ; and under their auspices that particular organization, in which Guy Averall had been serving, really enjoyed a very considerable portion of peace and quietness. Moldwell, who showed himself to be a sensible and well-conducted man, was still retained as 1st Sergeant of Company " E," and under the wise and beneficent management of the officer in charge, the cause of good morals and correct principles still continued to flourish. Drills were kept up at regular intervals ; non-commissioned officers were selected for their attention to duty, rather than for their bullying demeanor and physical strength; while rowdyism and ruffianism, in all their forms, were completely discouraged. In addition to all this, Captain Square was able to devise means of instruction and of amusement for his men. A garden for the use of the post was cultivated; books for a library were purchased ; a reading room with periodicals in it was opened ; and to crown all a Thespian society was organized; which after a while favored the residents of Fort Pleasanton, with those well known and highly venerated pieces " Box and Cox." " The Loan of a Lover," "Slasher and Crasher," and other performances of a similar character. In these dramatic performances, it deserves to be noted that Guy Averall himself took part, and on one occasion had the honor of acting Mr. Box, and on another "old Swizell " in the " Loan of a Lover," in both of which roles he endeavored, as in duty bound, to acquit himself with decent credit. At any rate this dramatic club was noted a great success by those who took part in it; and if the outside spectators were disposed, now and then to be critical, why no one, I'm sure, will deny them that privilege.

But the greatest change which took place in regard to Company " E," at this time, consisted in the remodelling of the female department. When the good Mrs. Daisy took her departure for Europe, she seemed perfectly willing to throw the veil of oblivion over the past ; and provided Mrs. Square were willing to give her a little assistance, in regard to Hector, she saw no reason why the latter lady should not accompany her. But as Square himself objected to this arrangement, it followed as a necessary consequence that Mrs. Daisy had to exist as best she could, while abroad; and that young Hector had to look out for himself without cousin Eleanor's assistance. This was an undoubted hardship, especially when it is recollected that the Brigadier had never been obliged heretofore to endure any annoyance of this sort. Still, she saw fit to submit to the new arrangement of affairs, with as good a grace as possible, and even seemed disposed occasionally to take no small amount of credit to herself for doing so.

In the meantime what can be recorded of the demeanor of Mrs. Square, now that she was installed in the place formerly occupied by her aunt in the Regiment? Briefly then, let us say that she conducted herself like a plain sensible woman, and we do not know that we can bestow on her any higher encomium than that. If we attempted to praise her the thing would have to be done by negatives. She did not boast of her high ancestry; she did not call the enlisted men her " dear children," and worry the very life out of them, at the same time, by her nonsensical tasks; the amount of personal service which she required from these latter was very small indeed; and as to this thing of throwing her arms round a young officer, and kissing him in public, in the way her aunt occasionally did, why Mrs. Square would as soon have attempted to fly. And yet in spite of these negative traits, both officers and soldiers were willing to vote their Captain's wife a genuine lady, and as such were disposed to show their fealty and allegiance to her by every means in their power. And in this connection we have only one question to ask—does not a good and noble woman make her influence felt in a thousand ways? Is there not an instinctive reverence for her, in the breast of every man whatever may be his rank or condition? And on the other hand, how often has rudeness been shamed and lawlessness put to flight by the appearance of a high-minded and sensible woman among those, who on ordinary occasions, pay very little attention to legitimate restraints? And no one, we are sure, more truly admired Mrs. Square, and rejoiced in her present happiness to a greater extent then did our old friend Guy Averall.

II.

ONE feature in the mental improvement of the subject of this narrative at this time is worthy of record. During the winter months, such personages as were good men and true, among the soldiers of Company " E, " of the Twenty-sixth Artillery, would frequently assemble in the room occupied by the first Sergeant, where the books belonging to the library were kept; and during these assemblages many excellent conversations took place, the subject being generally suggested by some event of current interest, some incident in the life of this or that speaker, or possibly the ideas that were presented in some volume which a member of the party had been reading. And here, without more ceremony, we beg to present an outline of the talk which took place at one of these meetings, as evidence of the character and mode of thinking of soldiers; those taking part in it being our old friends Sergeant Moldwell, and Privates Petersen, Hogan and Averall. The former speaks :

Moldwell. A cold Canadian evening, is it not. The wind has lately shifted round to the northeast, with the promise of a couple of feet of snow, on the ground, before morning. We need hardly expect a mail at this gait of going, for the next week or ten days, now that the Lake is frozen over.

Hogan. True, yet de'el take it—the fewer official letters I get, the fewer of them I'll have to answer. Beside which, with good quarters, and this rousing log fire before us, we need only cogitate on the doctrine of the Pythagoreans—that beans contain the soul of the world.

Moldwell. You are right, man—you are right. Beans, as you say, are very good food—when used discreetly. On such an occasion as this, nevertheless, I often think of the verse of Burns, which serves to describe the outside scene:

> When biting Boreas, fell and doure,
> Sharp shivers through the leafless bower,
> When Phœbus gives a short lived glower
> Far south the lift ;
> Dim, darkling through the flaky shower
> Or whirling drift.

Is it not a good thing though, that we have these books and that theatre to amuse us, else we might grumble, perchance, at these bleak winds and inclement skies. I have heard it said that the Icelanders amuse themselves, during such weather as this, by reciting their long songs and sagas; so it is to the inclemency of their skies that we owe the preservation of their literature. By the way, I fancy that last piece of ours, at the theatre, was quite a success; at least the audience, then present, seemed to be as well satisfied as usual, and as long as they don't complain, I'm sure we have no reason to find fault with them.

Petersen. Admirable, admirable, indeed. And that song, Hogan, which you gave us about "the widow McFegg, and her leg, which was washed and hung up on a peg, by a keg," was indeed an admirable thing. But confound it—I always seem to be in bad luck. I never attempted anything in the way of acting, but something or other is sure to go amiss.

Hogan. Amiss! my dear fellow. Why amidst the bustle and confusion of the stage, there is no one in the audience who notices your mistakes. You are the best actor in the whole company, as every person of sense will immediately allow.

Petersen. Yes, but on the very last occasion, when we appeared in public, I was sent into a garden to climb an apple-tree, in order to secure some of the fruit growing thereon. As Jimmy Twitcher, in the Golden Farmer, I performed the part to perfection ; got hold of the plunder, and was on the point of descending the tree, when, on a sudden, the branch on which I was walking gave way, my posterior was caught on a twig in descending, my unmentionables were rent in twain, exposing my naked pedestals to the audience ; and to crown all, the bottle of medicine which I had previously stolen, was smashed in the descent, and the cussed liquor came trickling down my legs, just as if I had been immersed in a shower-bath. To say the least, the situation was not a pleasant one, especially as the male portion of the audience chose to set up a roar at that instant, while the ladies held down their heads and pretended not to see anything. I am not one of your sensitive persons, who are easily embarrassed, but I did not feel quite at home, on the stage, at that instant, I assure you.

Hogan. No matter man, no matter man, you did the whole thing admirably. There is not a single person in the company who could act that piece any better than you. We intend having a five act comedy before long, the " Poor Gentleman," for instance, and you shall have the character of Doctor Ollapod in it, " at your very good service."

Petersen. Bravo! bravo! hurrah for the Fort Pleasanton Dramatic Club, of which we are all accredited members. And Hogan, you can give us the " Groves of Blarney " as an interlude, in your usual style, to which we all will be attentive listeners."

Averall. Is it not singular, as many pieces as we have played, that they are all of one pitch, either broad farce or low comedy. I have been reading Shakespeare of late, portions of which I have gone over twice. I like his plays immensely, I consider the perusal of them an epoch of my life. Cannot we have one or two of them on the stage, Hamlet or Othello, for instance, just by way of variety?

Moldwell. I admire your pluck, Averall, but as to this acting of the plays you mention, the thing is more easily said than done. Shakespeare is a genius by himself, as different from other dramatists, as the sun in his splendor above our heads, differs from the brightest star that may shine in the firmanent. In brief then, we cannot obtain actors who will do justice to the prominent characters in Shakespeare's works.   Your would be histrionic can spout Metamora, or saw the air as Spartacus ; but when he is required to define Hamlet, for instance, with his thought, his sense of calamity, and his wayward irresolution, the speech of the would-be Roscius fails him, his face will not convey the impression which Shakespeare evidently intended ; he is by turns either weak or bombastic, and the consequence is that those who have read Shakespeare in the solitude of the closet, turn away with infinite disappointment and disgust, and vow they will not go to hear that author murdered anymore.   Such, at least, has been my experience on all these occasions ; and many there are, beside myself, who will tell the same story in regard to the living theatre.   It is the old battle between the ideal and real.   The latter, however near it may approach, can never equal our notion of the former.

Petersen.   Which of the plays of Shakespeare do you admire the most ?

Moldwell.   A somewhat difficult question to answer, although as complete works of art, I have heard the palm given to Macbeth or Othello.   Any of them, however, contain food enough for reflection.

Hogan.   You are right sir, you are right, and if at any time, I have under my charge, an all prevailing genius who is resolved to woo the muse Melponene, I will explain to him the correct principles on which a tragedy should be written.   But here I have discovered something, which occurs in a drama, not written by Shakespeare, and which I should like to repeat to our lady Glumdalclitch, who seems to be always doating on those dear foreign potentates, of whom she so frequently speaks.

1

There was a king, right stately,
  Who had a great big flea,
And loved him very greatly,
  As if his own son were he.
He called the knight of stitches,
  The tailor came straightway,
" Ho ! measure the youngster for breeches
  And make him a coat to-day."

2

In silk and velvet splendid
  The creature now was dressed.
To his coat were ribbons appended ;
  A cross was on his breast ;
He had a great star on his shoulder ;
  Was a minister, in short ;
And his relatives, greater and smaller,
  Became fine people at court.

3.

The lords and ladies of honor,
  Fared worse than if they were hung.
The queen, she got them upon her,
  And all were bitten and stung.
And did not dare to attack them
  Nor scratch, but let them stick ;
We choke them, and we crack them,
  The moment we feel one prick.

Hurrah! for the Baron Von Goethe!   Best thing,
I'm sure, that he ever wrote."

*Petersen (who rises to his feet with an astonished
look).* Private Hogan, I'm somewhat afraid you
have forgotten yourself. The great Goethe, the immortal Goethe, if you please.

Hogan. Please allow me to explain. I do not
utter a word of disparagement against that divine

writer, and even if I did, the attempt would be simply ridiculous, on my part, but this I perceive, that there are a number of readers, both in England and America, who express the most unbounded admiration for the German, and some there are who are ready to laud every thing that he has written, both good and bad, as if it all were supremely exquisite. Now that to me savors of affectation, and against affectation, of all sort, I am the sworn foe. To illustrate what I mean, it may be mentioned, that a few days ago, while looking over a very respectable periodical, published in the city of Boston, I noticed an article on Wilhelm Meister, in which that work is praised to the skies, and in proof of this admiration, it is stated, by the author, that he has read the production of Goethe "three several times in succession," in order to discover its true intent, meaning and purpose. Now in the first place, let me observe, that a literary composition which requires to be read over and over again, in order to be understood, cannot by any possibility be a well written book; and, taking the critic on his own grounds, Wilhelm Meister is certainly deficient in one prime excellence, I mean, clearness of purpose. In spite of this warning, I nevertheless did attack the volume on the recommendation of my New England friend, and speaking as a barbarian, I must certainly say I was greatly disappointed in it. In no way does the production correspond with our notions of an English novel. The discussions in it are heavy, the plot is loosely constructed, the story is by no means interesting, and there is a certain grossness in nearly every one of the characters presented, which to my mind is perfectly astonishing. No wonder Lord Jeffrey condemns it. And yet our learned critic can say that this production of the great Goethe is simply unapproachable! A truce, I say, to such paltry and barefaced balderdash as this.

Moldwell. And yet, it must be recollected that Goethe has a whole nation at his back; for the Germans, one and all, seem to consider this Wilhelm Meister as a veritable *chef d'œuvre.*

Hogan. And I, for one, do not find fault with them if they discover beauties in the book, which I, as a stranger, am not permitted to see. But when I notice the extensive worship of every thing Teutonic, which now prevails, I am always tempted to think of one of Hans Andersen's tales.

Moldwell. Which one do you mean ?

Hogan. That one about the rogues and the cloth of gold, which according to the version I read, runs in this way. On one occasion, it is recorded, a couple of rogues came into a capital city, set up a loom, and declared they would commence immediately to weave a web of gold. "But," said they, "the web is of so extraordinary a texture, that any person who may be unqualified for the office he holds, cannot see anything but a piece of common cloth in the same." A few days after they had commenced operations, the King of the country, hearing of their skill, thought he would pay a visit to the strangers, and going into the house where they were, and looking at their warp and weft, he really thought the piece was nothing more than a web of ordinary cloth. But being afraid, at the same time, that any one would suspect him as unfit for his office, he in-

stantly exclaimed "what a beautiful web of gold !
What a beautiful web of gold !" And then, in order
to impress himself properly on the weavers, he handed
them a valuable gift, and took his departure. The
next day the chief vizier came on a similar errand,
and although he likewise could see nothing extraordinary in the web, yet rather than have it supposed he was unfit for the place he held, he deemed
it prudent also to exclaim "what a beautiful web of
gold ! What a beautiful web of gold !" And then
he gave his present, in like manner, to the rogues,
and away he started. In the same way, each official
in the city paid his visit, and offered his gift, while
in the mean time the two rascals were secretly laughing in their sleeves, at the way they had cheated these
mighty potentates At length a common fool was
brought in to see the wondrous web; but instead of
praising it, as was expected, this individual observed
that there was nothing remarkable in the cloth, as
far as he could see, and as to the gold which was
said to be there, he could not notice a particle of
that metal in its composition. "If that be your
opinion," said the weavers, "we are resolved to decamp as soon as possible, for depend on it, as soon
as it is suspected that *fools speak the truth*, the king
himself will discover we are nothing but cheats, and
it wont be long till we have to suffer, either from the
bowstring or bastinado." Now to my mind some of
our book critics, when they write for periodicals,
resemble the officials in this tale—in short, they are
afraid of saying a word against such a writer as
Goethe, lest they should be suspected as unfit for
their office.

Moldwell. A vera guide story—a vera guide story, and I think I understand the application. You mean to say that the German's volume is not a great volume, in the best sense of the word, nor his hero, Wilhelm, a great man, and that in all essential respects, any soldier now sitting in this room, who would write a true account of his mental development, from the time he commenced reading, Con Cregan for instance, to the present time, would give a much more worthy exhibit, take it all in all, than the great privy-councilor has left us. Well, sir, for the honor of the Twenty-sixth Artillery the point will not be disputed—the point will not be disputed, and this much I will say by way of explanation respecting Wilhelm's shortcomings, that at the time Goethe wrote, the social condition of Germany was such that any person in it, less than a baron was never thought of ; and even at the present time we cannot expect much elevation of sentiment in a country where rank is everything, and the personal pride of the plebeian is almost unknown. Yet after all deductions are made, we nevertheless must acknowledge that the German is indeed a giant in literature. Who is there, for instance, that has looked over a translation of his great work Faust, that has not been impressed with the power evinced in that poem. As an example of this I cannot help quoting the lines addressed to Margaret herself.

> Who dare express him,
> And who profess him,
> Saying, I believe in him !
> Who feeling, seeing,
> Deny his being

Saying, I believe him not !
The all unfolding
Folds, and upholds he not
Me, Thee, Himself

   *   *   *   *

Vast as it is, fill with that love thy heart,
And when thou in the feeling blessed art,
Call it Bliss, Heart, Love, God,
I have no name to give it !

Petersen. These are wonderful lines indeed ; and expressive of the thoughts of a great mind on a great theme. But hark ! there is the first call for tattoo, and we must now separate. This evening we have discussed the drama and Goethe; to-morrow we will take up some other matter as a proper subject for our cogitations. In this same room, then, we will have another social meeting.

   *   *   *   *   *

Such is a sample of the discourses which were held, at this time, among the enlisted men of Company " E," Twenty-sixth Artillery. Is it any wonder that under such influences and auspices as these, the mind of Guy Averall should be constantly and gradually improving ?

III.

The reader who has followed the thread of this narrative thus far, will probably enquire what became of Ryan and Lawless, the offenders in the case of the unfortunate Corporal Sullivan. The statement in this matter is but a brief one, but may serve to illustrate the beautiful uncertainty of the law. After remaining in the county jail at Jonesville, till the assembly of the circuit court, an application was made for a change of venue, on the ground that an unprejudiced jury could not be assembled in the place where Sullivan was killed, and this application the court saw proper to grant. The trial, by one expedient or another, was put off for a year ; and when it actually did take place, the jury did not see fit to convict the accused of a criminal act. A powerful argument was made in the case by the prosecuting attorney, who insisted that all the circumstances of the transaction pointed to the fact that Sullivan was the victim of a conspiracy on the part of Ryan and Lawless. In particular, he argued that if anything approaching to fair play had existed when they met for the purpose of settling their dispute, that Ryan would certainly have borne some marks of the resistance of Sullivan in the encounter. The contrary, however, was the case; Sullivan had been cut and gashed, in the most horrible manner. while the body of his opponent did not afford evidence of a single scar. But it was all to no purpose, the jury held to the opinion that as Sullivan had accepted a challenge to fight, the party who gave it was relieved from all responsibility as to the result, and as a consequence, the prisoners were entitled to their freedom. Both Ryan and Lawless had however been previously discharged from the United States service, by order of the War Department, and hence it followed that neither of these worthies, who had long been the pests of Company "E," ever afterwards joined that organization. What became of them finally was not known; but a report was circulated at one time, that Ryan was killed in a street quarrel in New Orleans ; and that Lawless, finally met with the fate he justly deserved, at a small town in the interior of Texas. But whether this was really so or not, we have no means of determining, we merely repeat the rumor for what it is worth, as the last intelligence ever received concerning the good Mrs. Daisy's "dear children." As to the unfortunate Kitty Traynor, her history may be dispatched in a few words. Shortly after the arrival of the Twenty-sixth Artillery at Fort Pleasanton, she somehow or other found her way to that station, and then entered the service of Mrs. Square, who treated her with every possible consideration. In the course of a couple of years she was married to Petersen, and made him a very good wife. But her old laughter-loving spirit had somehow disappeared; the murder of her first husband had evidently made an impression on her which could not be eradicated.

Meanwhile, it affords us much pleasure to state that the good Mrs. Daisy had a perfect feast of delight while abroad ; and the following letter, which was written by her, while visiting the city of Paris, will explain her feelings on this occasion in a more graphic way, than could possibly be done by any words which we might offer.

Hotel de L' Imperatrice,
Rue de Rivoli, *June 23d*, 18—

My Dear Friend :

Here we are in this delicious city of Paris, surrounded by all the elegance and pleasure that the world can possibly contain, and enjoying ourselves in a way that is perfectly delightful. I have visited the Louvre, I have promenaded in the garden of the

Luxenbourg, I have traversed the Place de la Concorde, and have inspected the interior of the Cathedral church of Notre Dame, and find the topographical situation of these places to be just as I had already depicted them. My own good Tom has accompanied me in these excursions, back and forward through the city; and although by no means enthusiastic as regards *la belle France*, I have yet found him to be a very useful guide and cicerone on all occasions. I attended the opera, the night before last, and saw the Empress there, and can assure you that the reports we have in America, concerning her, do not begin to do her justice. In my opinion, she is really one of the most beautiful and charming women that the world has ever seen; and if that churub of a son of hers, in whom I take such a profound interest, is only her counterpart, he must be a perfect angel in himself, and the glory also of his father. The Empress on the occasion referred to, sat quite near to me—indeed the box which she occupied was in the same tier as that in which I was placed, so that I had a very good opportunity of observing her, which I did in as quiet and unobtrusive a manner as I possibly could. I believe it is not considered etiquette to stare at august personages in Europe, through a lorgnette; I consequently was obliged to be somewhat discreet in the use of my glass. I however paid particular attention to the toilette of her Imperial Majesty, which I am enabled to describe in full. This consisted of a dress of white moire antique, trimmed with point lace, *berthe* and *manchettes*, looped with clusters of pale pink roses, and a wreath of the same flower in her hair.

27

The effect of the whole, I assure you, was perfectly elegant; and I am determined to provide myself with a similar outfit in as short a time as possible. To-morrow I will visit Worth, and the day after I am to be honored by a presentation at the Tuileries.

As to that good man, the Emperor, he accompanied his wife, and was received with much applause when he entered the box. Yesterday, I was fortunate enough to again catch a glimpse of him while crossing the Place de la Concorde. He was riding in a carriage, drawn by four glossy black horses, and preceded by a couple of officers, dressed in very elegant uniform. The Emperor bowed repeatedly to the crowd, as the carriage rolled past. This I consider a mark of gracious manners on his part; and shows at a glance that his Imperial Majesty most thoroughly understand the wants and wishes of the French people. Next Tuesday, being a holiday, the family are to hear mass at the Church of Saint Roch, which is on the Rue Saint Honorè, at a short distance from the Tuileries. Of course I intend to be there, for to worship under the same roof, with such exalted company, is a privilege of too high a character to be wilfully neglected.

As to the inferior order of French people, I like them ever so much, they seem so polite—indeed I have noticed that your genuine Parisian takes off his hat to every lady of his acquaintance whom he meets, without regard to her dress, and I have been told, without regard to her character also. As far as I have been able to observe the chief occupation of a Frenchman is to amuse himself, and certainly this city of Paris, affords him every opportunity of doing so. Seated by the side of his little table, watching the crowd that hurries past him on the boulevards, glancing perchance on the columns of the Siécle or Moniteur, how happy and contented the ordinary Frenchman seems! Then he has the theatre, the opera, the Musee de Cluny, which contains such a vast collection of objects from the most distant ages, the Louvre with its array of paintings, and the circus inside the Champs Elysées, where the most skillful riding and tumbling is exhibited for the benefit of the crowd. *Quelle belle ville que Paris*—for myself I live in a perfect whirl of delight. As to that famous *Jardin Mabille*, of which so many ridiculous stories have been told, I can only say I visited the place, in company with my own good Tom, and I can assure you found nothing but perfect propriety there.

This city of Paris, as I find by my own experience, affords an excellent opportunity of observing the customs of foreign nations; for in truth there are representatives of almost every country in the world to be found here. At the hotel where I am at present quartered, a Russian prince is said to be among the guests. He is a singular looking man, with a black moustache and a bald head. He always dines by himself, and the day before yesterday, I was creditably informed, that he had a live ox slaughtered for his especial benefit in the kitchen belonging to the establishment. I consider this very singular, although Tom, I am sorry to say, does not take one particle of interest in these charming little eccentricities. *Mais je vive en espoir*, I still have hopes that my own good husband, whom I love so very much, will yet be cured of a portion of his savagery, and then he will simply be to me—the best and dearest man that ever existed.

Your affectionate friend,

SOPHIA DAISY.

IV.

TIME wore on, and at length the enlistment in the case of Private Averall expired. He received his discharge from the service of the United States, with the word "unexceptionable," written in the space appropriated to the character which is given to the soldier. Averall was rather gratified at receiving this word of commendation from Captain Square; although, to tell the truth, he hardly thought he deserved the encomium on all occasions, for where is the soldier, living or dead, who has not been guilty, now and then, of his little sins of omission and commission. As his commanding officer nevertheless chose to say this much in his favor, Guy Averall did not object. He received his final documents with thanks, and after bidding adieu to his old comrades, and singing "Auld lang syne" in a select company consisting of Petersen, Moldwell and Hogan, the enterprising hero of this narrative prepared himself once more to take his chance of citizen life. But the attempt was not a thing of long duration for—

> The lad that to roaming is early inclined,
> To stick to one duty is never resigned.
> And to give a young gentleman right education
> The Army's the only good school in the nation.

To tell the honest truth, Guy Averall, after five

years' continued service in the ranks, found himself somewhat out of place among civilians, and as a natural consequence of this unenviable state of feeling, he came back, and shouldered the musket once more. His absence from the Army was spent in paying a visit to his old habitation in New Jersey; but, lack a day, his quondam employer, Mr. Gore, was dead; Mrs. Gore herself was living with her former *protégé,* John Henry Blasedell; the pretty Miss Jessie, now somewhat stout in person, was surrounded by two or three flaxen-haired children, and how could Guy Averall content himself while contemplating these mutations? To repeat what has been already said in this paragraph, before two months were over, our friend returned to the military station at Fort Pleasanton, expressed his willingness to again enlist, was examined in due form by the Surgeon, and before many more months were over was once more a "soldier laddie," under the guidance of Uncle Sam.

The second term of service which Averall performed was of a somewhat variegated nature. As regards his mental development he studied assiduously, so as to make considerable progress, not only in classical, but also in mathematical learning. At this time Guy made the acquaintance of both Homer and Horace in the original tongues, the two authors that seemed to him the most interesting of all those that have descended to us from antiquity, since they both afford pictures of society, different, it is true, from each other, but yet very real in regard to the respective periods which they describe. Nor was his duty as a soldier more laborious than that which

falls to the lot of the average enlisted man. As the
case stood, Guy's Company spent a while at Fort
Pleasanton, and was then ordered out on the Utah
expedition; and although the winter at Fort Bridger
was a very trying one, as every person who was at
that place will confess, yet with the establishment of
peace among the Mormons, the Twenty-sixth Artillery had a taste of garrison duty once more. At
this time, it may be observed, our friend received the
first instalment in the way of promotion, for at the
post of Fort Leavenworth he was made Corporal,
and in about four months afterwards he was advanced
to Sergeant, a position which Guy held for a considerable length of time afterwards. In the march between Fort Leavenworth and Laramie, made subsequent to his promotion, Sergeant Averall had an
encounter with a party of Sioux, for having been
sent out on the prairie in order to secure a supply of
hay for the horses of his Battery, the execrable savages almost overwhelmed the small party of men
who were under charge of our friend. But Guy, in
the first instance, retired to such cover as his wagons
afforded, and from thence he opened such a fire on
his enemies that after a little while these latter were
forced to decamp, with the loss of three or four warriors killed, and double that number wounded. For
his skill and bravery in this affair, Sergeant Averall
received the thanks of the officer in command of his
Regiment, while his name was subsequently mentioned
in General Orders. The only objection to the conduct of Guy in this matter came from a somewhat singular source. As subsequently appeared, the old rascal, who had attempted to swindle Averall in the mock

auctioneer's on Broadway, and afterwards acted as
the priest Manetho in P. T. Barnum's circus, eventually turned penitent, confessed his sins, ingratiated
himself with the Quakers, and was appointed a peace
commissioner to the Sioux, in which capacity he
wrote a terrific account of Guy's inhuman slaughter
of the Red men, a report which subsequently formed
the basis of a pathetic attack on the Army, by a
celebrated orator in Boston, who singled out Guy
Averall as the most inhuman personage that the
world had ever seen, and as such held him up to the
execration of humanity. But every one knows what
an artist in words is the justly celebrated Phillips.

It was only in his third enlistment that Guy
thought he had some reason to complain. The war
"of the Rebellion" had broken out; the Artillery in
common with the other branches of the service was
completely demoralized; in the Regiment in which
he had been serving some twenty or thirty appointments of officers had been made from citizen life;
when Averall conceived the foolish notion, that some
little attention was due those old soldiers who under
all circumstances had remained faithful to the flag;
and who had borne the burden and heat of the day
in Florida, in Utah, in the Indian country and else-
where. He was further emboldened in this notion,
for of those who had received appointments lately,
hardly one, as far as he was aware, knew anything
whatever of the ordinary routine of duty with troops;
the only exception, indeed, being a certain young
gentleman of his acquaintance, who having failed in
his first semi-annual examination at West Point, now
took the short cut to office, and received a commis-

sion without graduating at all. So with much fear
and trembling, Averall ventured to make known his
view of the case to the former Captain of his Company, now Major Square, when that kind-hearted
gentleman was pleased to say, that he really did not
know but Averall, take him all in all, would do no
discredit to a commission. "Still," said he, "we
officers are helpless in this matter—indeed I should
have taken occasion to present your name to the War
Department before now, but am creditably informed
that it would be useless for me to do so, as the wants
of the public are not yet satisfied. All I can say in
the connection therefore is, do your duty faithfully
in the field, and be assured as far as my personal exertions are concerned, your case will not be forgotten." So with this commendation, Guy Averall went
back to his Regiment; and advanced and retreated
with the Army of the Potomac, in a very gallant
manner, for a couple of years, at the end of which
time he again appeared before his old commanding
officer, who meanwhile had been promoted to the
position of Lieutenant Colonel.

"Well, Averall, what can I do for you?" was the
inquiry which Colonel Square now made. Hereupon
Guy was under the painful necessity of again re-
stating his case. "I don't pretend to be immaculate,
sir," said he, "I, no doubt, have my defects, as well
as anyone else; but this I will say, that if I have an
unfortunate love of books, it never has prevented
me from attending to my duty; and now, after fifteen years' service, and disqualifying myself for
almost every other occupation, I shall consider my
case a very hard one indeed if I find any number of

green striplings are placed over my head, and I, as an old soldier, am left out in the cold."

"Your claim is certainly a meritorious one," said Colonel Square, "but what can I do for you as long as I am destitute of personal influence at the Department? The trouble with our military system, as the case stands, is simply this, that it has never been sincerely contemplated that any one should be promoted from the ranks of the Army to the grade of officer, and as a consequence of this a person who recommends a soldier for a commission is regarded as doing an out-of-the-way thing; no matter how guarded he may be in the premises. As the case stands, you may get an appointment, and again you may not—the thing is all luck—my advice to you on the whole is, if you can use any congressional influence, do so, by all means, without delay, for any one of us old soldiers are only too conscious of the fact, that ten words from a Senator or Member of the House of Representatives will avail more in securing advancement, than if you fought in the field for half a century, and were covered from head to foot, with scars received in battle."

The words thus spoken, although containing little that was novel, produced quite an impression on Guy Averall. After thanking his old commander for his advice, he turned away, and while walking down Pennsylvania Avenue, he began to cogitate. "Well, well," said he, "it is somewhat hard after doing my very best to be honest, for a considerable number of years to find myself so utterly helpless and dependent as I am now. Yes, three successive enlistments in the Army, now almost completed; and to find myself placed under a lot of green boys, some of whom, to my knowledge, can hardly spell! I am sensible of the sad mistake I committed in separating myself from the great body of civilians when I first enlisted; had I commenced life in a proper form, attended a caucus, ran with a fire-engine, acted as a repeater at election time, or even denounced the effiete aristocracy of the old world, I might now be a free man, entitled to all the rights and privileges of an ordinary resident of the United States, instead of being the mere shuttlecock I now am. But never mind; once this enlistment expires, I will turn over a new leaf; and then if puffing and blowing and sounding my own trumpet is fit to effect anything, I will yet be a power in America."

Just at that moment, if the truth must be told, our friend felt somewhat indignant at what he was pleased to designate the unjust favoritism of Washington city, when turning the corner towards Lafayette Square, he saw a large tall woman coming down the street, and by her side was walking the young and gallant 'Lieutenant Daisy. Hector, for such he was, had grown during the last year to be a fleshy, dogmatic-looking fellow, with a stomach on him like a beer barrel. The mathematician was expatiating on the qualities of a certain *cotelette de bécasse a la suprême*, of which he had partaken the previous evening at a senatorial dinner, and whose excellencies were such as to satisfy the wants of the susceptible young gourmand. As to the lady who walked alongside of the officer, it is hardly necessary to say a word in regard to her identity. In a few seconds after he first saw her, our hero was engaged in making a most profound bow, while in front of him stood that very majestic personage, the Brigadier General himself.

"Why Averall, I am so glad to see you! What a very fine soldier you have become! A Sergeant too, I notice! Let me congratulate you. And how are all the dear children?"

"As well, madame, as could be expected," said Guy.

"I am very glad indeed to hear that," responded the lady. And what has become of that excellent old soldier—I mean Sergeant Moldwell?"

"He is at present stationed, as Ordinance Sergeant, at Fort Pike."

"Ordinance Sergeant at Fort Pike! why that is in Louisiana, is it not?"

"Yes, ma'am," said Guy.

"And that good man, Hogan, where is he now?"

"Hogan, at present, is employed as clerk in the War Department," responded Averall.

"Clerk in the War Department! And Petersen?"

"Practicing phrenology, madame, in Pittsburgh."

"Practicing phrenology in Pittsburgh. Why that indeed is wonderful. And what has become of that good man, Lieutenant Blodgett, who worked so hard at manufacturing the bugs?"

"Lieutenant Blodgett is the most lucky person with whom I am acquainted," was the answer. "He left his command, and started off to Washington a few days ago, and then by dint of sounding his own praises, he got an appointment in the volunteers as Brigadier General."

"The dear good child!" exclaimed Mrs. Daisy.

"Oh! how I did love that man! And, Averall, what position beside Sergeant, do you hold?

" The same, madame, that I have for a good many years, I attend to my duties, look after my squad, keep to myself in my tent, and now and then pore over a book. That is all, I assure you."

" Why that is too bad," said the lady. " In a democratic country like ours, and in such stirring times as these, when every one is advanced, they ought certainly to have given you some promotion."

" I have been foolish enough to think I was entitled to some, but

> Aspettare, e non venire ;
> Stare in letto, e non dormire ;
> Ben servire, e non gradire ;
> Son tre cose da morire.

To expect what never came, to lie in bed and not sleep, to serve well and not to be advanced, are three things to die of. Thus say the Italians."

" But Averall you shall not die, not if I have the means of preventing it. Your services, as orderly, during the time you were under Major Daisy's command were of too valuable a nature to be forgotten in that way, and beside all this, any person who quoted those dear Italian proverbs in the way you do, should not be allowed to die. Let me know what you want?"

" Well, Madam, to be candid, I have of late been in search of a commission in the Army," said Guy. " It may be a piece of vanity on my part, but I consider my general education as good, and my services to the government as valuable, as that rendered by the majority of those who have lately received appointments."

"And, indeed, I think so too," responded Mrs. Daisy. "I have always considered you as one of the most intelligent soldiers we have in the service."

"Oh, Madam," said Guy with a profound bow. "I certainly have no right to claim that distinction. There are many persons, now serving in the ranks, whose deservings and attainments are surely much greater than mine."

"Let me see, you are a native of Canada, are you not?" asked Mrs. Daisy.

"I am an Irishman, Ma'am, by birth," responded the other, "but spite of adverse criticism, an American, I trust, by feelings and habits, as every soldier, in the Army of the United States should be. I have no desire to live in any other country than the one where I now am."

"Well, let us see, have you ever spoken to any one in regard to your commission?"

"I have, Ma'am, to Colonel Square, but that officer regrets his inability to assist me in any very material way."

"The dear, good Colonel Square, I think him an admirable man. And his sweet, amiable wife! I consider her one of the most perfect persons who ever lived."

"I consider Mrs. Square a queen among women," responded Averall, who still retained no inconsiderable share of the loyalty he once felt towards that lady.

"And so do I too," was the rejoinder. "I consider Mrs. Square a real queen, and have always treated her as such. But reverting to our former subject, the service, Averall, and particularly the Artillery, is in a much better condition now, do you not think, than when you first joined the Army?"

"In many respects it certainly is," was the rejoinder. The officers and men seem to be very well disposed to each other at present ; and in addition we are now relieved in a great measure from the presence of these extremely lively gentlemen with whom we once were blessed. Such persons as Lawless and Ryan are not now very often met as non-commissioned officers "

"The poor dear children," exclaimed Mrs. Daisy. " I did love them so very much ; and only felt too much mortified when I understood that they both had been accused of the most horrible crimes. But let it pass. Averall, I am glad to hear you speak in the way you do, and now in regard to this commission that we have been discussing. I suppose, as you say, that Colonel Square has been exerting himself in your behalf, with very indifferent success, and such being the case, I presume I may be allowed to interfere. I will take your matter in hand and will see what can be done for you. Sergeant Averall, we ladies can usually effect our purpose in Washington, when we choose to put our shoulders to the wheel. I certainly think it a hardship that a few months recruiting duty, in the case of that dear child, Von Gingroski, the Polish count, should meet with a reward which your twelve or fifteen years of service cannot secure, and if Mrs. Colonel Johnson can get a commission for her *protégé*, by running to the Secretary, I certainly ought to secure a like favor for mine."

And after making the customary obeisance, and with these words as a final understanding, Guy Averall pursued the even tenor of his way, and the next evening he was with his battery on the Rappahannock.

Two days after this interview with Mrs. Daisy, the Captain of Guy's Company, the former Lieutenant Spruce, called him up to his tent, and handed him an official letter with a grin. Guy opened it, and found that it contained a notification of his appointment to the grade of Second Lieutenant. Poor Averall was never more surprised in his life. He positively had given up all notion of succeeding in the Army. Not to any merit of his own, either as regards length of service or general good conduct was his promotion due; but to the excellent Mrs. Daisy all his fortune in the Army was to be attributed, and the hero of this narrative was always proud to acknowledge the obligation.

After a pause of a few minutes Guy Averall attempted to speak. He thanked his immediate commander for his kind wishes in the matter and then added, " I have reason to think that a friend in Washington has assisted me in obtaining this grace, as the case now stands my duty is plain."

' " What is that ? " asked Captain Spruce.

" To serve that government which has entrusted me with its confidence in a loyal and honorable spirit ; to take proper care of the office with which I am invested ; and while remembering that control which it is my duty to exercise on all occasions, to never forget the rights and deservings of all conditions of men."

" Bravo ! bravo ! my dear fellow," exclaimed Spruce with a most engaging smile, " I admire your sentiments."

www.ingramcontent.com/pod-product-compliance
Lightning Source LLC
Chambersburg PA
CBHW032306280326
41932CB00009B/719